1783
TAX LIST
of
MARYLAND

—Part I—

Cecil, Talbot, Harford
and Calvert Counties

Compiled by
Bettie S. Carothers

HERITAGE BOOKS
2010

HERITAGE BOOKS
AN IMPRINT OF HERITAGE BOOKS, INC.

Books, CDs, and more—Worldwide

For our listing of thousands of titles see our website
at
www.HeritageBooks.com

Published 2010 by
HERITAGE BOOKS, INC.
Publishing Division
100 Railroad Ave. #104
Westminster, Maryland 21157

Originally published 1993

Other Heritage Books by Bettie S. Carothers:

1776 Census of Maryland

1783 Tax List of Baltimore County
Robert W. Barnes and Bettie S. Carothers

Index of Baltimore County Wills, 1659-1850
Robert W. Barnes and Bettie S. Carothers

Maryland Oaths of Fidelity

Maryland Source Records: Volume 1

All rights reserved. No part of this book may be reproduced or transmitted in any form or by any means, electronic or mechanical, including photocopying, recording or by any information storage and retrieval system without written permission from the author, except for the inclusion of brief quotations in a review.

International Standard Book Numbers
Paperbound: 978-1-58549-059-2
Clothbound: 978-0-7884-8398-1

TABLE OF CONTENTS

CECIL COUNTY.................................... 1

TALBOT COUNTY...................................34

HARFORD COUNTY..................................79

CALVERT COUNTY................................. 167

INDEX.. 203

INTRODUCTION

This volume of the 1783 tax assessment lists for Talbot, Cecil, Harford and Calvert Counties is an extremely helpful source volume for anyone doing research in those counties.

The lists, arranged by hundreds within each county, show the names of landowners, number of white persons in the household, the tracts of land owned by the individual and the number of acres in the tract. There are also lists of bachelors (with their securities) and paupers (anyone who owned less than 10 pounds worth of property.

Identifying individuals with common names is always a problem. After the Revolutionary War is an especially difficult one in which to work. Using these tax lists in conjunction with wills and deeds, it is much easier to distinguish between two or more individuals with the same name who lived in the same part of the county at the same time.

From time to time the researcher may find the name of a person with no "whites" listed but with some land. This usually meant that the person owned property in the hundred but lived elsewhere.

Adding to the book's usefulness is a map showing the approximate locations and boundaries of the hundreds of Harford County, drawn by J. H. Livezey.

The original lists are in the Scharf Collection at the Maryland Historical Society and the Hall of Records. Although the original lists also indicate how many slaves, what kinds of livestock, and how much gild plate the individual owned, the pertinent information for genealogical purposes has been abstracted here.

Robert Barnes

1783 TAX LIST

CECIL COUNTY MARYLAND

Agreeable to the act to raise supplies for 1783 by Richard Savin, assessor in the 1st District of Cecil County containing the Hundreds of Bohemia, West Sasafras and North Sasafras.

Owner or Claimor	Tract Name	Owner or Claimor	Tract Name
Jacob Truman Abbott	Truman's Park	Wm. F. Brazier	house & lott
Mary Abbott	Daniel Den	James Brice	Add. to Forest
Fanny Ailen	house & lott		Frisby Harris
Mordecai Allen	house & lott		Adventure
Wm. Barniby	house & lott		Hargroves Choice
Lewis Beard	Martins	Rebecca Brown	house & lott
Lewis Beard	Norland	Philey Caulk	Worlds End
John Beedle	Colition	Thomas W. Caulk	Wheeler Point
John Beedle	Pains Neglect	Samuel Chew	New Intersection
John Beedle	Friars Neglect		Frisby's Meadows
Raymon Beedle	Brice's Discovery		Frisby's Delight
Raymon Beedle	Carters Harbour		Pains Lott
Samuel Beedle	James' Adventure		Bennetts Grove
Samuel Beedle	Brice's Purchase	Nathaniel Chiles ?	Bucklers Hills
Samuel Beedle	pt. Essex Lodge	Alphonso Comegys	None So Good In
Stephen Beedle	Cox's Forest		Finland
Thomas Beedle	Beedle Promise	Wm. Comegys	Neighbours Neglect
Thomas Beedle	Vulcan's Loin	James Coppen	Coppens Chance
Thomas Beedle	Mekins Adventure		Resurveyed
Thomas Beedle	True Game		James' Lott
Thomas Beedle	Sparnels Delight		Pain's Lott
Thomas Beedle	pt. Horns Marsh		Silvanus Folly
Charles Blake	Rounds	John Corman	house & lott
Eliza. Bordley	Panther Rest &	James Cosden	Mulberry Mould
	Pullin's Refuge		Mulberry Dock

1783 TAX LIST OF CECIL COUNTY MARYLAND

Owner or Claimor	Tract Name	Owner or Claimor	Tract Name
Ann Cowarding	house & lott	Charles Heath	Heath's Range pt.
Benjamin Cox	Civility	Daniel C. Heath	Worsel Manor
John Cox	Bateman Loyal ?	Daniel C. Heath	Heath's Range pt.
John Cox	Mathiasons Park	Daniel C. Heath	house & lotts
John Cox	Concliuston	Augustine & John	Hendricksons Addit.
	Cox's Property	Hendrickson	Indian Range
Robert Craig	Hackston Pt.		Cockatrice pt.
Sarah Cunningham	Buntington Pt.	Wm. Hoops	Hackston
James Davis	house & lott	James Huches	Daniel Den
John Davis	pt. Frisbys Farm	James Hughes	Hackiston pt.
Joseph Davis	Kings Delight	James Hughes	Civility
Joseph Davis	Mary's Jointure	James Hughes	Happy Harbour
Joseph Davis	Knavery Outdone by		Hills Adventure
	Justice	Sarah & Jemima Hughes	Buntington
Rebecca Davis	pt. Frisby's Farm	Samuel Hutchinson	Homely
Rebecca Davis	pt. Level		Severson's Delight
William Davis	Rattle Snake Neck		Clemenson
	Cockakin Level	Nathaniel Hynson	Martins
	Kings Delight	Nathaniel Hynson	World End
	Tully's Lot	Nathaniel Hynson	Urison
Wm. Decoursey	house & lott	Gilbert Jackson	house & lott
Michael Earle	Swan Harbour	Wm. Jackson	Daniel Den
Michael Earle	Frogmore	Thomas Jones	Happy Harbour
Michael Earle	pt. Addition	James Long	house & lott
Barth. Etherington	Shrewsberry	James Louttit	Mt. Harman
	Jamora		Ward's lott
Thos. Etherington	Indian Range		Shillington
Thos. Etherington	Cockakin Addit.		Sheffeits
Bernard Evertson	house & lott		Hog Pen Neck
John Fashney	house & lott		Go Look
John Fisher	house & lott		Chance Pt.
Ezekiel Forman	Middle Place		Forlorn Hope
Sarah Frisby	Frisby's Meadows	Edward Lusby	Hazle Branch
Wm. Gooding	Worsel Manor	Robert Lusby	Larimore Neck pt.
Charles Gordan	Sarah's Jointer	Nathaniel McColister	house & lott
Francis Hall	Hackiston	James McGowan	house & lott
Francis Hall	Spry's Stills	John McGowan	house & lott
John Hall	Cox's Purchase	Thomas Marr	house & lott
John Hall	Marks Field	James Mathews	Pearce's Lott
Robt. Harrowood	house & lott	James Matthews	Andrews Square
Henry Hayes	pt. Essex Lodge	Wm. Mathews	house & lott

1783 TAX LIST OF CECIL COUNTY MARYLAND

Owner or Claimor	Tract Name	Owner or Claimor	Tract Name
Wm. Mathews	Cox's Forest	Mary Penington	Buntington
Wm. Mathews	Valentines Rest	Otho Penington	Heath's Range
Ann Mercer	Mt. Harmount	Robt. Penington	Carters Harbour
	Indian Range	Saml. Penington	Rich Lott
James Mercer	Larimore's Neck		Two Branches
	Mounts Field	Wm. Drake Penington	Beck's Meadow
James Mercer	Barbadoes	Benjamin Porter	Hazle Branch
John Mercer	Daileys Desire		Friars Hills
John Miller	Middle Neck	James Porter	Middle Ground
John Miller	Happy Harbour	James Porter	Bateman's Fugal?
Geo. Milligan	Corborought	James Porter	Kings Aim
	McGregory's Delight	Benjamin Price	Maiden Head
	Savins Rest		Locust Thickett
	Bank's	Eliza. Price	Wales Pt.
Isaac Money	Hard Ponds &	Henry Price	Rice's Intelligence
	Homely	Henry Price	Larimore's Neck
John Money	Mesapotamia	John Price	Pasture Point
John Money	Augustines Defiance	John Price	pt. Essex Lodge
	Larimores Neck Engl.		Carters Harbour
John Money	Sheffeits		pt. Good Luck
Samuel Money	Friars Hills		pt. Mill Pond
	Friars Neglect		Long Neglected
James Morgan	Level pt.		Swan Harbour
James Mortan	Mesapotamia		Brices Discovery
William Nelson	Bandon Bridge	Joseph Price	Mary's Part
William Nelson	Cox's Forest		Cockakin
William Nelson	Worsel Manor		Indian Range
	Woodbridge		Hendricksons Luck
	Vulcan's Loin	Noble Price	Clememon
Benjamin Nowland	Green Spring	Wm. Price	Dividings
Sylvester Nowland	Daileys Desire	Ann Ruley	Maiden Head
Hugh Patterson	house & lott	John Rumsey	Meadows
Casandra Pearce	Rounds		Rounds
	Addition to Rounds	John Ryland	Mulberry Mound &
	Pearce's Meadow		Mulberry Dock
Henry Ward Pearce	Locust Neck	Benj. Sappington	Smith's Addition
	Coliton Half		Brownings Neglect
	Poplar Neck	Augustine Savin	Kings Aim &
Saml. Pennington	Two Branches		Bums Meadows
Wm. Pearce	house & lott	Edward Savin	Hazle Branch
	Gibsons Green		Friars Hills
John Penington	Mulberry Mount		Augustines Defiance
	Mulberry Dock	John Savin	Indian Range
Joseph & Isaac Penington	Heath's Range	Margaret Savin	Dayley Desire

1783 TAX LIST OF CECIL COUNTY MARYLAND

Owner or Claimor	Tract Name	Owner or Claimor	Tract Name
Mary Savin	Larimones Neck Enl.	Richard Thompson	house & lott
Mary Savin	Bucklers Hills	Ezekiel Torman	Chance Addition
Mary Savin	Green Spring	Rachel Tully	Knavery Outdone by
Rich. Savin for			Justice
B. Benson	Money Worth		House & lott
Richard Savin	Center	Robert Vallow	house & lott
	Buck's Meadow	Edward Veazey	Salem Point
Richard Savin for			True Game
Wm. Savin	Green Spring		Abrahams ____
Richard Savin for			Veazeys Lott
B. Benson	Jones Venture	Edward Veazey	pt. Dividend
Richard Savin	Benjamins Level		Addition
Richard Savin	Indian Range	John Ward Veazy	Frisby's Farm
William Sears	Lott in Cecil Town		Add. to Frisby's Farm
Benjamin Severson	Seversons Delight	Rebecca Veazey	Carters Harbour
	Homely	Thomas B. Veazey	James Adventure
Richard Smith	Bennetts Grove		pt. Essex Lodge
Thomas Stephens	Panthers Rest	Benjamin Vickers	Augustines Defiance
Thomas Stephens			Friars Hills
for Canby?	Sidge Field		Larimore's Neck Enlarg.
Joseph Stockton	Virginity		Larimore's Addition
	New Garden	Benjamin Walmsley	Mt. Addition
	High Park		Shrewsbery
	Abraham's Promise	Rebecca Walmsley	Larimore's Neck Englar.
Edward Stoops	Rook & Pill		Augustines Defiance
	Micum	Sarah Walmsly	Clemenon
	Money Worth	John Ward, Esq.	Locust Thickett
	Middle Neck		Level Pt.
	Penny Worth	John Ward of	
	Philadelphia	Peregrine	Coxes Forest
John Stoops	Buntington		Pains Lott
	Rook & Pill		Wards Knowledge &
	Mapleton		Addition
Vachel Terry	Carters Harbour	John Ward Esq.	Indian Range
	Brices Discovery		Salem Pt.
	Hack's Addition		Strange
John D. Thompson	Long Lane		True Game
	pt. Addition	Peregrine Ward	Buks? Meadow
	Corsbough		Coliton
	Thompson's Interaction		Dayley Desire
	Dunbarr		Heath's Range
Richard Thompson	house & lott		Hendricksons Oversigh

1783 TAX LIST OF CECIL COUNTY, MARYLAND

Owner or Claimor	Tract Name	Owner or Claimor	Tract Name
Peregrine Ward	Green Field	Sarah Weaver	Heath's Outlet
	Frisby's Neglect	Thomas Whirington	Neighbours Neglect
	Kings Aim pt.	Alex. Williamson	Happy Harbour
Thomas Ward	pt. Happy Harbour	Hezekiah Wingate	Kings Aim
William Ware	pt. Happy Harbour		Frisby's Meadows
	Connecticut		pt. Frisby's Farm
	Conengim ?		Frisby's Prime Choice
	Neighbors Grudge	James Wroth	Hendrickson
	Neighbors Neglect		Mesapotamia
Wm. Ward Sr.	Sarah's Jointer		

A return of property by Richard Savin, assessor in the 1st District of Cecil County containing the Hundreds of Bohemia, West Sasafras and North Sasafras.

Name	# of white inhabitants	Name	# of white inhabitants
Jacob Truman Abbott	1	Stephen Beedle	7
Mary Abbott	4	tent. to J. Brady	
Wm. Abbott (single man)	1	Thomas Beedle	5
Charles Allen & Thompson	2	Benjamin Benson	5
Francis Allen	4	Jeremiah Benson	1
tent.to J. Brady		Sec. Henry Hendrickson	
Mordicai Allen	2	Isaac Blew	1
John Allman	6	Sec. John Cox	
James Anderson	2	Peregrine Bodle	5
Wm. Bakman-pauper	1	John Bonion	1
John Ballarman	2	Abigail Boon	6
Wm. Barnsby	10	Andrew Boyer &	
Wm. Baylis &		Ailorn Beck-paupers	1
Isaac Bahman	6	Abraham Boyer	7
James Beard	1	Thomas Bowings	5
Lambeth Beard	1	Deborah Brannan	6
Lewis Beard	2	William Brazer	3
Wm. Beard		James Brice	—
Sec. Lewis Beard	1	Rebecca Brown	6
Harman Beedle	1	James Broxon of John	1
John Beedle	4	Sec. John Broxon	
John Beedle	1	John Broxon, Jr.	10
Rayman Beedle	—	John Broxon, Sr.	2
Samuel Beedle	2	Thomas Broxon of John	1
Samuel Beedle	1	Sec. John Broxon	

1783 TAX LIST OF CECIL COUNTY, MARYLAND

Name	# of white inhabitants	Name	# of white inhabitants
Jam Bruaid	2	John Crouch	6
Henry Campbell	2	Mary Cunningham-pauper	2
John Cann	1	Sarah Cunningham	6
John Carey	4	James Davis	4
John Carnan	2	John Davis	1
Ebenezer Cartlow? pauper	3	Joseph Davis	7
		Morris Davis	9
Abraham Cartwright	6	Rebecca Davis	1
William Cataneck	1	William Davis Jr.	1
Isaac Caulk	3	William Davis Sr.	6
Pheby Caulk	3	John Dennis	1
Thomas Ward Caulk	8	William Decoursey tent. to J. Brady	4
Archibald Chain ___ B.	4		
Samuel Chew	1	Michael Earle	4
Nathaniel Childs	11	Thomas Empson	3
Philip Cline	5	Bartholomew Etherington	1
Alfhanso Comegys	8	Bartholomew Etherington Sr.	4
William Comegys	6	Benjamin Etherington	8
John Conely-pauper	5	John Etherington	5
Elisha Cooper	1	Spencer Etherington Sec. Thomas Etherington	1
Ephraim Cooper	1		
John Cooper	4	Thomas Etherington	2
Thomas Cooper	—	Thomas Etherington	3
James Coppin-free negro	6	Bernard Evertson Tent. to E. Heath	2
John Coppin	1		
James Cosden	1	John Fackney tent. to J. Brady	4
Ann Cowarding	1		
James Cowarding	1	James Fagan & Ruth Fitzgerald-paupers	6
Benjamin Cox	1		
Harman Cox	1	Daniel Farbad?	4
John Cox	7	Jonathan Fedis	1
John Cox Jr. Sec. Henry Hendrickson	7	John Fisher-tent. to J Brady	4
		John Fitzgerald	1
Capt. John Cox	11	Nathaniel Ford	6
Peregrine Cox	1	Ezekiel Forman	—
Wm. & Margaret Cox paupers	10	Sarah Frisby	—
		John Gafton & Vachel Gribon-paupers	6
John Craddock	1		
Robert Craig	7	Wm. Gafton & George Hart	1
Daniel Creadock	1	Benson Geers	5
Prichard Credock	9	Daniel Geers	6

1783 TAX LIST OF CECIL COUNTY, MARYLAND

Name	# of white inhabitants
John Geers	8
Major Joshua George	1
Henry Glassford -pauper	2
Jack Gold (free Mulatto) pauper	4
Isaac Gooding	7
William Gooding tent. to Sarah Barrington	6
Charles Gordon	—
Henry Griben	1
Robert Hadgion	6
Joseph Hague	5
Francis Hall	—
John Hall	4
William Hall	3
Thomas Hankey	5
Stephen Hare & (paupers) Jonathan Hollings	6
Henry Hayes	11
Ruth Hayes	3
Ruth Hayes	3
George Headney	5
Charles Heath	—
Daniel Charles Heath	—
Rebecca Hedges	1
John Henderion tent. to J. Thompson	2
Augustine & John Hendrickson	6
Bartholomew Hendrickson	1
Ephraim Hendrickson	1
Henry Hendrickson	8
John Hendrickson	6
Mathias Hendrickson	1
Mathias Hendrickson	4
Robert Hollowood	5
George Hott	6
James Hughes	3
Sarah & Jemima Hughes	—
Jesse Hukill	9
William Humphrey	3

Name	# of white inhabitants
William Husler	5
Samuel Hutchison	2
John Hynson-free negro	11
Nathaniel Hynson	6
Gilbert Jackson	1
William Jackson	2
Jacob Jennings &(paupers) Margaret Jones	10
Thomas Jones	3
James Kee	4
John Kerk	4
Garrit Kirk	4
John Lang-3 free negroes	1
John Lapel	4
Barbery Lee	4
William Leslie	5
John Lewis-pauper	1
Rev. John Lewis	1
James Logan & John Lester - paupers	7
James Louttit	4
Edward Lusby	5
John Lusby Sec. Robert Lusby	1
Joseph Lusby	5
William Lusby	4
James McCallam	4
Sarah McClay, Henry Matthews, John McKimmey-paupers	7
Nathaniel McCleland	1
Alexander McCloud	1
James McGowan	8
John McGowan	6
John McGregory	8
John McMilligan	1
Morris McMilligan -pauper	4
John Martin (cooper)	7
William Martin Sec. John Hyland Price	1
James Martin (cooper)	5
Arthur Matthews	1

1783 TAX LIST OF CECIL COUNTY, MARYLAND

Name	# of white inhabitants	Name	# of white inhabitants
James Matthews	1	Henry Ward Pearce	7
Dr. William Matthews	6	Henry Ward Pearce Jr.	1
Ann Mercer	4	William Pearce	7
James Mercer	7	Benjamin Penington	3
John Mercer	4	Ebenezer Penington	7
John Miller	1	Henry Penington & Elizabeth Price	2
George Milligan	4		
Robert Milligan	1	James Penington	5
Isaac Money	3	John Penington	4
John Money	11	John Penington	1
Rebecca Money	4	Joseph & Isaac Penington	5
Robert Money	1	Joseph Pennington	4
Samuel Money	1	Mary Penington	7
James Morgan	10	Otho Penington	8
John Morgan	1	Robert Penington	9
John Murphy	1	Samuel Penington	5
Rachel Neavil	1	William __ Penington	2
William Nelson	7	Thomas Pointworth-pauper	2
James Newill & Edw. Norton	8	Benjamin Porter	6
John Nicholas	7	Capt. James Porter	6
Benjamin Nowland	8	James Hance Powell	1
James Nowland	4	Benjamin Price	3
Jesse Nowland	1	Eliakim Price	4
John Nowland	2	Elizabeth Price	2
John Nowland Sr.	8	Henry Price	5
Nathan Nowland tent. to Eliza. Bordley	—	Hyland Price	7
		John Price	12
Nathan Nowland	8	John Hyland Price	6
Richard Nowland	1	Joseph Price	7
Sylvester Nowland	5	Lewis Price	3
Thomas Nowland	1	Nicholas Hyland Price	1
John Otherson	1	Noble Price	4
Otho. Otherson	5	William Price	5
Bartholomew Owens	7	Richard Reynolds	5
Benjamin Parsley & James Mercer	1	Richard Rich	2
		Andrew Rigs-pauper	6
Edward Parsley	3	George Road	6
Elizabeth Parsley-pauper	4	John Robert (heirs)	
Thomas Parsley	1	Robert Roberts-pauper	4
Thomas Parsley	3	Anable Robinett-pauper	6
Hugh Patterson tent. to J. Brady	8	Richard Robinett	1
		Thomas Robinett-pauper	4

1783 TAX LIST OF CECIL COUNTY, MARYLAND

Name	# of white inhabitants	Name	# of white inhabitants
John Rowls & Wm. Nelson	1	William Stoops	1
Catharine Rue-pauper	3	John Stuart-pauper	4
Ann Ruley	8	Joseph Sturgis	—
Seth Ruley	2	Jacob Sutter	2
Fredue Ryland	7	Ashbury Sutton	4
Fredus Ryland	1	Benjamin Sutton	1
tent. to Mrs. Pearce		John Taggard	6
John Ryland	10	Samuel Taylor	6
John Ryland Sr.	9	James Temple -pauper	2
Peter Ryland	1	Vachel Terry	6
Benjamin Sappington	7	John D. Thompson	6
tent. to Pregory heirs		Rev. William Thompson	14
Thomas Pearce Sappington	1	Saml. Todd tent. to Thos. Marr	6
Benjamin Saverson	6	Robert Truman	1
Thomas Saverson	1	Thomas Tull	4
Edward Savin	1	Edward Tully	1
Joshua Savin	1	Rachel Tully	2
Margaret Savin	1	Robert Valle-free negro	—
Peregrin Savin	1	Garrett Vansant-pauper	1?
Augustine Savin	8	Edward Veazey	7
John Savin	8	John Ward Veazey	8
Mary Savin	—	Rebecca Veazey	5
Richard Savin	4	Thomas B. Veazey	2
Catharine Scott	1	Benjamin Vickers	11
Wm. Sears-tent to F.__	2	George Vickers	9
Ephraim See	6	Geo. Vickers-tent. to	
John Shaw-pauper	3	Mr. Blake	—
Rebecca Shepperd-pauper	1	Ann Walmsley	3
John Silivain-pauper	4	Benjamin Walmsley	3
Dr. Richard Smith	—	Rebecca Walmsley	7
William Smith-pauper	4	Robert Walmsley	5
John Soaper	1	Sarah Walmsley	8
Robert Soper	6	Henry Ward	1
Edward Spencer-pauper	1	John Ward	3
William Sporat?	5	John Ward, Esq.	1
William Starkey	6	John Ward son of John	6
Thos. Stephens for Canby	1	John Ward son of Peregrine	7
Joseph Stockton	8	Peregrine Ward	7
Edward Stoops	1	Thomas Ward	1
John Stoops	11	William Ward Jr.	5
John Stoops for Stoops heirs	1	William Ward Sr.	—

1783 TAX LIST OF CECIL COUNTY, MARYLAND

Name	# of white inhabitants	Name	# of white inhabitants
Sarah Weaver	3	Alexander Williamson	6
Benj.Webb-Sec.John Geer	1	Hezekiah Wingate	6
James Welsh	1	James Wroth	6
William Whitley	5	Thomas Wroth	1
Jacob William	8	Sec. ____ Wroth	
Beruch Williams	4	John Wyley	9
Nathaniel Williams &		William Yardly	6
Peter Wingate	6	Robert Young	6

The 2nd District of Cecil Co., Maryland including the Hundreds of Middle Neck, Bohemia Manor and Back Creek.

Name	#	Name	#
Hannah Adare	3	Joseph Beastton	13
Caleb Alexander	9	Richard Beastton	10
Eli Alexander	4	Zebulon Beaston	8
William Alexander	5	Noble Beedle	23
Andrew Anderson-pauper	5	Nathan Biggs	—
John Archer		Sec.William Taylor	
Benjamin Arlergee	1	Thomas Biddle	—
Sec. John Arlergee		Sec. Thomas Biddle	
John Arlergee	6	Thomas Biddle (Elder?)	4
Adam Armstrong	1	Thomas Biddle	8
Sec. Edward Armstrong		Wilmor Biddle	1
Edward Armstrong Sr.	1	William Stoops-Sec.	
Edward Armstrong	3	Empion Bird	—
William Arrants	5	David Black	5
Elianor Baker	8	John Blanchfeld	1
Francis Baker	—	John Blanchford	5
Nicholas Baker		Joseph Blanchford	5
Sec. Wm. Veazey	1	William Bohaimen	8
John Barnaby	0	John Bouchell	2
Richard Barrington	3	Dr. Sluyler Bouchell	1
Michael Bassett	1	Sluyler Bouchell	1
Benjamin Bayard	3	Sec.Thomas Barnhill	
John Bayard	—	Thomas Bouchell	5
Peter Bayard	3	James Boulden	4
Samuel Bayard	6	James Boulden	—
Adam Bayles	5	John Boulden	1
Evan Beal	8	Lewis Boulden	5
Geo. & Andrew Beaston	6	Thomas Boulden	8

1783 TAX LIST OF CECIL COUNTY, MARYLAND

Name	# of white inhabitants	Name	# of white inhabitants
Isaac Bowen	1	William Davis	9
Sec. William Veazey		Nathaniel Dawson-Sec. James	1
Richard Bowen	8	Thomas Dixon	4
Richard Boulden	9	James Donoly	1
Benjamin Bravard	12	John Donoly	1
Thomas Bravard	3	Patrick Downing	1
Richard Briun	1	Wm. Veazey-Sec.	
Sec. William Veazey		John Elburn -pauper	5
Thomas Briun	1	Richard Ellis	4
Sec. Caleb Alexander		John Ellwood & Rich. Ellwood	2
John Bryan & John Biddle	2	Sec. Andrew Hughes	
Sec. John Thompson		Lanbert Elsbury	4
Samuel Buckworth-pauper	6	Ensor (heirs)	
Thomas Burnham	4	Rich. & Benj. Flintham	2
William Camlin		Sec. Sarah Flintham	
John Campbell	2	Sarah Flintham	6
Valentine Carperla	5	Edward Ford	5
William Cashore	3	John Ford	5
Jeremiah Carty	3	Mary Ford	1
John Carty	4	Richard Ford	1
John Chambers	4	Richard Ford of George	6
Nicholas Chambers	4	Richard Ford of John	3
Nathan Check	1	Richard Bouden Ford	5
Sec. Peregrine Check		Susannah Ford	1
Mary Chuck	4	Thomas Ford	6
Michael Churn	5	William Ford	1
John Clendenen	1	Sec. James Hukill	
Benjamin Allen-Sec.		James Foster	11
Moses Cochran	3	Benjamin Fowler	6
Jeremiah Conoly-pauper	2	Thomas French	4
Richard Corbaley	3	James Fulton	
George Craig	4	Joshua George	1
James Craig	1	Sidney George	1
James Craig	8	Robert Gilmore	2
John Craig	1	William Gilmore	1
Owen Craig-Sec. Wm. Veazey	1	Sec. Robert Gilmore	
William Craig	5	Amos Glenn	3
William Craig Jr.	1	Samuel Glenn	6
Andrew Crow	5	John Gordon	7
Robert Crozier	1	Prudence & Lydia Hall	3
Sec. ? Thomas Brown		Spencer Haltham	4

1783 TAX LIST OF CECIL COUNTY, MARYLAND

Name	# of white inhabitants	Name	# of white inhabitants
William Harley-pauper	5	Aaron Latham	5
Daniel Hatton	6	Sylvester Latham	1
James Haywood	1	James Lawrenson	8
Sec. John Hollings		Peter Lawson	4
Hannah Henderson	5	Archibald Lemmon	4
David Henry-Sec. John Craig	1	David Lewis	6
John Hershey (mill)	1	Isaac Lewis	2
Jonathan Hodgson	5	Thomas Lewis	8
Richard Hodgson	1	Ephraim Logue	7
Sec. William Veazey		Rosannah Lynch	6
John Hollings	3	James McBride	4
Jacob Hollingsworth	—	John McClary	4
Zebulon Hollingsworth	—	Mathew McCombs	6
Isaac Hooper	6	James McCorg	6
Jacob Hudson	7	Ephraim McCoy	7
Benjamin Hugg	6	Thomas McGlocklin	1
Jacob Hugg	3	Sec. William Veazey	
Andrew Hughes	5	Heck (Hector) McGowan pauper	2
Daniel Hughes	3		
Rowland Hughes	7	John McHenry (Baltimore)	—
Samuel Hughes	3	Joshua McKimms & James	2
James Hukill	6	McKims-Sec. Susannah McKims	
Jeremiah Hukill	8	Richard McKims	1
Josiah Hukill	7	Sec. Peregrine Vandergrift	
Peter Hukill	9	Duncan McKitridge	2
Spencer Hukill	3	Mr. Mackey	—
William Hukill	5	James Mansfield	2
Joseph Hunt	5	Jemima Mansfield	3
Robert Hunter-pauper	4	John Mansfield	5
William Jackson	9	Samuel Mansfield	3
John Jobion	—	Susannah Mekins	4
Francis Jones	1	Andrew Miller	10
Sec. William Thomas		Benjamin Miller	8
William Jones	6	Samuel Miller	7
Ann Kirk	5	Abraham Mitchell	—
Robert Kleinhoof-pauper	6	John Montgomery	11
William Kleinhoof	5	Gilliam Moore (Wm. ?)	5
William Kleinhoof, Jr.	2	Nathan Moore	1
Sec. Wm. Kleinhoof		Sec. Juliane Moore	
John L. Knight	6	Samuel Morrison	4
Sinclair Lancaster	10	Wm. Morrison-Sec. Wm. Veazey-1	

1783 TAX LIST OF CECIL COUNTY, MARYLAND

Name	# of white inhabitants	Name	# of white inhabitants
Charles Mullan-pauper	8	Isaac Scott	3
John Muller-pauper	7	Robert S. Scott	1
Joseph Murphey-pauper	2	Samuel Sharp	9
Samuel Nash	3	William Sheran-pauper	6
Ephraim Norwland	7	Edmond Shields	6
John Nudie	4	Laurence Simmonds	1
Nicholas Parisett	5	Jacob Simpers	2
Joseph Patterson	4	Benjamin Sluyter	5
Thomas Patterson	7	James Smith	1
Henry Pearce	—	Robert Sprosol	6
Benjamin Pearch	11	John Steel-pauper	2
Hyland Price	5	Ephraim Sterling	5
John Price	15	Jacob Sterling	4
Thomas Price	3	Joseph Stern	1
William Price	9	Sec. Thomas Ford	
William Price Jr.	8	Benjamin T. Stoops	3
James Pugh-pauper	4	William Stoops	10
John Pugh	4	John Stuart	3
Charles Quigley	2	John Stunstill	1
James Ratliff	2	Sec. Nicholas Chambers	
Robert Ratliff	1	Benjamin Taylor	7
Sec. James Ratliff		Jeremiah Taylor	5
John Rawlings	3	Joseph Taylor	7
John Rawlings	—	Joseph Taylor, Jr.	1
Selia Rawlings	1	Sec. Joseph Taylor	
Thomas Reynolds	12	William Taylor	2
Thomas Richardson	5	William Taylor	1
Elizabeth Rider	4	Sec. Jeremiah Taylor	
Joseph Rider	6	Benjamin Thomas	2
Jacob Robb	9	Joseph Thomas	—
Samuel Roberts	4	Joseph Thomas	4
Alexander Robison	1	Joseph Thomas Jr.	5
Sec. Ephraim Thompson		Isaac Thomas	1
Hugh Rolston	5	Quila Thomas	1
Daniel Ross	4	William Thomas	10
Tobias Rudolph	—	Abraham Thompson	1
William Rumsey	1	Ephraim Thompson	1
Benjamin Sappington	—	Ephraim Thompson	6
Richard Sappington	5	George Thompson	4
Thomas L. Savin	5	Richard Thompson	1
Alexander Scott	4	Robert Thompson	2

1783 TAX LIST OF CECIL COUNTY, MARYLAND

Name	# of white inhabitants	Names	# of white inhabitants
Robert Thompson	2	William Ward	4
George Vansant	5	Joseph Watson	
George Veazey	1	Martin Wert	—
Noble Veazey	4	Thomas Wert	7
Peregrine Veazey	7	Conrod West	3
Robert Veazey	1	Benjamin Whittam	8
Sec. William Veazey		Peregrine Whittam	9
Samuel Veazey	9	William Whittam	4
William Veazey	4	Wm. Whittam-Sec. Benj. Whittam-1	
Isaac Venimon	9	John Wimble-pauper	3
Adam Wallace	7	Peter Wingate	6
Thomas Wallace	3	Sarah Wood	
John Wamsley	5	Alexander Wright	6

Return of land by William Veazey, assessor of the 2nd District of Cecil County, Maryland containing the Hundreds of Middle Neck, Bohemia Manor and Back Creek.

Owner or Claimor	Tract Name	Owner or Claimor	Tract Name
Hannah Adair	pt. Alex. & Sligo	Dr. Sluyter Bouchell	pt. Laber tract
Caleb Alexander	pt. Rumsays Range and a lott	Benj. Bravard	pt. Buck Ridge
		Benj. Bravard	pt. Charles' Camp
Eli Alexander	pt. Hispaniola & Bullins Range	Benj. Bravard	pt. Lusk Orginal Range Sligo
Elianor Alexander	Buck Ridge & Luck	Benj. Bravard	pt. Jones'Green Spring
Edward Armstrong	pt. Boulding Rest	Benj. Bravard	pt. Frogs Quarter
Edward Armstrong	Fatigue	Thomas Bravard	pt. Hispaniola
John Atkin	Black Bridge & Luck	Thomas Bravard	pt. Glassgois
Francis Baker	pt. Laber tract	Wm. Buchanan	Buchanan's Endeavor
John Barnaby	no name given	Wm. Buchanan	pt. Rumsays Range
John Bayard	no name given	Wm. Camlin	no name given
John Bayard	pt. Laber tract	John Chambers	Two Sifters
Samuel Bayard	pt. Laber tract	Nicholas Chambers	no name given
Thomas Biddle &		March Check	no name given
John Fields	no name given	Peregrine Check	no name given
Thomas Biddle(Elk)	____ & Bristow	Richard Ellis	pt. Laberder & Ellis' Escheat Orginal
Thos. Biddle(Elkn)	pt. Geores Friendship		
Davis Black	_____	John Ford	no name given
James Bouldin	pt. Jones'Green Spring	Mary Ford	no name given
John Bouldin	pt. Bouldins Rest	Rich. Ford of Geo.	pt. Bouldins Rest
Richard Boulding	pt. Noble Wood	Rich. Ford of John	no name given

-14-

1783 Tax List of Cecil County, Maryland

Owner or Claimor	Tract Name	Owner or Claimor	Tract Name
Richard B. Ford	Bullins Range & ___ Alexander & Sligo & Bullens Range	John Nudee ___ Ogle Benjamin Pearce	pt. Laber tract pt. Nole Wood pt. Nole Wood
Susannah Ford	pt. Bohemia Sisters	Henry W. Pearce	no name given
Thomas Ford	pt. Bouldins Rest	Wm. Price Jr.	no name given
James Foster	pt. Jones'Green Spring	Charles Quigley	Quigley's Lodge
Charles Garden	pt. Divident	Tobias Randolph	Blanketeen Forest & Black Ridge & Ruck
Joshua George	pt. Middle Neck		
Sidney George	pt. Middle Neck	Thomas Richardson	pt. Hispaniola
Samuel Glenn	no names given	William Rumsey	Adjunition
Prudence & Lydia Hall	pt. Nole Wood	William Rumsey	pt. Dividend
Spencer Hattham	Blansford	Thomas L. Savin	Welsh Point
Soloman Hearsey	pt. Laber tract	Benj. Sappington	Foxes Starbour
Hannah Henderson	Thompson Town	Alexander Scott	no name given
John Holland	no name given	Ann Scott	pt. Laber tract
Jacob Hollingsworth	no name given	Sarah Scott	pt. Clifton
Zebulon Hollinsworth	Duck Neck	Benjamin Sluyter	no name given
Benjamin Huss	non name given	Benj. T. Stopps	pt. Nole Wood
Samuel Hutchison	Griffin	Benj. T. Stoops	pt. Georges' Friendship & Horn Point
Jacobs heirs	no name given & Dalifes	___ Taylor	pt. Buck Range
John Jobson	pt. Askmore	Jeremiah Taylor	pt. Alen & Sligo
John L. Knight	pt. Clifton	Jeremiah Taylor	Nash's Adventure
John Leach Knight	no name given	Jeremiah Taylor	Taylor's Lott
Aaron Latham	no name given		Taylor's Chance
Peter Lawson & Ensor heirs	pt. Bohemia Manor		Kirk Mintter pt. Rumsays Range
Rosannah Lynch	Askmore	Benjamin Thomas	Griffin
James McClorg	Blanketeen Park	Isaac Thomas	Griffin (2 tracts)
Mr. Mackey	no name given	Joseph Thomas	Griffin, a lott (2) sic
Noble Middle	pt. Georges Friendship	Joseph Thomas, Jr.	Griffin
Noble Middle	pt. Bristow and Bidles Intent	William Thomas George Thomson	Welsh Right pt. Newport
Andrew Miller	pt. Bohemia Sisters	Ephraim Thompson	pt. Bohemia Sisters
Benjamin Millor	no name given	Geo. Thompson	pt. Kirk Miston
Benj.Millor & Rich.Ford of John	pt. Two sisters	Richard Thompson Robert Thompson	no name given no name given
Abraham Mitchell	pt. Newcastle Back Landing	Adam Wallace	pt. Newport & no name Blanketeen Park
John Montgomery	no name given	Thomas Wallace	pt. Laber tract
Samuel Nash	Nash's Adventure	William Ward	pt. Askmore

1783 TAX LIST OF CECIL COUNTY, MARYLAND

Owner or Claimor	Tract Name	Owner or Claimor	Tract Name
Joseph Watson	no name given	Thomas Wirt	no name given
Martin Wert	pt. Armstron's Fortune	Alexander Wright	no name given
Benjamin Whittam	no name given		

The Return of John Oglevee, assessor in the 3rd District of Cecil Co, Maryland containing the Hundreds of North Millford and East Nottingham.

Name	# of white inhabitants	Name	# of White inhabitants
George Alexander	9	Jesse Brown	8
Isabella Alexander	5	John Brown	2
John Alexander	6	Messer Brown	2
Josiah Alexander	8	James Cambill	8
Sarah Alexander	8	Alexander Campbell	3
Charles Anderson	1	Daniel Carionear	4
Jacob Anderson	9	Francis Caruthers	5
John Anderson	2	Walter Caruthers Jr.	5
Ann Armstrong	4	Jonas Chambers	12
John Armstrong	6	Benjamin Chandlee	9
William Armstrong	9	Benjamin Chandlee Jr.	5
George Ash	4	Elijah Churchman	9
Nicholas Ash	5	George Churchman	9
Henry Askin	8	John Churchman	—
Nancy Bailey	6	James Cochran	3
John Barnaby	6	Robert Cochran	9
David Barr	7	Elijah Cole	3
William Beam	9	John Cross	11
William Birk	7	George Cully	9
Hugh Black	3	Henry Cully	3
James Boggs	9	Samuel Cummins	5
Richard Bond, Esq.	7	John Cuncoa	6
Richard Bond Jr.	2	Mathew Cunningham	6
Samuel Bond Jr.	4	James Davison-pauper	3
Samuel Bond Sr.	3	John Davison	5
Enoch Bonsal	7	William Davison	7
Ebenezer Booth	7	George Day	8
Jonathan Booth	9	John Douglass	6
William Boyd	9	George Downey	8
George Bradley	7	Samuel Duff	10
Thomas Broom	1	John Eakin	—

1783 TAX LIST OF CECIL COUNTY, MARYLAND

Name	# of white inhabitants	Name	# of white inhabitants
John Eavens	3	Widow Hollingsworth	1
John Ellgis	5	Zebulon Hollingsworth	8
Rebecca Emmitt	2	Zeb. Hollingsworth for Wm. Montgomery	—
James? E. England	7		
Samuel Evans	9	Zeb. Hollingsworth for James Black	—
Henry Ewing	14		
Robert Ewing	2	George Horner	4
John Fee	5	Samuel Huet	3
James Fife	2	Benjamin Huff	6
James Finley	6	Thomas Huggins	4
James Garrett	3	Mary Hughes	4
Elisha Gatchel	4	Thomas Jacobs	1
Jacob Gatchell	2	John Jeans	10
Jeremiah Gatchell	8	Cornelius Jewell	4
Nathan Gatchell	4	Archibald Job	8
Samuel Gatchel	4	Daniel Job	1
William Gibson	9	John Johnson	3
Thomas Giles	3	John Johnson	9
Joseph Gilpin	11	John Johnson (weaver)	5
Joseph Gilpin for Cates heirs	—	Thomas Johnson	6
Samuel Gilpin	2	Hugh Jordan	3
Rachel Ginn	6	Thomas Jordan	3
Francis Gittear	4	James Kilgore	1
George Glass	3	Thomas Kilgore	4
Sterrett Gray	7	William Kilgore	5
Thomas Guileland	8	Mary Kirsh	3
James Hall	—	Timothy Kirsh	10
John Hall or Hull	4	George Lawson	3
Widow Hambleton	—	John Lawson	11
Ruben Harden	3	John Leach-pauper	6
George Harriss	3	Richard Lewis	10
Thomas Hervey	6	Hugh Logan	7
James Hibbett	4	Hugh Longwill	3
Samuel Hill	5	Robert Longwill	5
Samuel Hill	3	William Longwill	2
Thomas Hill	7	Joseph Louraign	1
Henry Hollingsworth	—	John McClintough	3
Jacob Hollingsworth	4	James McCowen	6
Levi Hollingsworth	—	Alexander McCoy	3
Stephen Hollingsworth	—	Henry McCoy	4
Thomas Hollingsworth	—	John McCuncoa	2

1783 TAX LIST OF CECIL COUNTY, MARYLAND

Name	# of white inhabitants	Name	# of white inhabitants
John McCutchen	8	Jacob Reynolds	—
William McKew	6	Benjamin Ricketts	10
James McKibbin	4	David Ricketts	5
John McKnight	3	John Ricketts (cooper)	5
David Mackey	5	John Ricketts (flint)	9
James Mackey	5	John Thomas Ricketts	3
Capt. James Mackey	8	Daniel Robinson	12
John Mackey	3	Henry Robinson	3
William Mackey	5	John Robinson	4
William Mackey	7	Elisha Rogers	3
Thomas Manuel	4	Rowland Rogers	7
Thomas May	2	Thomas Rogers	12
Edward Maybon	5	William Rogers	5
Joseph Mehaffy	7	Hezekiah Rowls	5
Abraham Mitchel	6	Jacob Rudolph	4
John Mitchel	3	Mitchel Rudolph (pauper)	5
William Mitchel	5	Thomas Rudolph	7
William More	3	Tobias Rudolph Jr.	1
Jonathon Mullan	5	Widow Rumsey	8
Willem Mullen	5	John Scott Jr.	4
John Murry	2	Capt. John Scott	8
John Oglevee, assessor	13	Thomas Scott	10
Elizabeth Oldham	7	Thomas Scott	
Jacob Oldham	4	William Scott	3
Moses Oldham	1	William Scott	—
Richard Oldham	6	Thomas Sharp	9
Robert Oldham	7	Elizabeth Shepherd	3
Thomas Owings		Thomas Simpers	3
Michael Nowland	4	Geo. & Wm. Singleton	8
Edward Parker	6	Joseph Singleton - pauper	3
Henry Passmore	1	Forgus Smtih	10
Richard Passmore	2	James Smith	8
Samuel Peak	8	Hezekiah South	7
William Pearce	6	Samuel Stall	6
David Perry	8	James Steel	8
Cornelius Post	7	Margaret Steel	7
William Price		Joseph Tannor	5
William Ralition	6	Edward Taylor	3
Charles Ramsey	7	Christian Thomas	7
John Read	4	Henry Thomas	1
Alexander Read	7	Isaac Thomas	7
Henry Reynolds	7	William Thomas	6

1783 TAX LIST OF CECIL COUNTY, MARYLAND

Name	# of white inhabitants	Name	# of white inhabitants
Robert Thomson	2	Baruch Williams	—
Andrew Tool	3	Charles Williams	4
Joseph Trimble	6	Benjamin Willson	9
Thomas Underhill	6	William Willson	5
John Waggoner	7	Alexander Wilson	3
Andrew Wallace	2	George Wilson	5
David Wallace	6	Joseph Wilson	11
Joseph Wallace	—	Philip Wilson	3
Joseph Watts	4	Samuel Wilson	8
George Wallace	2	Samuel Wilson	4
Edward Wear	7	Thomas Wilson	8
Samuel Whan	9	Samuel Winhut	11
Abner White	4	Archibald Woods	5
Edward White	8	Alexander Work	4
John White	9	James Work	8
Jonathan White	8	Samuel Work	4
Ralph Whitecar	5	Donaldson Yeates	7
		Robert Young	3

SINGLE MEN

Alexander Armstrong
Archibald Armstrong
John Badders
Moses Badders
Abraham Broom
John Cambel
Edmond Channel
Michajah Churchman
Mordecai Churchman
James Currey
Levi Davis
Gray Douglass
John Eakin
Nathaniel Erzbey

William Fletcher
George Gartrill
Robert Haywood
John Jameson
William Jameson
George Johnson
William Johnson
William Kerney
Joshua Loutit
Samuel McElroy
John Mills
Charles Neel
Jeremiah Oldham
Roger Parrott
George Princil

Ruben Ricketts
Elijah Rogers
Joseph Rogers
Henry Smith
William Smith
Peter Springer
John Taylor
William Terry
Andrew Thomson
Sampson Toutchstone
Thomas Underhill
James Willson
Thomas Willson
John Wright

1783 TAX LIST OF CECIL COUNTY, MARYLAND

Paupers of the Third District

Name	# of white inhabitants	Name	# of white inhabitants
Widow Badders	5	William McCarting	8
William Bairfoot	6	James McKneel	5
Jeremiah Baker	_	William Mason	2
James Bohannan	6	Robert Mills	3
John Brown	5	William Nutt	7
John Carrold	6	Samuel Parker	2
Samuel Clenaougham	4	Widow Passmore	3
William Cloward	8	John Patterson	3
William Cooley	7	William Patterson	3
Benjamin Everet	9	Zebulon Phillips	8
William Foster	4	Thomas Read	3
Samuel Gilpin	_	Abel Ricketts	2
William Gold	6	Andrew Robinson	4
Abel Hanna	8	William Thomson	6
Widow Hill	2	Samuel Veazey	_
Francis Hokes	4	John Ward	_
John Hopkins	3	Joseph Warrisin	
Mary Hunter	2	Benjamin Williams	5
John Hynott	5	Adam Willson	7
Widow Leason	2	Benjamin Willson	5
Mathew Leins	4	James Willson	2
John Lowry	7	John Woodrow	9

The Return of Abraham Cazeir, assessor of the 4th District including the Hundreds of South Milford and Elk.

Name	# of white inhabitants	Name	# of white inhabitants
John Adams	3	Jacob Ashbaugh	4
Edward Agnew	3	John Barr	8
Cornelius Aion	6	Robert Barr	6
Fredus Aldridge	11	James Barrock	2
Thomas Allford	1	James Bathorn	7
John Anderson	7	Francis Bay	5
Thomas Armstrong	4	Timothy Bayles	5
Alexander Arnet	1	Lawson Beard	4
Sec. J.___Means		William Beck	7
Harman Arrants	5	Alyland Beedle	8

1783 TAX LIST OF CECIL COUNTY, MARYLAND

Name	# of white inhabitants	Name	# of white inhabitants
Empson Bird	6	Joshua Donohs	—
Peter Bouldin	3	Joseph Dugan	8
Jonathan Bowen &		Ann Elliott	1
Mathew Burns-paupers	7	Rees Evans	—
John Boyd	4	Archibald Foster	9
Nathan Boyd	8	James Foster	4
Augustine Boyer		Jese Foster & Wm. Fulton	7
Cornelius Bradley	5	John Foster Jr.-pauper	8
John Bristow	7	John Foster Sr.	3
John Bristow Sr.	5	William Foster	3
Rachel Bristow	5	David Frew	2
John Brown	5	William Fulton	11
Patrick Brown-pauper	4	John George	6
William Brown	8	Nicholas George	3
Willson Buck-pauper	4	Edward Gerish-pauper	6
Henry Buntol	5	Daniel Gillespie	3
James Campbell	6	Samuel Gillis'	2
John Campbell	4	Samuel Gilpin	
Abraham Cazier, assessor	—	John Glass	8
William Chaniel	1	Mary Granger & Wm. Grace	5
sec. John Curlet?		paupers	
Bennett Chew	—	Isaac & James Hall	7
Peter Close	3	Robert Hart	5
John Cochran	7	Thomas Hart	6
James Cook	2	William Harvey	10
James Couden	—	Robert Hempfield	5
Philip Creamer	4	Stephen Honny	4
Isaac Crouch	10	Jonathan Hill	6
James Crouch	5	John Thomas Hitchcock	4
John Crouch	2	Nicholas Hitchcock	4
Sarah Crouch	11	Thomas Hitchcock	6
Stephen Crouch	1	William Hitchcock	7
Sec. Robert Hart		Isaac Holt	6
John Curlet	5	John Hopkins	2
Sampson Currer	2	Richard Hukill	11
William Currer	3	William Huston	5
Adam Dabson	4	Edward Hyland	6
Elisha Darumple-pauper	3	Isaac Hyland	4
Wm. Dawson & James Dugan	9	Nicholas Hyland	3
paupers		Stephen Hyland	5
Thomas Dixon	1	Nathan Ireland	3
Sec. Nicholas Hyland		Henry Jackson	7

1783 TAX LIST OF CECIL COUNTY, MARYLAND

Name	# of white inhabitants	Name	# of white inhabitants
Elisha Johnson	6	James McColley	2
Jacob Johnson	8	John McColley	6
Josiah Johnson	5	Samuel McCowan	3
Mathias Johnson	3	John McCraken	7
Simon Johnson	3	Hugh McCray	10
William Johnson	4	Thomas McCreery Jr.	9
Charles Jones	1	Thomas McCreery Sr.	6
John Jones	8	John McDowell	1
Mary Jones-pauper	3	Mathew McGlocklin	6
Moses Jones	9	Thomas McGriffin	1
Robert Jones	5	Thomas McCreery-Sec.	
Samuel Jones	5	Benjamin McKinney-pauper	5
Thomas Jones	1	James McNinch	7
John Kanky	13	John McWorton	5
John Kanky, Jr.	1	Samuel Maffitt	
John Keitley	9	Jacob Manley	10
Ebenezer Kelly	1	Gawin Mathis	5
Sec. John Foster		Henry Maulden	1
George Knight	6	James Maulden	5
John Lewis		William Maulden	1
Samuel Lewis	4	Benjamin Means	1
James Little	5	Sec. Thomas Jones	
Joseph Lort	6	John Means	8
John Low	6	Amos Miles	1
Elisha Lowry	1	Sec. Peter Bouldin	1
Sec. Henry Jackson	1	Thomas Miller	5
James Lowry	1	William Miller	3
Mary Lowry	1	Easter Money	5
William Lowry	1	Alexander Moody Jr.	2
Sec. Jesse Manly		Alexander Moody Sr.	4
Jacob Lum	8	John Moody	4
Michael Lum	6	Alexander Moor	1
James Lutton	3	Sec. Benjamin Maulden	
Robert Lutton	4	James Morrow	4
Anthony Lynch	6	John Muckclose	10
James Lynch - Pauper	5	Thomas Murphy	5
William Lynch	3	John Nash	9
Hannah McBride	3	John Neavil & Lucy Nash paupers	9
William McClure	8	Thomas Owings	8
Ann McColley	6	William Passmore	4
Daniel McColley	7		

1783 TAX LIST OF CECIL COUNTY, MARYLAND

Name	# of white inhabitants	Name	# of white inhabitants
Robert Patterson	4	Thomas Short	12
Nathan Philips	9	George Simpers	8
Nicholas Philips	1	John Simpers	11
Jesse Price	4	Thomas Simpers	3
John Price	4	Adam Short & Stephen Testor	8
Sarah Price	5	paupers	
Thomas Price	6	Henry Smith	7
Jonathan Proctor-pauper	5	Joseph Smith	5
John & Andrew Read	_	Joshua Smith	7
Samuel Redgrave	5	Michael Smith	6
Robert Redman-pauper	6	Robert Smith	5
Jonathan Richardson-pauper	3	Lydia Sparowgrove-pauper	6
Josiah Richardson	7	Henry Stalcup	3
James Roach	6	Henry Stedman	6
Philip Roach	_	John Taylor	6
Henry Ross	4	Mathew Taylor	5
Jacob Rudolph	_	James Thacknay	7
Benjamin Rumsey	_	Rachel Thacknay	6
Jane Rumsey	_	Joseph Thomas	_
John Rumsey	_	William Veaz'ey	5
Sabina Rumsay	_	Zekiel Veazey	3
John Russell	1	Thomas Wallace	9
Sec. Thomas McCreery		James Warram	6
Isaac Rutter	1	William Watson	6
Sec. Philip Roach		John Weston	_
Samuel Rutter	5	John Willson	2
Ann Savin	18	Thomas Willson	7
James Scott	3	Hezekiah Wingate	_
Moses Scott	8	Donaldson Yates for	_
Mary Seagers	8	Alexander Johnson	
James See	4	William Young-pauper	3

1783 TAX LIST OF CECIL COUNTY, MARYLAND

Return of land by Abraham Cazeir, assessor in the 4th District including the Hundreds of South Milford and Elk.

Owner or Claimor	Tract Name	Owner or Claimor	Tract Name
Fredus Aldridge	Two Necks	Adam Dobson	Good or Bad
	St. John's Manor	Josuah Donoho	pt. Elk Manor
John Anderson	pt. Concent	Rees Evans	Concent
Cornelius Armstrong	-Gorec	Jessee Foster	St. John's Manor
Thos. Armstrong	Rumsey's Discovery	John Foster	pt. Breerton
Jacob Ashbaugh	Lum's Venture	John Foster	Johnson's Add.
	pt. Maney Range	William Foster	Plumbpoint Fork
Robert Barr	_illy Broon	David Frew	Nether Lands
Timothy Bayles	pt. Elk Manor		Storey's Meadows
	Clay Bank	William Fulton	pt. Providence
Lawson Beard	Drum Green	John George	Highlands
William Beck	Wasp Nest	Nicholas George	pt. Highlands
William Beck	pt. Story's Meadows		pt. Truimph
Augustine Boyer	Land Oar & Meadows	Samuel Gilpin	Little Angelzo
	Stoney Chase	Isaac & James Hall	Partners Parcel
John Bristow	pt. Hylands Discovery		Halls Discovery
Rachel Bristow	pt. St. John's Manor		Halls Venture
Wm. Brown	Simper's Meadow-pt.		Hollingsworth Parcel
Henry Butell	Racoon Range	Robert Hart	pt. Triumph
Abraham Cazier	St. John's Manor		pt. Highlands
Bennett Chew	Comucent?	William Hervey	Buck's Head Hill
James Cosden	St. John's Manor		Hervey's Purchase
	pt. Lum's Venture	John Thomas Hitchcock	-Hope Well
	pt. Maney Range	Isaac Hott	pt. Breerton
Isaac Crouch	Purchase		Cennes Desire
	New Amster	Edward Hyland	pt. St. John's Manor
	pt. Johnson' Add.	Isaac Hyland	pt. Highlands
Sarah Crouch	pt. Triumph	Nicholas Hyland	pt. Highlands
Sampson Currier	Hope Well	Stephen Hyland	pt. Highlands
Tempson Currier	Small Hope		White Marsh
William Currier	pt. North East Manor		St. John's Manor
	Deer Harbour	Henry Jackson	St. John's Manor
	pt. Story's Meadow	Alexander Johnson	Gorce
	Capris Intent	Elisha Johnson	Benbebers Forest
	Currier's Lot	Jacob Johnson	Fedred pt.
	Currier's Add.		Johnson's? Purchase
Adam Dobson	Hollings Point	Mathias Johnson	Johnson's Fancy
	Angelzo	Jacob Johnson	Law Meadows
	Visirs Lott	John Jones	pt. Forest
	Successor	John Kanky	St. John's Manor

1783 TAX LIST OF CECIL COUNTY, MARYLAND

Owner or Claimor	Tract Name	Owner or Claimor	Tract Name
John Lewis	St. John's Manor	Josiah Richardson	pt. NorthEast Manor
William Linch	pt. North East Manor	James Roach	pt. NorthEast Manor
Jacob Lum	pt. St. John's Manor	Philip Roach	pt. NorthEast Manor
	Lum's Venture	Benjamin Rumsey	Bailey
	Maney Range		Collers Town
	Hyland's Discovery		Round Stone
Michael Lum	pt. St. John's Manor		Witters
Robert Lutton	Philips Neglect		pt. North East Manor
John McCrakan	pt. St. John's Manor		pt. St. John's Manor
Thomas McCreery	Chambers Venture		Jones' Discovery
	Concent	Jane Rumsey	New Hall
Samuel McGown	Casson's Forest	Johh Rumsey	pt. Rumsey's Discovery
James McNinch	Good Neighbour		Antago
Samuel Maffitt	pt. Benbebers Forest	Sabina Rumsey	Ant Castle
	pt. Good Neighbour	* Jacob Rudolph	no name
	Gorce	Samuel Rutter	pt. Elk Manor
	Maffitts Division		pt. Clay Bank
	Maffitts Restitution	Ann Savin	St. John's Manor
Jacob Manley	Steels Head	Mary Seagers	pt. Lum's Venture
Benjamin Maulden	Mt. Collester		pt. Maney Range
William Maulden	Collers Town	George Simpers	pt. North East Manor
Thomas Millers	pt. Ant Castle	John Simpers	New Spain
Alexander Moody	pt. Elk Manor		Simper's Choice
John Moody	pt. Elk Manor		Successor
James Morrow	North East Manor		Simper's Meadows
	pt. Wasp Nest	Thomas Simpers	no name
Thomas Murphy	pt. Elk Manor	Robert Smith	pt. Gorec
William Passmore	Concent	Henry Stedman	Eagles Nest
Nathan Philips	pt. Breerton	Mathew Taylor	Brown Point
Thomas Price	pt. Elk Manor	James Thackray	Triumph
	pt. Breerton	Joseph Thomas	Fedred
John Ramsey?	North East Manor	William Veazey	pt. St. John's Manor
John & Andrew Read	Kingsley		pt. Hyland's Discovery
Samuel Redgrave	Elk Manor	Thomas Wallace	Hollingsworth's Purchase
			Chambers Venture pt.
			Pt. Providence
* James Warram	pt. N.E. Manor	Hezekiah Wingate	pt. Breerton
* John Weston	Rumsey's Discovery	Donaldson Yates	Concent Resurvey

* out of alphabetical order

-25-

1783 TAX LIST OF CECIL COUNTY, MARYLAND

1783 Tax List returned by Basil Williams, assessor in the 5th District of Cecil County, Maryland; containing the Hundreds of Susquehannah South, Charles Town, and West Nottingham. All living in Susquehannah Manor unless otherwise indicated.

Owner or Claimor	Tract of Land	Owner or Claimor	Tract of Land
Richard Abram		John Jack	
Arthur Alexander		Thomas Jonny Jr. & Sr.	
John Alexander		Edward Justice	
Jeremiah? Baker	Clay Fall?	Robert Lesloy or Lesley	
John Beard		John Lesley	
Charles Brookins		Mathew & Saml. Logan	
Eliza Brumfield		Thomas McClary	
Mary Brumfield	Sonua	James McCormack	
Jane Caldwell	Cavan	Saml. & Wm. McCullough	
John Cameron		John, Saml. & Wm. McKeown	
John Carswill		Jacob McVey	
George Cathor		Jacob McVey of John	
John Cathor		John McVey Jr. & Sr.	
Samuel Clark		James Milligan	
William Corbott		Edward Murphy	
Thomas Cord		Stephen Newell	
Moses Cralstone		Robert Orr	
John Crookshanks		James Orruk	
Isabell Cunningham		Frances Owens	
John Cunningham		Thomas Russell (weaver)	
Jeremiah Currer		Thomas Russell Esq.	
William Domigan		William Simcoe	Anna Catherina
Joseph Edmunson		William Simcoe(glebe) pt. of Clay Hall	
William Edmunson		John Slycer	
Joseph England		Widow Slycer	
James Glascow		John & Wm. Stinson	
John Golloughor		Capt. Wm. Thomas	
John Green		John Thompson	
William Green		John Underhill	
Tod & Wm. Guffoy		Wm. Waruthers	
James Hagany		Mary Welcheouk & Co. (North East Works)	
John Hall (weaver)		Andrew Wellocks	
John Hall, Jr. & Sr.		Andrew Welsh	
Thomas Hartshorne		Jesse White	
George & Michael Hedrick		Samuel Wiggins	
Robert Hill		Thomas Williams	
John Hudson	Carpenters Point	James & John Wilson	
John Hutchingson		David Worly	

1783 TAX LIST OF CECIL COUNTY, MARYLAND

Paupers in South Susquehannah Hundred

John Baker Jr.
John Baker Sr.
Wm. Colosdy?
Hugh Crosson
Michael Dougharty
James Gardner
Robert Harvey?
John Irwin
James MC Cullough

SINGLE MEN IN SOUTH SUSQUEHANNAH HUNDRED

James Antriam
John Beard
James & Wm. Caldwell
John Caruthers
William Cather
James Channels (negro)
James Cord
David Cothan ?
George England
David Gardnor
Wm. Glascow
John Iller
James Jack
Wm. McVey
Samuel Martin
Richard Newell
Zebulon Oldham
Joseph Pew
Stephen Severson
James Wellaks
David Worley

1783 Return for West Nottingham Hundred, Cecil County, Maryland.

Thomas Allen
William Allin
Henry Anderson
James Banns Sr.
James Barclay
William Barclay
John Blackburn
John Borland
Jackim Brackley
Elisha Brown
Jacob Brown Jr.
Jacob Brown Sr.
Joseph Brown Jr.
Joseph Brown Sr.
Samuel Brown
Edward Burns
John Butterfield
John Churchman
James Crawford
William Cole
Jessee Coulson
John Coulson
Joseph Coulson
Thomas Coulson
John Crawford
James Cummins
James Davidson
John Dickson
James Eagin
James Eakins
David Edmiston
James Emiston
John Emiston
James Evans Jr.
James Evans Sr.
John Forguson
Richard Hall
Isaac Haynes
Job Haynes
John Haynes
Nathan Haynes
Phebe Haynes
Sarah Haynes
Widow Haynes
William Haynes
Robert Hindman
Samuel Hindman
David Job
William Johnson
John Kelly
Nicholas Kelly
Abner Kirk
Jacob KIrk
John Kitpatrick
William Kitpatrick
John Knight
William Knight (Adm. ?)
William Knight Jr.
William Lee
Rosannah Love
James Maxwell Esq.
John MC Clain
John McCollough
James Merchant
Joseph MIfflin
James Miller

1783 TAX LIST OF CECIL COUNTY, MARYLAND

West Nottingham Hundred, Cecil County, Maryland

- Robert Moorguiss
- Robert More
- Joseph Nesbitt Jr.
- John Patrick
- Thomas Patton
- Thomas Patton
- David Poak
- Andrew Ramsey
- Patrick Reash

- Isaac Reynolds
- Jacob Reynolds
- Jesse Reynolds
- Joseph Reynolds
- Samuel Reynolds
- Sarah Rich
- Stephen Rich
- William Rogers
- Robert Scott
- Elisha Sedwell

- Hugh Sedwell
- Jacob Sedwell
- Joseph Sedwell
- Widow Sedwell
- John Tebbs
- Andrew Wark
- Richard Wells
- John Welsh
- Robert Welsh

SINGLE MEN IN WEST NOTTINGHAM

- William Alexander
- James Banns
- Joseph Banns
- Andrew Brackly
- David Brackly
- John Butterfield Jr.
- William Cord

- Robert Evans
- Hugh Ferguson
- Thomas Ferguson
- Robert McClain
- James McCollough
- Samuel McCollough

- Ferdinand More
- Joseph Nesbitt
- David Potts
- Andrew Reagh
- James Reat
- Ezekiel Reynolds
- Aron Wark

CHARLES TOWN

- Nathaniel Baker
- Thomas Baker
- James Barley
- Edward Bearsley
- Richard Bennet
- Thomas Boggs
- George Brown
- Frances Brumfield
- James Campbell
- Robert Cathor
- Richard Chew
- Jeremiah Collins
- David Corbett
- Samuel Coultor
- James Cunningham
- James Dougherty
- Benjamin Ferguson
- Robert Finny

- Dr. William Gibson
- Rose Gilmore
- Widow Ginthor
- William Gorrish
- Andrew Grubb
- John Hamilton
- John Hamelton Jr.
- John Hamelton Jr.
-     200 acres Senaca Pt.
- Patrick Hamilton
- James Hassan
- Peter Hersch
- John Huddabuck
- Edward Jackson
- Peter Jaquith
- Samuel Kilpatrick
- William Lambard
- Robert McMullin

- Samuel McNair
- Edward Mitchel
-     Pt. of Seneca
- Major Samuel Moffett
- James Monwow
- Sarah More
- Jacob Northerman
- John Northerman
- Nathan Norton
- Mary Palmer
- Edward Parker
- John Peter/?
- Elizabeth Pritchard
- heirs of Dr. Rigar
- Rope Walk Co.
- Baruch Williams
- Wm. Winchester
- William Work
- James Wylie
- Thomas Yeoman

1783 TAX LIST FOR CECIL COUNTY, MARYLAND

SINGLE MEN IN CHARLES TOWN

Nathan Bennett	James Hart	Thomas Owens
Robert Cather	William Howell	George Smith
William Glascow	Dr. Harford Montgomery	Henry Yonole
	Edward Morton	carpenter

The Return by Samuel Durbin, assessor in the 6th District of Cecil Co., Maryland containing the Hundreds of Susquehannah and Octarara. Everyone listed is living on the Manor unless otherwise indicated.

Owner	Tract of land	Owner	Tract of land
Robert Akens		Alexander Ewing	Harmans Rambled
Arthur Alexander			High Park
Wm. Arbuckle	pt. Daugherty's Desire		Davisons Fancy
	Fagru's ? Chance	Amos Ewing	
	Emmory's Endeavour	Moses Ewing	
	Manor	Patrick Ewing	Barren Forest
John Bankhead		Samuel Ewing	pt. Dividings 1/3 mll
Andrew Barrett	Anchor & Hope		and land
William Bateman		Thomas Ewing	
Joseph Boon		Capt. Wm. Ewing	pt. Dividings, Long Lane
Francis Boyd			Add. to Long Lane,
Robert Calahan			Huckleberry Meadow
James Cambell			mill and land
Samuel Carr	Peck's Island	Robert Finley	
Richard Chew		Benjamin Foster	
Philip Cole		Joseph Freazer	Teague's Forest
Jacob Coonrod	Russell Owen	Alexander Fulton	Penna. claim resurveyed
Jane Corbett			Emmory, Satisfaction,
William Craig			Doherty's Desire
John Cresswell	Ryecrats Choice		Haims 30 acres
Elizabeth Crockett		Richard Gay	pt. Loves Arrowood
John Cromwell	Success		pt. Loves Addition
William Currier		Samuel Gay	
Jacob Death	Glasshouse	James Gillespie	pt. Holland
William Dixon		Nathaniel Gillespie	Mt. Gillespie
Andrew Dunbarr	pt. Loved	Samuel Gillespie	Greenberry
Samuel Durbin, assessor	Perry Neck	William Gillespie	pt. Loves Addition
		William Glassco	
Amos Evans		John Glenn	Muddy Springs
John Evans		Jane Grier	

1783 TAX LIST OF CECIL COUNTY, MARYLAND

Owner	Tract of land	Owner	Tract of land
Richard Griffen	pt. Glasshouse & Man	Ann Meek	
William Griffen	pt. Glasshouse & Man	Samuel Miller	Steelmans Delight
William Grimes	Penn Brook.		Condemned for mill
Elihu Hall Sr.	pt. Boldings Dispatch Halls Lot, and Halls Choice	Edward Mitchell Mary Mitchell John Murphy	Gotham Bush
Elihu Hall of Elijah	pt. Halls Lott	James Nesbitt	Widows Lott
Jonathan Hartshorn	pt. Holland	Robert Nesbitt	Widows Lott
John Hawkins		Patrick O Flinn	
David Henderson's heirs		David Patten	
Michael Helm	Penna. claim	William Patten	
Joseph Higgons		John Patterson	
Alexander Hillis	Hillis Delight	Samuel Patterson	
James Hunter		John Patrick	Dry Spring
Wm. Hutchman		Henry Plaxico	
Edward Jackson		John Poke	Tomb
Thomas Johnson	Larkins Desire	Andrew Porter	Smiths Fort
Thomas Kelly		George Porter	Teagues Delight
Andrew Kidd		James Porter	Porters Choice
James Larrimore		Robert Porter	
Hugh Lyon	Widow's Lott	Samuel Porter	Good Neighbours, Struggl
James Love			Good Luck
John Lyon	Widow's Lott	Stephen Porter	mill and land
Robert Lyon		David Price's heirs	
Robert Love	Emmory's Satisfaction	Jacob Reynolds	
Thomas Love	pt. Hopewell, Loves Addition, Loves Arrowood, Barronett Limited	Richard Reynolds Geaoge Rhey Wm. Rowland	Rutherford's heirs, Add. to Glasshouse, Barren Forest
John McCall			
John McClain	McClains Folly	John Ryan	
John McCoy	Johnsons Adventure, Halls Choice	Tolbert Shipley David Smith	Perry Neck
Thomas McDowell	Heney Island, Notri Dame	James Spear Thomas Steel	Widows Lott
John McHarrey		John Sterrett	Widows Lott
Robert McMaster		John Stump	Harts Delight, Gotham Manor
James McMullin			
Samuel McMullin		Stephen Suttin	pt. Holland & Larkins Desire
Joseph McNealey			
John Marcus Jr.		John Taylor	
Robert Marcus Sr.		John Tigart	

-30-

1783 TAX LIST OF CECIL COUNTY, MARYLAND

Owner	Tract of Land	Owner	Tract of Land
Philip Thomas	Amshire Warrant	Andrew Ware	
Elizabeth Troy	Troys Folly	Joseph Watson	Sinclear's Purchase
Rich. Thomas' heirs	Perry Point	George Welsh	
Samuel Thomas	pt. Perry Point	James Welsh	
Isaac Dico Watson	Palmers Island	Robert Welsh	
	Sinclears Purchase	Charles Whitelock	
John Walker	Halls Choice	Charles Whitelock, Jr.	
Robert Walker	Walkers Delight		
Thomas Walker	PD		
Thomas Wallis	Larkins Desire		
	pt. Holland		

Recorded by Samuel Durbin, assessor in the 6th District of Cecil Co., Maryland containing the Hundreds of North Susquehannah and Octarara.

Name	# of white inhabitants	Name	# of white inhabitants
Robert Akins	6	Jane Corbett	1
Arthur Alexander	4	Joseph Cothon	3
William Arbuckle	—	Robert Craig	1
James Bankhead	3	William Craig	6
John Bankhead	4	John Cresswell	2
Andrew Barrett	6	Elizabeth Crockett	8
William Bateman	7	John Cromwell	1
John Bell	1	Vincent Cromwell	6
Robert Bell	10	William Currier	4
Joseph Boon	4	Jacob Death	4
Francis Boyd	7	Robert Dickison-pauper	3
Patrick Cahey	6	William Dixon	9
Robert Calahan	—	Alexander Dougherty	5
Moses Cannon	12	Andrew Dumbarr	4
Samuel Carr	6	Samuel Durbin, assessor	7
Saml. Carr & Susannah Cazier	11	Amos Evans	4
		John Evans	5
Thomas Chandler	3	Alexander Ewing	9
Richard Chew	4	Amos Ewing	3
Wm. Clark & John Carr paupers	5	Moses Ewing	4
		Patrick Ewing	11
Sandries? Cohorn	3	Samuel Ewing	8
Philip Cole	—	Thomas Ewing	8
Jacob Conrod	10	Capt. William Ewing	5

1783 TAX LIST OF CECIL COUNTY, MARYLAND

Name	# of white inhabitants	Name	# of white inhabitants
William Ferguson	5	Robert Knox	5
Robert Finley	7	Edward Lafferty	6
Wm. Flanagan-pauper	2	George Lashley	5
Benjamin Foster	3	James Larrimore	7
Joseph Frazor	—	William Linton	1
Charles Freel Sec. Wm. Griffen	1	John Little-Sec.Wm.Little	1
		William Little	9
Alexander Fulton	5	Mathew Lockwood-pauper	7
Richard Gay	8	William Logan	9
Samuel Gay	5	Margaret Long-pauper	1
James Gillespie	10	James Love	1
Nathaniel Gillespie	1	Robert Love	10
Samuel Gillespie	6	Thomas Love	9
William Gillespie	6	William Low	
William Glass	2	Hugh Lyon	8
John Glenn	7	James & Joseph Lyon	2
Jane Greer	1	John Lyon	4
Richard Griffen	4	Robert Lyon	
William Griffen	8	John McCall	6
Elihu Hall Jr.	4	James McCan	3
Elihu Hall Sr.	11	John McCan-pauper	4
Elihu Hall of Elijah	7	William McCandley-pauper	6
William Hamby	6	Henry McCann	4
Jonathan Hartshorn	7	John McClane	2
Joshua Hartshorn	1	John McCoy	13
John Hawkins	8	Alexander McCullough	7
Michael Helm	7	Thomas McDowell	5
Henry Helman-pauper	4	John McHarry	4
David Henderson heirs	4	Joseph McHealey	5
Joseph Higgins		Henry McKeever	7
Abraham Hillis	7	Neal McKeever	2
George Hines	8	Samuel McLary	5
James Hunter	7	Robert McMaster	10
William Hutchman	5	Samuel McMullen Jr.	3
Edward Jackson	8	James McMullin	4
Isaac Johnson & George Kevin-paupers	9	Samuel McMullin Sr.	2
		Murty Mahan	3
Thomas Johnson	6	John Marcus Sr.	5
Thomas Kelly	6	Robert Marcus	4
Andrew Kidd	7	Ann Meek	2
Saml. Kinnman & John Lynch paupers	8	John Miller Sr.	5
		Samuel Miller Esq.	6

1783 TAX LIST OF CECIL COUNTY, MARYLAND

Name	# of white inhabitants	Name	# of white inhabitants
Edward Mitchell	8	John Sidwell-pauper	5
Mary Mitchell	1	David Smith	7
John Moore	8	James Spear	5
Margaret Moore-pauper	4	James Steel	5
Ruleph Morgan	8	John Sterrett	5
Robert Morrow	4	John Stump	4
John Murphy	3	James Suan	5
Moses Newill-single man	1	Stephen Sutton	6
James Nisbitt	4	John Taylor	9
Robert Nesbitt	3	Thomas Taylor	6
David Patten	7	Philip Thomas	—
William Patten	10	Samuel Thomas	2
John Patterson	6	Saml. Thomas for Rich. Thomas heirs	—
Samuel Patterson	6		
John Patrick	—	John Thompson	8
Henry Plaxico	10	James Tibbs	1
John Poke	5	Sec. James Porter	
Andrew Porter	4	John Tigart	4
Andrew Porter Sr.	7	John Touchstone	8
George Porter	6	John Tower	2
James Porter	3	Elizabeth Troy	1
Robert Porter	5	John Tullam	1
Samuel Porter	3	Andrew Walker	8
Stephen Porter	8	John Walker	5
David Reynolds-pauper	3	Robert Walker	3
Fanny Reynolds-pauper	4	Thomas Walker	8
Jacob Reynolds Sr.	1	Andrew Ware	5
Richard Reynolds	5	Robert Ware	2
Robert Rowland	5	Allen Waters	5
William Rowland	10	Isaac Dico Watson	5
John Ryan	5	Joseph Watson	4
James Scott & Hanah Reyley paupers	5	George Welsh	4
		James Welsh	8
Samuel Scott	1	Robert Welsh	8
Talbut Shipley	—	Charles Whitelock	8
		Charles Whitelock Jr.	3
		Robert Williams	6
		John Wood	6

Single Men: Saml. Marcus, Robt. Marens, Jr., Wm. McClure, Joshua & Wm. McCoy.
Paupers: James Barr, Wm. Beard, Joseph Benjamin, James Bennitt, Solomon Blake, Thomas Bryan, Jonathan Grant, Timothy Guinea, Rich. Hill, Thomas Hill, Wm. Harrey Gustavus Henderson, Stephen Horner, Wm. Mahan, Henry Miller, James Thompson, Adam Tullam, Wm. Welsh.

1783 TAX LIST OF TALBOT COUNTY, MARYLAND
Bay & Mill Hundreds

Name	Tract Name	# of white inhabitants
Samuel Alcock	Gaskins Point	5
Rebecca Aldron	pt. Yaffords Neck	—
	Andersons Island	
	Blandons Addition	
Moses Allen	Abrahams Lott	—
	Mill Road 2nd Addition	
	Groughton	
Alex Anderson	pts. of tracts names unknown	2
Thomas Ashcroft	Beach	7
	Davenport	
John Auld	pt. Elliotts Folly	6
	pt. Aulds Security	
Mary Auld	Newport Glasgow	
Hannah Austin	Austins Trial	8
	Burgess' Add.	
	Neighbors Hand Off Add.	
	Neils Advantage	
	Austins Chance	
	Stoney Lot	
James Ball	Upor Holland	16
Thomas Ball	Balls Resurvey, formerly called Long Neck	8
Henry Banning Esq.	Conjunction Resurvey	9
	pt. Matthew Circumvented	
Jeremiah Banning Esq.	pt. Halls Neck	1
	pt. Hopkins Point	
	Chance	
	Taylors & James' Discovery	
James Barnes	pt. Caulk's Add.	9
Andrew Barrow	pt. Tilghmans Fortune	8
	Hardins Endeavour	
James Barrow	Ashby	10
	Betty's Cove	
	York	
	Betty's Add.	
Thomas Barrow	Ashby	7
	pt. Hardins Endeavor	
Elizabeth Bartlett	pt. Ratcliff Mannor	6
John Bartlett	pt. Ratcliff Mannor	7
Richard Bartlett	pt. Ratcliff Mannor	6

1783 TAX LIST OF TALBOT COUNTY, MARYLAND
Bay & Mill Hundreds

Name	Tract Name	# of white inhabitants
William Benny	pt. Faulknors Square	2
Nicholas Benson	Bensons Enlargement	7
	Bogs Hole	
Perry Benson	Bensons Choice	14
	Benson's Enlargement	
	Bogs Hole	
Elizabeth Blades	Matthew Circumvented	5
John Blades	Matthew Circumvented	5
Zadock Bolfield	pt. Hazzard & Coventry	9
	pt. Haphazzard Addition	
	Powels Island	
	pt. Batchelors Range Add.	
Daniel Bridges	Budon	10
John Bruff	2 lotts in St. Michaels Town	9
Sarah Burk(for life)	pt. Coventry	9
	Mucklomore	
	Comolias Range	
	pt. Jacob & Johns Pasture	
Frances Cardiff-in Dover	pt. Lawstock	---
Charles Carroll Esq.	Poplar Island	---
Wm. Marsh Catrup	Cottingham	7
	Jacob & John's Pasture	
	Neglect	
John Caulk	Lawstock	6
	pt. Caulks Add.	
	pt. Tilghman's Fortune	
	Hazzard Spring	
	Arcadia	
Peter Caulk	pt. Lewis Point	10
James H. Chamberlaine, Esq.	Sheephead Point	---
	pt. The Gore	
	pt. Braintree Addition	
	pt. Partnership	
	pt. Necessity	
Samuel Chamberlaine Esq.	Four Squares	---
Samuel Chamberlaine Esq. as guardian for Thomas Chamberlaine	pt. Hookland	1
	pt. Yorkshire	
	pt. Cumberland	

1783 TAX LIST OF TALBOT COUNTY, MARYLAND
Bay & Mill Hundreds

Name	Tract Name	# of white inhabitants
Samuel Chamberlaine, Esq. as guardian for Thomas Chamberlaine (Continued)	Clay Addition pt. Rockey Hook & Add. pt. Plaindouling Endeavor Grundy's Lott Resurveyed Cabbin Rock Contention Bishoprich pt. Chance Goose Neck Intention Bartlotts Inheritance Boudon's Enlargement Eaton's Add. pt. Lobs Corner	
Samuel Chamberlaine Esq. as friend for Henry & Saml. Nichols, minors	Galloway Resurvey Kimbles Industry pt. Batchelors Range Add.	—
Samuel Chamberlaine Jr.	Rest Content Goodwins Addition	—
Joshua Clark's heirs	Tilghman's Fortune Dayley's Delight	—
George Collinson	Rehobath Rehobath Point	8
John Colston	pt. Waterford Fox Harbour	8
James Colston	pt. Cove Hall pt. Clays Hope	8
John Colston	pt. Tilghman's Fortune	5
Henry Colston	Cove Hall Fort Venture Clays Hope	1
Benjamin Cooper	pt. Miles End	5
William Cooper	pt. Miles End	7
Haddaway Cooper	pt. Miles End	7
Thomas Cummins	pt. Knave Keep Out	5
William Cummins	pt. Knave Keep Out	10
Charles Daffin	pt. Belfast & Add. Campers Neck Chance Kemps Lot & Addition	—

1783 TAX LIST OF TALBOT COUNTY, MARYLAND
Bay & Mill Hundreds

Name	Tract Name	# of white inhabitants
Charles Daffin (cont.)	pt. Hemersby	
	pt. Lewis Point	
William Davis	Fairplay	7
	pt. Mainsail	
George Impey Dawson	Lawstock	—
	Cudleton & Addition	
Impey Dawson	Cromwell Resurvey	6
James Dawson	Batchelors Range	4
	pt. Galloway	
John Dawson	Shriglay Fortune	9
Ralph Dawson	Jones Lott & Add.	6
	pt. Grafton Mannor	
	Hazzard	
Robert Dawson	Larremores Neck & Add.	7
Sarah Dawson	Dawson's Compasion	5
Ann Dixon	Collingham	—
John Dixon	Carters Plains	3
	pt. Neglect	
William Dixon	pt. Controversy	11
	Ashby	
John Dorgin	3 lotts in St. Michels Town with one Smith's Shop	—
John Dougherty	Barracks Discovery	
	Carters Farm	
John Dougherty for Wm. Ratcliff	Jacob & John's Pasture Poplar Level	—
James Earle Downey	Ashby	7
	Sheephead Point	
	Bodfields Endeavor	
Joseph Downy	Wisbitch	3
	Maybot	
Richard Downy	Yaffords Neck	7
Edward Elliott	Elliotts Purchase Escheated formerly called Macamher & Glover	7
Thomas Esgate	Hopkins Point & Add.	9
	pt. Partnership	
	pt. Haphazzard	
David Fairbanks	Good Hope	12
	Fairley	
	Fairbanks Chance	

1783 TAX LIST OF TALBOT COUNTY, MARYLAND
Bay & Mill Hundreds

Name	Tract Name	# of White Inhabitants
Elizabeth Fairbanks	pt. Belfast	—
	Fairley	
	Fairbanks Chance	
Fileman Fairbanks	Camper Neck	4
	Fairbanks Chance	
Isaac Faulkner	name unknown	7
Levy Faulkner	Neighbors Keep Out	8
	Faulkner's Folly	
Ann Fideman	Fideman's Discovery	4
George Foreson	Foreson	—
Howes Goldsborough Esq.	pt. St. Michaels Freshrun	7
	pt. The Gore	
	Newman's Thicket	
	Good Chance	
	pt. Carters Forest	
	pt. Carters Rose	
Mrs. MaryAnn Goldsborough-	Ashby	5
(for life)	Chance	
	Peters Rest	
	Fox Harbour	
	Newmans	
Robert Goldsborough Esq.	Bantry	6
	pt. Ashby	
	pt. Preserue	
William Goldsborough Esq.	pt. St. Michaels	—
	pt. The Forrest & Add.	
	pt. Cottingham	
	Newmans	
	Atkinsons Chance	
Thomas Groves	6 lotts in St. Michaels Town	3
John Haddaway	Fishburn Landing	4
Oakley Haddaway	pt. Miles End	5
Robert Haddaway	Harrisons Security	6
William Haddaway	Bartram	6
	pt. Luskey Haddaways Add.	
William W. Haddaway	pt. Haddaways Lott	3
	pt. Grafton Mannor	
Phil Hambleton	pt. Mt. Missory	7
	pt. Hurtlebury Garden	
	pt. Middle Neck	
	pt. Sherwoods Island	

1783 TAX LIST OF TALBOT COUNTY, MARYLAND
Bay & Mill Hundreds

Name	Tract Name	# of white inhabitants
Capt. William Hambleton	Newport Glassgow	10
	Martingham	
	Cambridge	
	Hambletons Addition	
William Hambleton	Milestone	6
Joseph Harrington	Harringtons Delight	4
	Adventure	
	pt. James Rogross	
Mary Harrington	Hatton Garden	5
	Point Lookout	
Francis Harrison	pt. Onions Range	7
James Harrison	pt. Sparowes Point	8
	Haphazzard	
	Foresoil	
	Poplar Neck	
Joseph Harrison	Mt. Missory	12
	pt. Crooked Intention	
Thomas Harrison, Assessor 1st. District	pt. Crooked Intention	5
	pt. Taylor & James' Discovery	
	Chance	
	Elliotts Lott	
	Elliotts Folly	
Thomas Harrison Jr.	name unknown	5
William Harrison	2 lotts in St. Michaels Town	4
John Harriss	pt. Ashford	8
	Long Neglect	
William Hart	Braintree	4
Ann Harwood	pt. of Addition	2
Mary Harwood	pt. of Addition	4
	Ratcliff	
William Hindman Esq	Harrington	4
	Kirkhoun	
Henry Hollyday Esq.	Ratcliff Mannor	13
	pt. Tilghmans Fortune	
	pt. Discovery	
	Turkey Park	
William Hooper	pt. Yaffords Neck	—
	Prosecution Meadows?	
	Glade & Addition to Glade	
	Comple Close Add.	
	Stamfords Folly & Hermitage	

1783 TAX LIST OF TALBOT COUNTY, MARYLAND
Bay & Mill Hundreds

Name	Tract Name	# of white inhabitants
William Ennalls Hooper	Mowand Gaskit Watson Watsons Addition	—
Francis Hopkins	Hopkins Point	8
Joseph Hopkins	pt. Ray's Point Snellings Delight Edward Hopewell Benson's Enlargement Skinners Discovery	8
Joseph Hopkins Jr.	pt. Hopkins Point	4
Richard Hopkins	pt. Hopkins Point	7
Susanna Hopkins widow of Thomas	Ray's Point pt. Adventure pt. Skinners Discovery	5
James Hughes	name unknown	5
John Hunt	Larramores Addition	7
Peter Hunt	Content Divinest Andrew	4
Benjamin Kemp	Wolf Harbour Boston Addition pt. Blaton Miles End	12
John Kemp	pt. Blaton	8
Magdalene Kemp	pt. Blaton	—
Thomas Kemp	Benson's Enlarged	9
James Kennady	name unknown	7
Anthony Kerby	Swamphole	12
John Kersey	Wobbley Sarocks Neck pt. Miles End pt. Fishburn's Landing	7
Blanch Lacompt	pt. Cumberland	3
Daniel Lambdin	Sandy Lott Bridges	8
Robert Lambdin	Summerton Winterton Wm. & Mary's Addition pt. Grafton Mannor	10
Wrightson Lambdin	Turkey pt. Onions Range Roberts Addition pt. Frittes Neck	8

1783 TAX LIST OF TALBOT COUNTY, MARYLAND
Bay & Mill Hundreds

Name	Tract Name	# of White inhabitants
John Leeds Esq.	Wade Point	1
	Haddon	
	Onions Range	
James Leonard	pt. Hopkins Point	8
	pt. William & James	
	pt. Partnership	
John Leonard	pt. Partnership	7
	pt. William & James	
Edward Lloyd Esq.	pt. Lawstock	5
James Lowe	Grafton Mannor	8
	Piney Neck	
	pt. Ratcliff	
Rachel Lowe	Addition	5
James Lowrey	Lawstock	10
Mary Lusby or Lurty (for life)	Old Women's Folley	—
John McDaniel	Fishburn's Lott	7
Patrick McQuay	Divine St. Andrew	5
	Paradice	
	Bampshire	
Foster Maynard	pt. Yaffords Neck	7
Francis Morling	Braintree & Addition	3
	Morlings Chance	
	Spring Close	
	Morlings Neglect	
James Morsoll	pt. Turkey	4
	Wrightsons Addition	
John Nesmith	Harden's Endeavor	7
	pt. Ashby	
Robert Newcomb	Robt. & Mary Resurveyed formerly called Harbour Rouse	7
	pt. William & James	
Henry Nichols Esq.	Maiden Point & Addition	—
	Weather Range	
Andrew Orem	pt. Elam	—
Hugh Orem	pt. Elams Addition	7
	pt. Fox Harbour	
	pt. Fox Hold	
	pt. Fox Den	
	___ Wasteland	
	pt. Ashford	

1783 TAX LIST OF TALBOT COUNTY, MARYLAND
Bay & Mill Hundreds

Name	Tract Name	# of white inhabitants
Rachel Orem	pt. Foxhold & Waterford	8
George Porter	Wellers Good Luck	
John Porter	pt. Friths Neck	12
Jonathan Porter	pt. Hopkins Point	6
Joseph Porter	Hamersby	8
John Potts for James Ratcliff-Jacob & John's Pasture		
Robert Richardson	pt. Boach ?	7
	Elliotts Lott	
	Davenport	
Thomas Richardson	name unknown	4
William Ridgway	pt. Westland	3
Janathan Rigby	Maxwell Moore	10
	pt. William & James	
	James Lookout	
	Partnership	
Philemon Rigby	Foxhole	3
	Crawford	
	Rigby's Folley	
	Anderby & Addition	
Thomas Rigby	Lamberton	5
	Rigby's Choice	
John Roaugh	pt. Grafton Mannor	8
Parthona Robson	pt. Partnership	5
John Rolle Esq.	Rolles Range	8
	Hooper Ensoll	
	Dorothy's Enlarement	
Robert Rolle	Robins Neck	4
	Sandy Bite	
	Hall's Fortune	
	pt. Grafton Mannor	
John Ross	Benson's Enlargement	
	Skinners Lott	
	Benson's Chance	
Benjamin Sands	pt. Sand's Lott	
	Chance Enlarged	
Mark Sewell	Bellfast	7
John Shanahan	Benson's Enlargement	8
	Sarah's Garden	
	Chance	
Nicholas Sherwood	Neglect	8

1783 TAX LIST OF TALBOT COUNTY, MARYLAND
Bay & Mill Hundred

Name	Tract Name	# of white inhabitants
Thomas Sherwood Esq.	Daniel & Mary Resurvey	4
	Cabbin Neck	
	Potters Lott	
	Potters Delight	
John Skinner	pt. Hopkins Point	8
Mordukey(Mordecai)Skinner	pt. Yafford Neck	3
Phil Skinner	Skinners Point	12
	Englargement	
	Skinners Addition	
	Skinners Discovery	
Thomas Smith	pt. Grafton Mannor	9
Jonathan Spencer	2 lotts in St. Michaels Town	___
Mary Spencer	pt. Onion's Range	___
Perry Spencer	Matthew Circumvented	6
	Edward Hopewell	
Philemon Spencer	pt. Fairplay	9
	pt. Mainsail	
Christopher Spry	Maxwell More	___
Charles Stewart	Long Neck	4
	Long Point	
	pt. Benjamin's Lott	
Mabel Tennant	Matthew Circumvented	4
Philemon Thomas	Claybourns Island	___
William Thomas	Cottingham	8
John Thompson	2 lotts in St. Michaels Town	3
	pt. Bentlehay James Progress	
	pt. Chance	
	pt. James Progress	
	pt. Parsley Neck	
	pt. Beach Elliotts Lott	
	pt. Elliotts Folley	
Thomas Tibbles	Tibbles Addition	4
	Sheepshead Point	
James Tilghman Esq.	Fausley? Edmonds Range	2
	Sharp	
	Chance	
	Dixons	
	Faulsey Meadow	
	Bryons Lott	
	Carters Plains, Range & Forest	
Lloyd Tilghman	Sherwoods Neck	___

1783 TAX LIST OF TALBOT COUNTY, MARYLAND
Bay & Mill Hundreds

Name	Tract Name	# of white inhabitants
Matthew Tilghman Esq.	Rich Neck & Addition	9
	Coopers Lot	
	Bradford Resurveyed	
	Union & Wells	
	Three Necks	
	Mabel & Addition	
	pt. Lawstock	
	pt. Elliotts Lott	
	pt. Elliotts Folley	
	Aulds Security	
	Davenport	
	Auk Lott	
Thomas Townsend	pt. Bensons Enlargement	
Ann Trippe	Cudlington	—
Edward Trippe	Hurtlebury Garden	—
John Valliant	pt. Cumberland	6
Garey Warner	pt. Carters Farm	
William Watts	Rigby's Discovery	12
Thomas Wayman	Ankdown?	12
Joshua Wilkinson	pt. Stephens? Point	3
Sarah Wrightson	Clay Neck	7
	pt. Onions Range	
	Jurdins Folly	

A List of People in Bay and Mill Hundreds not owning land.

Name	# of white inhabitants	Name	# of white inhabitants
Thomas Aldredge	—	Aaron Atkinson	10
George Applegarth	5	Joseph Atkinson	5
George Applegarth	6	Rebecca Aulderson	3
Robert Applegarth	8	James Austin	4
Thomas Applegarth	3	John Austin	8
William Applegarth	3	Thomas Austin	5
Francis Armstrong	8	John Ball	
David Auld	5	William Ball	5
Hugh Auld	2	William Barney	10
Philemon Auld	11	Samuel Barrow	
Samuel Auld	4	John Barwick	4
Sarah Auld	6	Richard Batsey	5
Thomas Auld	2	James Benny	6

1783 TAX LIST OF TALBOT COUNTY, MARYLAND

Name	# of white inhabitants	Name	# of white inhabitants
John Benny	5	Thomas Faulkner	7
William Biscot	—	James Freeman (negro at Ann Dixons)	—
Edmund Blades	11	Traverse Garland	—
John Beal Bordley Esq.	—	Rachel Goldsborough	3
Thomas Brassays	10	James Gooland	3
William Bridges	7	John Gorsage	7
Abraham Bromwell	4	Charles Gossage	8
William Burgess	2	Robert Gossage	5
Gorman Cade	6	James Grace	7
Duncan Cambell	4	Jane Grace	8
Thomas Camper	8	Mary Grace	7
William Camper	7	William Grace	9
Francis Cardiff	4	Thomas Greenhawk	3
James Carroll	7	Daniel Haddoway	—
Isaac Chambers	13	James Haddaway	6
Jonathan Closly	3	Mary Haddaway (widow)	6
Jonathan Coburn	4	Robert Haddaway	6
Solomon Coburn	8	Thomas Haddaway	7
Carter Cockayne	3	William Hambleton 3rd	3
Aliso Coleston	—	Joseph Harrington	4
James Collinson	10	Mary Harrington	5
John Cooper	6	Edward Harris	12
James Coudon	7	James Harris	5
William Coudon	6	Risdon Harris	3
Richard Covey	7	Benjamin Harrison	7
James Cray	5	James Harrison of James	3
John Crier	6	James Harrison Jr.	7
Charles Crookshanks	—	Joseph Harrison	8
Elizabeth Cummins	5	Joseph Harrison Jr.	7
Henry Davis	10	Joseph Harrison for Senoritia Reid	—
Hugh Dawson	5	Robert Harrison	6
Margaret Dawson	—	Solomon Harrison	3
Nicholas Dawson	5	Thomas Harrison Jr.	5
Thomas Dodson	8	William Harrison	7
Joseph Downey of James	6	Elizabeth Harwood	—
Joseph Downey Jr.	5	Rachel Harwood	3
Elijah Duling	10	Rizdon Harwood	4
Joseph Duling	3	Robert Harwood	—
John Durgan	6	Thomas Harwood	4
John Eaton	8	James Hindman Esq.	—
Daniel Fairbanks	4	William Hindman Esq.	4
James Fairbanks	7		
Philomon Fairbanks	4		

1783 TAX LIST OF TALBOT COUNTY, MARYLAND

Name	# of white inhabitants	Name	# of white inhabitants
John Hobbs	4	John Leddenham	4
Henry Hollyday	13	Nathaniel Leddenham	7
Thomas Honey ?	5	John Leonard	3
James Hook	3	John Caulk Leonard	6
William Ennalls Hooper	—	Jonathan Leonard	6
Downey Hopkins	—	William Level	6
Joseph Hopkins	8	James Lowrey	10
Lambeth Hopkins	7	John Lowry	3
Mary Hopkins	4	Joseph Lowry	10
Robert Hopkins	3	Robert Lowrey	3
Susannah Hopkins	5	Archibald McNeal	9
Wm. Hopkins by M. Harwood	5	Richard Mansfield	9
William Hopper	—	Arthur Marshall	7
James Hawbanks	4	Joseph Marshall	5
James Hughes	5	Meredith Marshall	5
George Hunt	4	Richard Marshall	5
James Hunt	2	Eleanor Massey	
John Hunt	—	David Matthews	4
Joseph Hunt	2	Rebecca Matthews	5
Peter Hunt of John	4	Thomas Matthews	8
Peter Hunt of Peter	8	William Matthews	7
Samuel Hunt	3	William Melward	4
Elijah Jackson	5	Thomas Nash	11
George Jefferson	11	Samuel Neighbours	8
Thomas Jefferson	5	Samuel Neighbours Jr.	8
Robert Jones	6	Thomas Neighbours	10
Jacob Keithly	5	John Norwood	3
James Keithly	5	Thomas Ogden	7
Lydia Kemp	10	Nicholas Orem	
Ebenezer Kennard	7	William Orem	8
James Kerby	5	William Parrish	5
Thomas Keys	4	William Pearsay	3
Thomas King	2	William Pearson	8
Lambert Kirby	3	Ann Perkins	4
Daniel Lambdin of Wm.	4	John Plummer	12
Robert Lambden	4	Daniel Richardson	9
Robert Lambden Jr.	4	Henry Richardson	9
Alexander Larramore	6	Peter Richardson	16
John Larramore	—	Moses Rigby	7
Jonathan Larramore	5	Aaron Ringrose	2
Massey Larremore	6	John Robinson	4
Edward Leddenham	4	Lambert Robinson	—

1783 TAX LIST OF TALBOT COUNTY, MARYLAND

Name	# of white inhabitant	Name	# of white inhabitants
Thomas Robinson	6	Elisha Stewart	8
Andrew Robson	8	John Stocker	5
Thomas Robson	5	Elijah Stoker	5
Robert Sands	5	John Swan	6
Thomas Sands	6	John Sweatman	2
William Sears	10	Rachel Tar	5
Basil Sewell	10	William Thomas	8
Diana Sewell	7	Henry Tibbles	5
Henry Seymore	10	John Tibbles	11
Joseph Seymore	7	Ephraim Quik Trippe	—
Charles Sherwood	8	Edward Turner	2
Philip Sherwood	8	Charles Vickers	8
William Sherwood	9	Samuel Vinton	6
Alexander Sinclear	10	Edmund Wayman	—
A____ Smith	4	Frances Wayman	7
Archibald Smith	5	William Weaver	7
Elisha Smith	8	Esther Welch	4
Mary Smith	2	William West	12
Jonathan Spencer	10	Sarah Weston	5
John Spry	1	John Willowby	7
Richard Stanfield	6	Robert Winterbottom	6
		Jonathan Winters	7
		Alice Worlds	5

A LIST OF SINGLE MEN AND THEIR SECURITIES IN BAY AND MILL HUNDREDS.

Single Men	Security
Thomas Aldredge Jr.	Hugh Auld
Robert Applegarth Jr.	Robert Applegarth Jr.
Solomon Atkinson	John Tibbles
David Auld Jr.	
Thomas Ball Jr.	Thomas Ball
William Barnes	James Barnes
David Barrow	Thomas Barrow
John Barrow	Thomas Barrow
Richard Barrow	Andrew Barrow
James Benson Jr.	Perry Benson
Thomas Blades	John Blades
John Blakoney	James Ball
Allen Brerely	Joseph Hopkins Jr.
William Bucklor	Robert Richardson

1783 TAX LIST OF TALBOT COUNTY, MARYLAND
Bay & Mill Hundred

Single Men	Security	Single Men	Security
John Camper	Richard Mansfield	Wm. Jones of Robt.	Thomas Wayman
John Carter	Phil. Auld	Wm. Jones of Benj.	Thos. Wayman
Stephen Catrup	Henry Holloday	Benjamin Kemp Jr.	Benjamin Kemp
Daniel Caulk	James Barnes	John Lambdin	Robt. Lambdin
John Caulk Jr.	Peter Caulk	Wm. Lambdin	Robt. Lambdin
James Choosly	Thomas Brassey	James Larremore	Saml. Hunt
Robert Choosly	William Catrup	Joseph Larremore	Philip Rigby
Jeremiah Coleston	Henry Coleston	James Hopkins Leonard	James Leonard
Aliso Cray	Henry Coleston	Thomas Leonard	John Leonard
James Crouch	John Nesmith	John Lowe	James Lowe
Ephraim Cummins	Eliza. Cummins	John McNulty	Thomas McNulty
James Cummins	Eliza. Cummins	Patrick McQuay Jr.	Patrick McQuay Sr.
Nicholas Cummins	Thomas Cummins	Thos. McQuay of	
Ralph Dawson Jr.	Ruth Lincicome	Catharine	Robert Haddoway
Robert Dawson	Sarah Dawson	Elijah Marshall	Rich. Marshall
William Dawson	Sarah Dawson	Joseph Norwood	James Cray
Joseph Edgar	Peter Caulk	Thos. Pearson	Robt. Richardson
Henry Elliott	John Shanahan	John Plummer Jr.	Alex. Larremore Jr.
James Flemming	John Flemming	Philemon Plummer	John Plummer
John Flemming	John Flemming	Joseph Porter Jr.	Joseph Porter
Daniel Gorsage	Joseph Harrington	Nathan Porter	James Ball
John Grace	Jane Grace	Robert Reddish	Eph. Toope(Trope)
Wm. Grace Jr.	Wm. Grace Sr.	Daniel Richardson	
John Haddaway	Thos. James Lowry	Nathan Richardson	Peter Richardson
John Haddaway	Sarah Dawson	Thos. Richardson	Peter Richardson
Peter Haddaway	Thos. Haddaway	John Scott	Peter Caulk
John Hall	Benj. Thomas	James Sears	
Jonathan Harris	John Harris	Joseph Sewell	Thomas Robson
John Harrison	Solomon Harrison	Thomas Sewell	Diana Spencer
Jonathan Harrison	Thos. Harrison	William Sewell	Foster Maynard
Joseph Harrison	Joseph Harrison	John Seymore	John Colston
Robert Harrison	Solomon Harrison	Matthew Shaw	John Dougharty
Wm. Harrison	J___Harrison	Wm. Shaw	John Dougharty
John He___	Wm. Haddaway	Alex. Sinclair Jr.	Alexander Sinclair
John Hewey	Wm. Pearson	Jonathan Sinclair	
John Hewey Jr.		Wm. Sinclair	Alex. Sinclair
Thomas Hollyday	Henry Hollyday Esq.	Jonathan Small	Isaac Faulkner
Hugh Hopkins	Thos. Harrison Jr.	Henry Snelling	Gorman Cade
James Hopkins	Henry Banning	Marmaduke Spencer	Phil Spencer
Joseph Hopkins	Thos. Harrison	Rich. Spencer	Perry Spencer
James Jones of John		Francis Spry	
John Jones		James Thompson	Isaac Chambers
Robert Jones of Benj.		Geo. Townsend	Thos. Townsend

1783 TAX LIST OF TALBOT COUNTY, MARYLAND
Bay & Mill Hundreds

Single Men	Security	Single Men	Security
Thos. Townsend Jr.	Perry Benson	Griffin Williams	
Hugh Watts	Wm. Watts	John Winterbottom Jr.	Will Mason
John Weaver	Lydia Kemp	Thos. Winterbottom	Daniel Bridget
Benjamin West	William West		

A list of all persons whose property does not amount to ten pounds and the number of white inhabitants in the family. Bay and Mill Hundreds.

Name	# of white inhabitants	Name	# of white inhabitants
Ann Austin	3	Alex Larremore	4
Edittown Barwood	4	Catharine Larremore	6
Peter Brown	4	Richard Linsmore	6
James Burk	6	John Liddle	4
Ann Coburn	4	John McNulty	3
Anna Coburn	3	Anthony Mahony	7
Peter Cole	4	William Mason	3
Sambest Condon	4	Lewis Matthews	6
Henry Connolly	5	Richard Miller	5
Benjamin Crisp	3	Rachel Pickering	6
Rebecca Crisp	4	Elizabeth Porter	5
Mary Cummins	5	James Porter	4
Edward Davis	6	John Hughs Porter	7
Alice Dawson	3	Joseph Riddish	5
Henry Dorrit	7	James Rimmer	6
Catharine Edgar	4	John Seymore	4
Rebecca Eubanks	4	William Shields	4
Rhoda Fairbanks	3	Sarah Snelling	3
John Greenaugh	4	Ralph Smith	4
William Haddaway	7	Moses Stains	8
James Harrison	9	Mary Stokes	3
William Harrison	8	Rebecca Suitor	4
William Hopkins	5	James Swan	6
John Horney	6	Jonathan Tar	4
Martha Hull	2	Jane Umbey	2
Rachel Jackson	3	Jonathan Valliant	3
Thomas Job	3	William Valliant	7
Saeah Kemp	5	Solomon Vinton	6
Thomas Kilmore	5	Elizabeth Wells	5
Mary Lancashire	2	John Winterbottom	2

1783 TAX LIST OF TALBOTT COUNTY, MARYLAND

District II including the Hundreds of Island, Tuckahoe and Kings Creek; taken by Joseph Bentley, assessor.

Owner	Tract Name	# of acres	# of white inhabitants
Charles Allen	name unknown	60	6
Moses Allen	Gatterby Moore	206 1/2	
Anthony Banning	pt. Daniels Rest	108	—
	pt. Walker's Tooth		—
Francis Baker	Bite the Biter	35	10
	Bakers Pasture	34	
	Skipton	300	
	Finneys Hermitage	236	
James Baker for Berwick heirs	Bibb	63	4
	name unknown		
James Barnwell	pt. Mill land	22	12
	pt. Oxford	308	
	pt. Rich Farm	50	
Mary Barnwell	pt. Bedworth	150	6
	Dixons Lott	30	
	Barnwell's Addition	66	
	pt. Hatten Hope	77	
	pt. Mt. Hope	77	
	pt. Oxford	30	
	Rich Farm Addition	70	
	pt. Partnership	42	
Benjamin Benny	pt. Benny's Resurvey		10
	pt. Benny's Addition		
	pt. Rumsey Forest		
	pt. Benny's Thicket		
	pt. Morgan's Addition		
	Misfortune		
	pt. Morgan's Neglect	619	
James Benson	pt. Fishing Bay		13
	pt. Huntington Range		
	pt. Huntingtons Mistake		
	pt. Neglect	373 1/2	
Joseph Berry	pt. White Marshes	190	9
George Berwick	pt. Stevens Plains	50	2
	pt. Christophers Lott	100	
Wm. Berwick for Vickers heirs	pt. Adventure	61 3/4	10
	pt. Fork	133 1/3	
James Bell	pt. Rock Clift	110 1/2	7
George Beswick	pt. Stevens Plains	150	2

1783 TAX LIST OF TALBOT COUNTY, MARYLAND
Island, Tuckahoe & Kings Creek Hundreds

Name	Tract Name	# of acres	# of white inhabitants
William Blake	Huntington Range & Fishing Bay	4	10
	pt. Benney's Resurvey	4	
William Blake for Young heirs	Carslakes Content & pt. Bartram	165 1/2	8
Anthony Booth	pt. Bloomsberry	50	4
Sarah Booth	pt. Bloomsberry	50	6
William Bordley	Loyds Gift	136	
	Lloyds Kindness	332	
	Norington	767	
	pt. Stevens Plains	50	
Samuel Bowman	pt. Johns Neck	350	2
	pt. Middle Spring	41 3/4	
	pt. Williams Lott	40	
Broadaways heirs	Sams Fields	102	—
	Rama Resurveyed	128	
	Broadaway Meadows	85	
	Straw Bridge	40	
John Bracco, Esq.	pt. Batchelors Branch	73 1/2	7
	Bennetts Neglect	18	
	Thief Keep Out	40	
	Triangle	18	
	Halls Range	148	
	pt. Partnership	10	
	pt. Limerick	8	
	Youngs Neglect	40	
Burgess heirs	pt. Beaver Neck	241	—
Sarah Burk for Stainers heirs	pt. Widows Chance	76	—
	Discovery	77 1/2	
John Catrop	pt. Mt. Hope	86	4
Ruth Catrop	pt. Mt. Hope	84 1/4	
Wm. Marsh Catrup	Adams Hazzard	45 1/2	—
James Lloyd Chamberlaine for Thomas Chamberlaine	pt. Chesnut Bay	561	
Saml. Chamberlaine	Conjunction & The Hazzard	427 1/3	—
Daniel Christian	Matthews Chance	121	6
Edward Clark's heirs	pt. Parkers Farm		—
	pt. Parrotts Lott		
	Parkers Farm Addition	374	

-51-

1783 TAX LIST OF TALBOT COUNTY, MARYLAND
Island, Tuckahoe, Kings Creek Hundreds

Name	Tract Name	# of acres	# of white inhabitant
Joshua Clark	Saloup	167	11
	pt. Hampton & Parkers Range	120	
Joshua Clark's heirs	Clark's Folly	101	
	pt. Johns Neck	118	—
John Clayland	Turners Discovery	30	
	Wold Pit Ridge	50	—
John Cockran	Tilberry	376	3
	pt. Coventry	100	
Nathaniel Cooper	Dudley's Choice	100	2
	pt. Hampton	50	
	pt. Rich Range	100	
	pt. Strawbridge	61	
Charles Crookshanks	Fentry	156	
	Lotts Corner & Long Point	—	—
Dardens heirs	Blessland	100	
Da	Dardons Serops	12 1/2	—
	pt. Turkey Neck	116	
	pt. Kingsbury	130	
	Kings Creek Addition & Marsh	90	
Mary Dawson	pt. Johns Hill	30	5
William Dawson	Huntington & Huntingtons Add.		9
	& pt. Neglect	318 3/4	
John Dickenson	pt. Addition	31	
	pt. Buckingham & Kelding	196 1/2	—
	pt. Hambletons Park	131 1/2	
Samuel Dickenson	pt. Mt. Hope	369 (Darlington)	
Isaac Dobson for	Beaver Dam Neck	71	10
Garey's heirs	pt. Elizabeths Enlargement	8 1/2	
	pt. Partnership Hazard	127	
	Strawberry Fields	100	
Mable Dobson	pt. Fork	66 2/3	
Catherine Dudley	pt. Advantage	18	8
	pt. Beaver Neck	100	
John Elbert	pt. Grantham &		
	pt. Lloyd Costin	291	—
Edward Eubanks	pt. Hatton Hope	163	
	pt. Mt. Hope	35	—
Jonathan Faulkner for	pt. Buckley	233	6
Thos. Cumerford heirs			
Faulkners heirs	pt. Chesnut Bay	100	
John Fauntleroy	Smiths Clifts	491	6
	pt. Dudley's Clifts	50	
	Harrow Green	5	

1783 TAX LIST OF TALBOT COUNTY, MARYLAND
Island, Tuckahoe, & Kings Creek Hundreds

Name	Tract Name	# of acres	# of white inhabitants
John Fauntleroy(cont.)	House Point	21	
John Ferns for John Goldsborough	Kennadays Hazard & Add.	52	—
Eleanor Fitzpatrick	Dirty Weeden & pt. Triangle	52	3
Rigbey Foster	pt. Advantage	50 3/4	7
John Fountleroy	pt. Chesnut Bay	234	—
Joseph Frampton	pt. Framptons Beginning	40	7
Robert Frampton	pt. Framptons Beginning & Forrest & Dyke	34	4
Thomas Frampton	Collins Pasture	50	8
	Framptons Chance	34 3/4	
	Lovedays Purchase	15 1/4	
Henry Garey	Dudley's Inclosure & pt. Highfield	136 1/2	10
Jonathan Garey	pt. Partnership Hazard & pt. Beaver Dam Neck	140	—
William Garey	pt. Advantage	500	7
Jeremiah Garland	Dundee	133 1/3	5
Joseph George for Berry's heirs	pt. White Marshes Mill land	190 30	—
Jacob Gibson	Gibson's Addition	9 1/2	4
	pt. Nobles Meadows	207	
Jacob Gibson's heirs	pt. Champingham & Bendon pt. Edmonton pt. Leith pt. Todd Upon Dewin	267 1/2	—
John Gibson	pt. Lloyd Costin (with spinning house) pt. Rebeccas Garden	260 6	5
John Gibson 3rd for Millers heirs	pt. Planters Delight pt. Hambletons Park	35 137	—
Jonathan Gibson	Edmonton Champingham & Bendon & Add. pt. Leith Todd Upon Dewin	270 1/2	7
Woolman Gibson	pt. Champenham Addition Champenham & Bendon pt. Edmonton pt. Leith pt. Todd Upon Dewin	71	4
Woolman Gibson Jr.	pt. Lloyd Costin pt. Rebeccas Garden	56 144	4

1783 TAX LIST OF TALBOT COUNTY, MARYLAND
Island, Tuckahoe, & Kings Creek Hundreds

Name	Tract Name	# of acres	# of white inhabitants
John Goldsborough	pt. Advantage	100	—
	Chamber's Adventure	118 3/4	
	Goldsborough's Triangle	45	
John Goldsborough's heirs	pt. Somerly		—
	pt. Warwick	347	
	Four Square	520	
Mary Ann Goldsborough	Rich Range	232 1/3	—
Robert Goldsborough	pt. Hambletons Park	131 1/2	—
	pt. Addition	31 1/2	
	pt. Widows Chance	60	
	pt. Buckingham & Kelding	196 1/2	
John Gordon	Timber Neck Point	60	—
	Walkers Tooth & Corner	140	
Rev. John Gordon	Doctor's Gift &		2
	Daniels Rest	112	
	pt. Partnership	96	
	pt. Addition	50	
Samuel Gore	pt. Dunsmore Heath	100	2
	Frampton	122	
Walker Gore	pt. Dunsmore Heath	100	3
Richard Greenhawk	pt. Buckley	200	6
James Gregory	pt. Turners Chance	50	8
John Gregory	Gregorys Outlet	16 1/2	13
	Poplar Level	116	
William Gregory	pt. Turners Chance	50	7
John Hall for Carslakes heirs	Newnams Lott & Nobles Chance	129	11
Robert Hall for Millers heirs	pt. Planters Delight	62 3/4	—
Joseph Hartley	pt. Hopewell		7
	pt. Batchelors Hope		
	pt. Bartram		
	pt. Kennemonts Delight		
	Beaver Dam Neck	300	
William Hayward	pt. Smiths Clifts	146 1/4	—
Miss Ann Maria Hemsley	Hemsley on Wye	1306	2
Hemsley & Kinnard	pt. Wilton	70	—
Giles Hicks	pt. Somerly	50	4
Margrett Higgs	Pottingham	100	—
	Skinners Swineyard & Skaggs Springs	233	—
Robert Hill or Hall & Millers heirs	pt. Addition	75	—

1783 TAX LIST OF TALBOT COUNTY, MARYLAND
Island, Tuckahoe & Kings Creek Hundreds

Name	Tract Name	# of acres	# of white inhabitants
Ann Hindman	pt. Addition	229	—
	Jordans Hill	157	
	Upper Range	56	
Henry Holliday	Hemsley's Brittania	113	—
Jonathan Hopkins	Garey's Beginning	12 1/2	4
Jackson heirs	Finneys Range	226	—
	pt. Weterton	170	
James Jackson	Stafford Moor	80	—
Robert Jadwin	pt. Parkers Range	118	9
Richard Johns	pt. Parkers Park	250	6
Mary Johnson	pt. Rich Farm	380	5
	pt. White Marshes	380	
John Keets for			
Callahans heirs	pt. Britanna	100	9
Alice Kemp	Nobles Addition	207	5
	pt. Finneys Hermitage	66	
Parrott Kerby	Dunns Range	100	7
Ann Kirby	Kirbys Venture &		7
	Kirbys Outlook	53 1/2	
David Kirby	Jacobs Beginning	50	2
David Kirby Jr.	Kirby's Interest		8
	Kimrick		
	Turners Range	130	
Michael Kirby	Kirbys Addition	154	7
Michael Kirby Jr.	pt. Buck Range	99 1/2	4
Richard Kirby	Kirbys Venture	123	4
Robert Kirby	pt. Parkers Range	70	9
Rachel Lane for	Fields Inheritance	219	5
William Dunning			
Anna Maria Lloyd	Partnership	1200	—
Col. Edward Lloyd	Addition	350	—
	Addition	50	
	pt. Addition	150	
	Addition survey for Hawkins	100	
	Bettys Branch	325	
	Bettys Dowrey	75	
	Bennetts Kind Caution	323	
	Bennetts Lloyd	384	
	Batcheloir Point	100	
	Brasserton	100	
	Bennetts Point	54	
	Bodwells Indian Neck	913	

1783 TAX LIST OF TALBOT COUNTY, MARYLAND
Island, Tuckahoe & Kings Creek Hundreds

Name	Tract Name	# of acres	# of white inhabitants
Col. Edward Lloyd (continued)	Crouches Choice	214	—
	Carslakes Content	60	
	Carters Inheritance	40	
	Dirty Weeden	100	
	pt. Dundee	133 1/3	
	Dudley's Lott	50	
	Faulkner's Folly	100	
	Fortunes Addition	52	
	Fortune	150	
	Grunny	400	
	Grange	150	
	Garey's Delight	50	
	Garey's Securtiy	124	
	Grasons Discovery	106 1/2	
	Henrietta Marias Discovery	216	
	Holm Hill	62	
	Hope Chance	50	
	pt. Kings Forrest	75	
	Knightly Addition	50	
	pt. Kings Plains	79	
	Knave Keep Out	50	
	Kings Neglect	111 1/2	
	Kings Forrest	75	
	Kings Plains	79	
	pt. Linton	600	
	Long Neglect	133	
	Lloyds Add. to Braerly	380	
	Lloyds Add. to Woolman	119	
	Lloyds Lott	141	
	Lloyds Park	946	
	Meirigate	300	
	Meirigate Addition	267	
	Mojety Addition	100	
	Marion	130	
	Morgan St. Michael	300	
	Nathans Point	50	
	Outlett	220	
	Personage	100	
	pt. Personage Addition	50	
	Roberts Infancy	65	
	Roadway	50	

1783 TAX LIST OF TALBOT COUNTY, MARYLAND
Island, Tuckahoe & Kings Creek Hundreds

Name	Tract Name	# of acres	# of white inhabitants
Col. Edward Lloyd (continued)	Satters Marsh	100	
	Scotts Close	200	
	Soldiers Delight	100	
	Sweatnams Hope	120	
	Smiths Clifts Point	258	
	Sarahs Lott	50	
	Todd Upon Dewin	80	
	Thumley Grange	500	
	Town Road	50	
	Timber Neck	160	
	Tanners Hope	50	
	Triangle	55	
	Woolmans Hermitage	55	
	Woolmans Inheritance	310	
	Woolmans Hermitage	109	
Richard Bennett Lloyd	Improvements	323	—
Lovedays heirs	pt. Middle Spring	160	—
	pt. Johns Neck	350	
Thomas Loveday	pt. Middle Pt. Swinyard & Lovedays Discovery	217	—
Sarah Lowther	Elizabeths Enlargement	39 1/4	6
	Forrest & Dykes	116 1/4	
Thomas Martin	pt. Parkers Park	250	—
Thomas Martin Jr.	pt. Johns Hill	15	8
Elizabeth Maxwell	Stevensons Purchase	882	
	Whetstone	150	
William McCallum for Thomas Loveday	Lovedays Marsh	66	5
Mary McKinnis	pt. Neglect	35 2/3	3
Millers heirs	Stevens Lott	35 2/3	
	Nobles Chance & Newnams Lott	200 1/2	
Milltonton heirs	Epsom	100	—
Thomas Morgan	pt. Morgans Neglect	98 1/2	3
	pt. Rumsey Forrest	40	
William Morgan	pt. Chestnut Bay & pt. Dudley's Clifts		7
Francis Morling	pt. Widows Chance	320	—
Needles heirs	pt. Kellum	201	4
Edward Needles	Needles Adventure & pt. Rock Clifts	220	

-57-

1783 TAX LIST OF TALBOT COUNTY, MARYLAND
Island, Tuckahoe & Kings Creek Hundreds

Name	Tract Name	# of acres	# of white inhabitants
John Needles	pt. Rock Clift & pt. Kellum	150	
Tristram Needles	pt Broad Lane	50	6̄
	pt. Kellum	50	
	pt. Highfield	50	
Henry Nichols	Long Acre	150	
	Thorps Chance	79	
Nehemiah Noble	Lambert & Britanna	71 1/2	
Phillip Norris	Kirbys Adventure	98	5̄
Andrew Oram Sr.	Francis' Delight	106	8
Andrew Oram for Vickers heirs	Rich Range & pt. Hampton	218	—
	Richards Necessity & Rich. Triangle	27	
Rebecca Oxenham	Moorfields	282	2
John Ozment	pt. Neglect	72	
Thomas Ozment for Dudley's heirs	pt. Kingston	47	8̄
	Dudley's Addition	154	
Isaac Palmer	pt. Dunns Range	100	10
	Moorfields Addition	40	
Aaron Parriott	pt. Johns Neck	25 3/4	8
	pt. Kingston	185	
Mary Parriott	pt. Johns Neck	25 3/4	6
	pt. Kingston	132	
Perry Parrott	Dobsons Advantage	28	7
	Worgans Reserve & Parrott Resurveyed	444	
Peter Parrott	pt. Francis' Plains	12	6
	pt. Rock Clifts	50	
Richard Parrott	pt. Bartram	100	7
	pt. Bartram & Carslakes Discovery-100		
	Halls Addition	12	
	Kimmemonts Delight	50	
Robert Pickering	pt. Halls Range	197	4
Ewell Plummer	pt. Austin	100	
George Plummer	pt. Austin	100	7̄
John Porter	New Begin	91 1/4	
Howell Powell Jr.	pt. Advantage	21	4̄
Howell Powell	pt. Bever Neck		
	Powells Meadows		—
	Powells Misfortune	206	
Joseph Rathel	Browns Lott	200	7

1783 TAX LIST OF TALBOT COUNTY, MARYLAND
Island, Tuckahoe & Kings Creek Hundreds

Name	Tract Name	# of acres	# of white inhabitants
Thomas Ray	Batchellors Branch Addition	61	4
	Dundee	114	
James Register	Parrots Reserve & pt. Francis' Plains	195	6
John Register	Kingsbury, Darlington & pt. Acton	108 1/4	9
Samuel Register	pt. Acton	108 1/4	6
Sam Register for for Willsons heirs	Kingsberry & Darlington pt. Middle Spring & pt. Kingsbury	177 1/4	—
John Reid	pt. Parkers Farm	130	6
	pt. Hampton	30	
Jacob Ringgold	Harrisses Range	361	—
Edward Roberts	pt. Dudley's Clifts	79	5
	pt. Robert's Purchase	200	
John Roberts	pt. Roberts Purchase	176	—,
	pt. Coventry	150	
	unpatented land	105	
Thomas Roberts	pt. Roberts Purchase	195	1
Miss Elizabeth Robins (Betsey)	pt. Rich Farm	14	—
	Holm Hill	434	
	pt. Fragment	13 1/2	
	Smith's Clifts	201	
Parrott Roe	pt. Advantage	8 1/4	5
William Rose	Arcadia	150	10
John Shannahane	pt. Hawks Hill Addition	50	—
	Fishers Hazard	18	
	Fishers Range, Contention & Stapleton	281	
Henry Sherwood	Bensted or Chamber's Add.	14	13
	Turners Lane	26	
	Cox's Hazard	103	
Hugh Sherwood of Huntington	Addition	80	—
	pt. Fishing Bay	12	
	pt. Huntington	138	
Capt. Hugh Sherwood	pt. Kellum	229	—
Andrew Skinner	pt. Tanners Choice	384 1/2	3
Richard Skinner	Tanners Choice	384 1/2	4
Richard Smith	pt. Rumsey Forrest	130 1/4	—
Sylvesters heirs	pt. Johns Neck	39	—
James Thomas	pt. Buck Range	102	5

1783 TAX LIST OF TALBOT COUNTY, MARYLAND
Island, Tuckahoe & Kings Creek Hundreds

Name	Tract Name	# of acres	# of white inhabitants
John Thomas	Mitchells Lott	77 1/2	8
	Little Britain	17	
	Benney's Resurvey	25 3/4	
	Winkleton	185	
John Thomas Jr.	pt. Mitchells Lott	122 3/4	4
	pt. Widows Chance	77 1/2	
Samuel Thomas for Hutchings heirs	Turkey Neck & Addition	270	—
	pt. Middle Spring	25	
	pt. Mill land	35	
John Thornton	Moorfields Addition	65	5
Edward & James Tilghman	Elizabeths Venture	596	—
Peregrine Tilghman	Hope	100	8
	Lloyds Discovery	96	
	Widows Chance	50	
	Michaels Discovery	100	
	Pickburne	200	
	Scotland	50	
	Talisaron	100	
	Adjunction	50	
Richard Tilghman	Henerietta Maria's Purchase	412	6
	Court Road	138	
	Chanie	100	
	Knave Stand Off	50	
Thomas Tilton	Ferrolls Branch	7	6
	pt. Hawks Hill	50	
	Catrups Security	13	
	pt. Mt. Hope	80	
William Troth	pt. Acton	294	6
	pt. Burlington & pt. Bennington	46	
Sarah Turbutt	pt. Blessland	410	6
	Boggs Marshe	100	
Edward Turner Jr.	pt. Worgans Reserve	20	8
	pt. Johns Hill	205	
John Turner	pt. Harrow Green	206	4
	pt. Smiths Clifts	198	
	pt. Johns Hill	90	
Joseph Turner	Turners Discovery	97 3/4	6
Sarah Vickers	pt. Dunns Range	64	3
	Vickers Venture	145	
	Piciadilly	209	

1783 TAX LIST OF TALBOT COUNTY, MARYLAND
Island, Tuckahoe & Kings Creek Hundreds

Name	Tract Name	# of acres	# of White inhabitants
Wallace heirs	pt. Nobles Chance	82	--
Wellington heirs	Betty's Chance	100	--
Park Webb	Highfield Addition		6
	Berry's Range & Dudley's Inclosure & Add.	260	6
William Whitby	pt. Lovedays purchase	11 1/4	3
George Williams	David's Ridge	80	4
Daniel Willson	pt. Middle Sprigg	127	4
	White Oak Swamp	100	
	pt. Williams Lott	94	
	Swineyard	25	
George Willson	Dudley's Domain	13 1/2	7
	pt. Maxwells Addition	4 1/2	
	Sibland Dudleys Chance, Maxwell Sibland & Sibland Addition	459	
Moses Yell	pt. Hampton &		7
	pt. Parkers Range	130	

A list of land owners in District II, including the Hundreds of Island, Tuckahoe and Kings Creek. This list includes the number of white inhabitants and the number of acres owned; none of this land has been named.

Name	# of acres	# white inhabitants	Name	# of acres	# white inhabitants
Lambert Booker	100	--	Nathan Kerby for Hugh Bi__e	--	6
James Burkham	54	--	Nicholas Loveday	353	4
Rebecca Burkham	112	4	William Loveday	353	6
John Chambers for Boswickes heirs	134	5	William Matthews	80	8
Mary Dudley	60 1/4	4	Jeremiah Nicols	150	--
Richard Dudley	84 3/4	9		218	
William Dudley	60 1/4	7	William Price	54	5
Robert Goldsborough Jr.	89	--	William Ratholl	54	5
Wm. Goldsborough	312	--	Thomas Roberts Jr. for Boswicks heirs	134 1/2	8
Richard Harrington	54	7	Miss Betsey Robins	200	--
James Kemp Jr.	150	8	William Shawhann	14 3/4	
John Kemp	177 1/2	1	William Warren	175	13

1783 TAX LIST OF TALBOT COUNTY, MARYLAND
Island, Tuckahoe & Kings Creek Hundreds

Name	# of white inhabitants	Name	# of white inhabitants
Isaac Anderson	5	Thomas Crail	7
William Austen	6	John Crowder	6
Thomas Banister	5	Robert Davis	6
Margaret Barnwell	—	Jesse Dobson	1
Margaret Barrow	—	George Dudley	—
John Bell	5	Robert Dwiggins	10
Mary Barnwell Jr.	—	William Edmondson	5
___Walker Benny	8	Joshua Elbert	9
William Bent	6	Patrick Ewing	—
Richard Beswicke	4	Jeremiah Fairbanks	6
John Blake	5	Aquilla Fallen	5
Peter Blake Jr.	4	Greenbury Faulkner	7
William Boils	7	Joshua Faulkner	7
Samuel Booker	—	John Fendall	7
Joseph Bowley	12	Robert Ferguson	8
James Bracco	—	John Ferus ?	4
John Bridges	6	David Fitzpatrick	6
Richard Bruff (lott)	5	John Floyd	5
Jane Burkham	1	George Foreson	—
Elizabeth Bullen	—	James Foster	5
Henry Bullen	4	Richard Frampton	5
Sarah Bullen	3	Jacob Gannon	4
James Busney (mulatto)	—	Thomas Gannon	11
Moses Butler	7	Charles Gardiner	7
Joseph Callahan	12	John Gardner	7
James Carey	2	George Garey	3
Griffin Chambers	5	Richard George	11
Martha Chance	1	Hephrebale Gild	5
Daniel Chapman	8	John Gore	5
John Chevers	5	Abell Grace	10
Arthur Clark	5	Ruben Gray	6
Robert Clogg	4	Joseph Grayham	5
Dr. John Coats	4	Richard Grayson	5
John Cockroll	7	George Hall	6
John Colbert	10	John Hardcastle	3
Robert Cole	7	Richard Harrington	4
Thomas Colner	7	Christopher Hart	10
Charles Cook	6	William Hazeldine	6
Mary Cooley	4	John Higgins	9
Nehemiah Cooper	2	William Higgins	8
John Cotner	5	Mark Hinesley	2

1783 TAX LIST OF TALBOT COUNTY, MARYLAND
Island, Tuckahoe & Kings Creek Hundreds

Name	# of white inhabitants	Name	# of white inhabitants
Christopher Hughes	7	Richard Milton	1
James Jones	7	Ross Morgan	8
McMurdy Jones	2	John Murphy	5
Robert Jones	3	John Charles Nabb	8
William Jones	7	Abner Newnam	9
James Kemp	3	David Newnam	8
James Kendrick	11	Elizabeth Nicols	4
James Kennaday	—	Jacob North	10
William Kent	5	Richard Norton	7
Benjamin Kerby	1	Thomas Nutwell	8
John Kerby Jr.	6	Edward Parkinson	7
Hopkins Kinnamont	5	Elizabeth Parrott	5
Joshua Kinnard	6	Salah Parrott	4
Philip Kinnemont	5	Sluytor Parrott	7
Daniel Kirby	5	Michael Pinkind	6
Hynson Kirby	4	George Plummer	7
William Kirby		James Plummer	13
David Lambdon	11	Solomon Plummer	8
Richard Larremore	6	Thomas Plummer	12
John Lee	4	Phileminon Porter	4
Greenwood Log	6	Thomas Porter	10
Conrad Lewis Lotherman	4	William Porter	9
William Loveday	6	John Post	6
Thomas Loverton	4	Levy Pourson	5
Morgan Lucas	7	Nathaniel Pratt	6
Ann Lundergin	5	Samuel Price	4
Dennis McCormick	5	Vincent Price Jr.	4
Josiah McGuire	6	William Price	5
William McKim	2	Wm. Price (Schoolmaster)	6
Mary McKinnis	3	William Reid	10
John McQual	7	William Reid Jr.	7
Jeremiah McQuay	2	Charles Ridgeway	—
Jeremiah McQuay Jr.	5	James Ridgway	6
William Maddree	9	John Ridgeway	8
Lewin Mansfield	2	Joseph Ridgway	5
Sarah Mansfield	7	Moses Ringrose	4
John Martin	5	Benjamin Roberts	3
James Matthews	5	Benjamin Roberts Jr.	5
John Merchant	3	Perry Roberts	5
John Merchant Jr.	8	Rebecca Roberts	—
Isaac Millington	7	Thomas Roberts Jr.	8

1783 TAX LIST OF TALBOT COUNTY, MARYLAND
Island, Tuckahoe & Kings Creek Hundreds

Name	# of white inhabitants	Name	# of white inhabitants
Thomas Roberts	8	Cornelius Taylor	4
James Robinson	6	William Taylor	6
Thomas Robinson	3	John Thomson	5
John Royals	4	Thomas Tier	3
William Sangston	6	Richard Tilghman 4th	—
James Seth	—	Henry Troth Jr.	2
Vachel Severe	5	Dr. Charles Troupe	2
Samuel Sewell	5	Samuel Turbutt	3
Jonathan Shanahan	8	James Turner	7
Abraham Sheron	6	Thomas Turner	11
Benjamin Shields	9	Sarah Vickers	3
Samuel Small	7	Jehu Warren	2
John Smith	6	Benoni Watson	10
William Start	8	Thomas Watson	6
Charles Stewart	7	George Williams	4
Thomas Stewart	9	Christopher Willson	7
William Strawhan	10	George Willson	7
James Sweat	1	James Willson (cooper)	7
Harrington Sylvester	8	Thomas Whitby	7
		John Winstanley	4
		William Winstanley	4
		Benjamin Wootors	7

A list of the free able bodied male inhabitants in District II who are subject to the fifteen shilling tax. (Single Men) Island, Tuckahoe, and Kings Creek Hundreds.

Single Men	Security	Single Men	Security
Nathan Allen	Francis Baker	Griffin Callahan	Joseph Callahan
Cloudsbury Amshir	John Gregory	Thomas Catrup	
John Beale	John Nabb	William Chapman	
Thomas Benny	Thomas Turner	Joshua Clark Jr.	Peter Parrott
James Berry Jr.		Solomon Coventon	George Plummer
Siskes Blake		Robert Cross	
William Blake		John Dawson	
John Bond (a free mulatto)		John Dixon . Jr.	
William Bonsly	Isaac Millington	John Dobson	Isaac Dobson
Nathan Boswicke	George Boswicke	Steven Frisby	Joshua Kinnard
James Bowman		James Gallahan	
Christopher Bruff		Jonathan Garey	
James Bullon		John Gibson of Woolman	
John Burgess		John Greenhawk	Samuel Sewell
Joseph Bush	James Gregory	Robert Griffin	

1783 TAX LIST OF TALBOT COUNTY, MARYLAND
Island, Tuckahoe & Kings Creek Hundreds

Single Men	Security	Single Men	Security
William Hardcastle	William Porter	Andrew Price	Rebecca Burkham
Loadman Harrington		Gilbert Price	Samuel Price
James Hazledine	Wm. Hazledine	John Ray	
Nathaniel Hopkins		David Register	
Woolman Howey		James Royals	John Royals
Manassa Kane	William Mossly	Richard Spencer	____Parrott
Alexander King		Nathan Sewell	
James Kinnard	Joshua Kinnard	John Shepperd	William Maddree
Morris Kirby	Richard Kerby	John Sherwood	Richard Dudley
Abner Krosby	Francis Baker	Philip Sherwood	
Ephraim McQuay		George Smith	
James Marchant		Richard Start	
Daniel Merrick	Henry Garey	John Vickers Thornton	
Richard Millington	Isaac Millington	William Tomlinson	Thomas Ozmont
Thomas Morgan Jr.		William Tormoint	
John Murphew Jr.	Samuel Turbutt	William Troth Jr.	
Phill Nutwell		Orson Turner	Joseph Turner
Jonathan Ozmont		William Spencer Wales	
James Parrott		Ennion Williams	
Thomas Parrott		Henry Williams	George Smith
Nathan Porter	Isaac Dobson	Isaac Williams	
		James Willson Jr.	

Brooke & Third Haven Hundreds

Samuel Abbott Jr.	Samuel Abbott	William Gore	Page Nash
James Alexander	Hannah Alexander	William Hart	Samuel Chamberlaine
John Alexander	Hannah Alexander		
Daniel Bartlett Jr.	Daniel Bartlett Sr.	Wm. Hayward Jr.	Wm. Hayward
John Birkhead	Charles Pickering Sr.	David Hill	Will Meluy
John Bind	William Bind	John Holmes Jr.	John Holmes Sr.
Joseph Bowdle	Henry Bowdle Sr.	Wm. Holsby Jr.	John Holsby Sr.
Samuel Budkley Sr.	Will Manadier	John Hopkins	Owen Troy
Joseph Carey	Henry Carey	James Hunter	Jonathan Clash
Moses Carr	Joseph Carr	John James	Henry Bowdle Jr.
Lemen John Catrup	Robert Neal	Roger Kelly	Jane Barnett
James Chaplin	Francis Chaplin	Alexander McClayland	Wm. Clark Jr.
Richard Clark	Jane Barnett	Nicholas Meads	James Dickinson Esq.
George Cook	John Stevens	Jacob Mitchell	Matthew How
John Frampton	Henry West	Saml. Mullikin Sr.	John Newman
Andrew Giles	James Delahay	Saml. Mullikin Jr.	Wm. Mullikin
Isaac Gilpin	John Dickinson	Francis Neal	Solomon Neal

1783 TAX LIST OF TALBOT COUNTY, MARYLAND
Brooke & Third Haven Hundreds

Single Men	Security	Single Men	Security
Joseph Neal	Solomon Neal	Joseph Price	Foster Price
Edward Northwood	Wm. Northwood	David Proctor	William Perry
Wm. Northwood Jr.	Wm. Northwood	Fisher Rakes	Thomas Price Sr.
James Parrott	John Pritchard	Robert Spedding	Edw. Mann Sherwood
John Parrott	Peter Webb	Richard Stub	Sarah Slack
Chas. Pickering Jr.	Chas. Pickering	Wm. Walker(carpenter)	John Reader
John Price	Thomas Price	David Williams	William Akers
		William Witlock	Pollard Edmondson

Name	# of white inhabitants	Name	# of white inhabitants
Richard Adley	6	James Buckly	6
John Akers	6	Thomas Buckley	4
Thomas Anderson	5	Allen Burgess	8
William Anderson	5	Andrew Callender	4
John Ardery	4	John Cane	8
John Armstrong	7	Henry Carey	4
William Arrendal	4	Samuel Chamberlaine	8
James Arrington	6	John Chapman	3
Thomas Baker	4	Jane Claremont	7
John Baleson	4	John Clark	6
Jane Barnett	9	William Clark	6
Peter Barnett	4	William Clark Jr.	11
Robert Bass	3	Jonathan Clash ?	9
William Beaver	2	Samuel Coburn	7
William Berridge	5	John Cockey	6
William Bind	6	Henry Collins	12
John Blake	7	William Commens	5
Thomas Blanch	2	Mary Cook	5
Henry Bowdle Jr.	5	Solomon Corner Sr.	—
John Bowdle	3	William Corner	6
John Bradshaw	1	Richard Coward	—
Moses Brimfield	6	Isaac Cox Jr.	2
Perry Brimfield	4	Jane Cox	—
William Brimfield	5	William Cox	1
Dorothy Brown	3	Isaac Craddick	6
George Brown	2	James Dandy	4
Robert Brown	6	Henry Darden	8
William Brown	12	Henry Delahay Jr.	5
Arnold Buckly	4	Nathan Denny	8
Henry Buckly	—	John Dickinson	
		Stephen Drummond	6

1783 TAX LIST OF TALBOT COUNTY, MARYLAND
Brooke & Third Haven Hundreds

Name	# of white inhabitants	Name	# of white inhabitants
James Duling	6	Joseph Jones	7
John Duling	3	Pierce Jones	7
Samuel Eason	7	Joseph Kemp	6
John Edwards	6	Solomen Kemp	5
John Erven	7	James Kennaday	3
Richard Ewley	2	Emery Kerby	5
John Fairhurst	3	John Kersey	9
Joseph Farrington	10	Oliver Lee	3
Thomas Fairhurst	2	William Lee	2
James Ferguson	—	John Love	7
John Flemming	12	Thomas Love	8
Thomas Flemming	6	David Lucas	6
Elizabeth Freeman	7	Thomas Lyles	5
Mary Framton	3	James McCarty	2
Mary Goldsborough	6	Thomas McClayland	8
Charles Gully	3	Alexander McKinsey	5
William Hambleton	3	James McMahon	4
Matthew Hardikin	5	James McMahon Jr.	8
James Harding	5	William Mackie	2
Henry Harrison	5	John Mansfield	3
Joseph Harding	2	William Marshall	10
William Harrison	7	Henry Martin Jr.	6
Richard Hayward	—	John Mason	2
Thomas Higgins	6	William Meiny	2
Capt. Francis Holmes	8	James Merrick	3
James Holsby	8	Matthias Merrick	7
John Holsby	7	Jane Mitchell	2
John Holsby Jr.	4	Rachel More	5
William Holsby	8	William Mullikin	5
James Hopewell	2	Daniel Murray	3
John Hopkins	8	Page Nash	7
James Horney	3	John Nicols	6
John Hill	5	John Noconam	10
James Jackson	4	John Noels	5
Catherine Jenkins	—	Lambert Norris	6
George Jenkins	2	William Northwood	8
Samuel Jenkins	8	John Paddison	—
Walter Jenkins	3	Joseph Parsons	4
John Johnson	5	Deborah Perry	—
David Jones	5	John Porter	4
Evan Jones	7	Foster Price	9

1783 TAX LIST OF TALBOT COUNTY, MARYLAND
Brooke & Third Haven Hundreds

Name	# of white inhabitants	Name	# of white inhabitants
James Price	5	James Stanley	5
Nathan Price	3	Rachel Stapleford	7
Thomas Price Jr.	7	_____ Start	6
Vincent Price	6	John Stevens	5
James Priestly	4	John Sylvester	8
Samuel Pritchard	5	Nicholas Thomas	2
Mary Rakes	6	Rebecca Tibbles	2
Thomas Rakes	3	James Tobin	8
John Rathol	5	Edward Trippe	9
John Reader	2	George Troth	9
Thomas Reid Sr.	5	Owen Troy	13
Jesse Richardson	1	John Tucker	2
Perry Riestly	7	Thomas Turner	6
John Ritchard	8	James Wainwright	9
Thomas Roach	5	Daniel Walker	5
David Robinson Jr.	2	Francis Walker	5
Henry Robinson	2	James Walker Jr.	
Thomas Robinson Sr.	4	Richard Walker	4
Robert Robson	5	Wm. Walker(shoe maker)	10
Michael Rogers	4	William Walker 3rd	5
Abraham Severe	13	Garey Warner	5
Thomas Sewell	7	Thomas Watts	9
John Singleton	2	William Weaver	3
John Skinner	7	James Webb	7
Matthew Slow	2	March Welch	3
Samuel Small	4	Henry West	5
Theophilus Small	10	Samuel White	6
Edward Smith	7	Thomas White	5
Elizabeth Smith	5	Thomas Wickersham	9
Francis Smith	7	John Wilson Jr.	4
Levin Spedding	3	Rebecca Woods	2

Name	Tract Name	# of acres	# of white inhabitants
Samuel Abbott	pt. Flemmings Threshes	171	6
	pt. Beaver Dam	66 2/3	
	pt. Manors Lott	66 2/3	
Moses Adams	pt. Hatfield & Hatfields Add	80	2
	Adams Add.	70	
William Akers	pt. Bullen	480	8

1783 TAX LIST OF TALBOT COUNTY, MARYLAND
Brooke & Third Haven Hundreds

Name	Tract Name	# of acres	# of white inhabitants
Hannah Alexander	pt. Wales, pt. Lowe Good Luck		8
	pt. Alexanders Choice, pt. Irish Freshes	184	
William Allen	pt. Sutton Grange	120	7
William Arrington	pt. Middle Neck	100	6
	pt. Studs Point	50	
	pt. Coxes Remmant	35	
Aaron Atkinson Jr.	1 lott		3
Col. Jeremiah Banning	Barnstone Chance	229	—
Rachel Barclay	Cumberland & Chame, Help Home & Solomon's Beginning	172	2
Richard Barnaby	2 lotts in Oxford		8
Richard Barnett	pt. Discovery	150	10
Ruth Barnett	pt. Patricks Plains	90	9
	Mullicans Delight	52 3/4	
Thomas Barnett	pt. Catlin Plains	100	5
Thomas Barnett(Dorset Co)	pt. Lowes Ramble	50	—
Daniel Bartlett	pt. Hambletons Park	170	4
Daniel Berry	1 lott		3
James Berry	pt. Rigbys Marsh	300	7
	Hackney Marsh	82 1/2	
William Berry	pt. Bozmans Add.	27 1/2	5
	pt. Chance	27 1/2	
Col. Christopher Birckhead	pt. Little Bristol	930	12
	pt. Lives Ramble(Lowes)	100	
	Dicks Marsh	200	
	pt. Nomini	200	
	pt. Discovery	56	
Lambert Booker	pt. Tilghmans Fortune	88	3
Henry Bowdle Sr.	pt. Taylors Ridge	100	—
	Marshey Point	50	
	Peter Denny	50	
Stephen Bowdle	pt. Bullens Chance	125	4
Tristram Bowdle assessor	Hoghole	268	1
	Hoghole Add.	3	
	Coxes Remmant	85 1/2	
Rev. John Bowie for Elizabeth Martin	Michdins Hall	200	2
	Martins Purchase	5 1/4	
	pt. Hier Dier Lloyd	200	
John Bozman	Tates Lott	618	—
	Piney Point	150	
	pt. Bozmans Add.	192	

1783 TAX LIST OF TALBOT COUNTY, MARYLAND
Brooke & Third Haven Hundreds

Name	Tract Name	# of acres	# of white Inhabitants
Lucretia Bozman	Rich Range	300	3
	Delph	100	
	Boons Hope	100	
	Spring Close	50	
	Stridham	18	
Edward Bromwell Jr.	pt. Goldsborough	87	12
Edward Bromwell Sr.	2 lotts in Oxford	——	4
Jacob Bromwell	1 lott in Oxford		6
Spalding Bromwell	2 lotts in Oxford	——	
Sarah Brown	pt. Parkers Pt. & Enlargement	115	—
	pt. Lowes Ramble	53	—
Elizabeth Browning	pt. Hier Dier Lloyd	150	
Major Joseph Bruff	1 lott at Court House	——	7
Elizabeth Bullen	pt. Lords Gift	200	1
	pt. Napps Lott	105	
	12th Prospect	45	
Joseph Bunting	pt. Dover	123	3
Elizabeth Canner	pt. Wooley Manor	233	1
Sailes Canner	Fosters Chance & pt. Wooley Manor	418	7
Joseph Carr	Millers Purchase	100	9
	pt. Lowes Ramble	44	
James Lloyd Chamberlaine	pt. Jobs Content, pt. Cooks Hope, pt. Desire & pt. Heworth	801 1/2	10
	Ginnings Hope	832 1/4	
	Romains	732 1/2	
	pt. Canterberry Mannor	210	
	pt. London Derry	382	
	Cornelius Coolspring	100	
	Surprise	40	
	Discovery	20	
	2 lotts at Talbot Courthouse		
	3 lotts at Oxford		
Samuel Chamberlaine	pt. Nether Foster	130	10
	Room	145	
	Heir Dier Lloyd	385 3/4	
	Heir Dier Lloyd	427 1/2	
	11 lotts at Oxford		
William Chaplain	Broad Oak	300	11
	Endfield	88	
	Suttons Grange	33	
	pt. Reedly	159	
	pt. Intention	18	

1783 TAX LIST OF TALBOT COUNTY, MARYLAND
Brooke & Third Haven Hundreds

Name	Tract Name	# of acres	# of white inhabitants
Francis Chaplain	pt. Intention	81	4
	pt. Reedly	80	
Ann Clark(Caroline Co.)	lott at Talbot Courthouse	___	8
Lambert Coburn	pt. Kings Sale	42	7
John Connolly	pt. Edmondsons Cove	5	6
	pt. Mullicans Choice	125	
Daniel Cox for Eliza.Thomas-pt. Double Ridge		280	2
Isaac Cox	pt. Taylors Ridge	100	4
	Hutchensons Add.	50	
	pt. Balden	30	
	pt. Bennetts Threshes	149	
Noah Corner	1 lott	___	5
Solomon Corner for Coleman heirs - 1 lott at Courthouse		___	7
Bridget Coward	Thirds of Plimhimmon	166 1/3	7
	Thirds of Morgans Add.	11	
Thomas Coward	pt. Plimhimmon	333 1/3	3
	1 lott at Oxford	___	
	pt. Morgans Add.	22	
	pt. Judiths Garden	90	
	pt. Combsberry	40	
Charles Crookshanks	8 lotts in Oxford	___	___
Charles Crookshanks for James Nicols	pt. Heworth	205	5
Joseph Darden	pt.Inclosure,pt.Easons Lott & Easons Neck	250	___
	Dickensons Lott	216	
Stephen Darden	pt. Bennetts Frishes	273	
	pt. Balden	80	
Thomas Dawson	pt.Cooks Hope Manner	200	___
James Delahay	pt.Hier Dier Lloyd	100	7
Henry Delahay	Hull	70	5
Mark Delahay	Robinsons Discovery formerly called Poplar Hill	66 1/2	6
Thomas Delahay	Delahays Fortune	100	5
Peter Denny	pt.Heworth & Cumberland	73	8
	Clifton	200	
	Hickory Ridge	12	
	Pt.Cumberland from Chance	6	
	Dennys Content	73	
Daniel Dickenson	Boston Clifts	270	8
Daniel Dickenson for John Harrisson	Dover Marsh	348	___

1783 TAX LIST OF TALBOT COUNTY, MARYLAND
Brooke & Third Haven Hundreds

Name	Tract Name	# of acres	# of white inhabitants
James Dickinson Esq.	Timothys Lott	403	2
	pt. Bozmans Add.	38	
	pt. Tates Lot	3	
	East Otwell	400	
James Dickinson Jr.	Hatten	374	3
	Frankfort St. Michaels	616	
Samuel Dickenson	Samuels Lott	500	7
	Crosierdere	220	
	pt. Hier Dier Lloyd	101	
	Powells Island	55	
	pt. Wales	46	
Mary Domahoy	Yorkshire	63	6
John Duncan	pt. Barmston	5	6
Pollard Edmondson	Edmondsons Difficulty	903	6
	Tilghmans Fortune	524	
	pt. Enlargement	50	
	pt. Heworth, pt. Desire	64	
	Jacks Cove	50	
Pollard Edmondson for	Upper Range	46	7
McManuss heirs	Upper Dover	114 3/4	
	pt. Mt. Hope	44	
Joseph Foster	Cornwell	100	—
	Joseph Lott	100	
	pt. Lowes Rambles	48	
Greenbury Goldsborough	pt. Hier Dier Lloyd	342	6
John Goldsborough (Dorset Co.)	Hogsden	100	—
	Parks Marsh	318	
	Marshy Peak	132	
	Thief Keep Out	36	
Nicholas Goldsborough	Groseet	150	2
	Parlett	100	
	Otwell	500	
	Addition	80	
	Duplication Point	20	
Nicholas Goldsborough for Thomas Goldsborough	Lott in Oxford	___	8
Thomas Gordon	Hobsons Choice	150	9
	Hunting Hill	170	
	pt. Parkers Pt. & Enlargement	130	
John Hancock	1 lott	___	2
Edward Harrison	pt. Timber Neck	87	3
	Harrisons Chance	41	

1783 TAX LIST OF TALBOT COUNTY, MARYLAND
Brooke & Third Haven Hundreds

Name	Tract Name	# of acres	# of white inhabitants
John Harrison	pt. Timber Neck	87	6
	Harrisons Chance	41	
Wm. Harrissons heirs	pt. Huntchings Addition	163	7
	pt. Pitts Range	200	
William Hayward Esq.	pt. Marshey Point	300	3
	pt. Canterberry Manor	173 1/2	
	pt. Turners Point & Graves & Buckingham	444 1/2	
	pt. Lower Dover	241	
John Helsby Sr.	pt. Parkers Point & Enlargement	75	7
John Heron	1 lott		6
Richard Hickson for Elizabeth Martin	pt. Wales, pt. Alexanders Choice & pt. Irish Thicket, pt. Lowes Good Luck.	368	10
John Higgins Jr.	Borams Range	177	7
Ann Hindman	1 lott		2
Henry Hollyday	pt. Buckingham, Pt. Providence	800	—
John Holmes	pt. Sutton	127	5
Dennis Hopkins	pt. London Derry	103	8
James Hopkins	pt. Nomini	100	7
James Hopkins	pt. Hambletons Park	70	8
Moses Hopkins	pt. Hambletons Park	70	2
John Jacobs for Jones heirs	Chase Help	2 1/2	5
	pt. Hawks Hill		
Alexander James	pt. Coxes Add.	56	2
	pt. Barmstone	44	2
Mary Jenkins	Lords Chance	100	8
	pt. Swamp Neck	27	
	pt. Shore Ditch	36	
	pt. Parishs Ridge	238	
Matthew Lewis Jenkins	pt. Powicks Ridge	121	9
Thomas Jenkins	pt. Double Ridge	120	5
	pt. Sutton Grange	180	
	pt. Powicks Ridge	121 1/2	
	pt. White Phillips	99	
Randolph Johnson	Turbuts Fields (by escheat called)	168	9
	Bite the Biter	206	
	pt. Lowes Rambles (by Escheat called) Johnson's Discovery	101 3/4	
James Jones	pt. Miners Lott	33 1/3	5
	pt. Beaver Dam	33 1/3	
Thomas Jones	lott		6
Thomas Jordan 3rd	pt. Edmondsons Freshes	100	7

1783 TAX LIST OF TALBOT COUNTY, MARYLAND
Brooke & Third Haven Hundreds

Name	Tract Name	# of acres	# of white inhabitants
Thomas Jordan 3rd for	pt. Edmondsons Freshes	200	—
Benjamin Kemp	pt. Lowes Rambles	150	4
Quinton Kemp	1 lott	___	3
Robert Kemp	pt. Catlin Plains, pt. Buckroe	150	3
	pt. Abbington	100	
	Walnut Garden	50	
	Hicks Addition	100	
	pt. Mullicans Delight	11	
David Kerr	Browns Park	119	—
	pt. Timber Neck	64	
John Littleton	pt. Jamacia	100	8
James Lloyd	Rumbley Marsh	300	7
	Buckland	250	
	Partnership	310	
Dr. Robert Lloyd	Gurlington	435	
	pt. Goldsborough	113	
	pt. Murray	150	
Mary Lurty	1 lott in Oxford	___	3
Alexander McCallum	pt. Desire & Haworth	289	1
	pt. Enlargement	50	
	McCallums Addition	14	
	Chance Help	35 1/2	
William McCallum	1 lott in Talbot Courthouse		—
Daniel McGinney	Piney Point	250	2
John McMahan Sr.	pt. White Phillips	42	4
Richard McMahan	pt. Lowes Ramble	80	9
Phillip Mackie	pt. Bullen, pt. Broad Oak, Pt.Homerby-250		4
	Newling	140	
Edward Markland	1 lott in Oxford	2	
John Markland	pt. Plimhimmon	100	5
	3 lotts in Oxford	___	
Elizabeth Martin	1 lott in Oxford		
Henry Martin Sr.	pt. Bullens Chance	125	6
	pt. Conjunction	25	
Mary Martin	pt. Hier Dier Lloyd		
	Shore Ditch	10	
	Rich Neck & Rich Neck Add.	322	
	Hard Measure	25	
Nicholas Martin	pt. Hier Dier Lloyd	332	8
	pt. Hard Measure	37	
	Wilderness	160	
	pt. Cormsberry & Riches Park	300	
	3 lotts in Oxford	___	

1783 TAX LIST OF TALBOT COUNTY, MARYLAND
Brooke & Third Haven Hundreds

Name	Tract Name	# of acres	# of white inhabitants
Robert Martin Jr.	Bullens Chance	100	4
Robert Martin Sr.	pt. Powicks Ridge	100	6
Solomon Martin	Crooked Ramble	75 1/2	10
	pt. Shore Ditch	37 1/2	
	pt. Swamp Neck	50	
Dr. William Maynadier	pt. Goldsborough (resurveyed)	170	7
	Tatterhurst	35	
	Maynadier Lott	24	
	Marshland	70	
	Timothys Lott	25	
	Fotterels Discovery	93	
	Flemmings Freshes	33	
	Wilderness	75	
	Jones' Interest	40	
John Mears	White Chappel	45	6
James Mullican Jr.	1 lott	——	7
James Mullican Sr.	1 lott		6
Jessee Mullican	pt. York	201	6
	pt. Yorks Destruction	40	
	pt. Powicks Ridge	6	
Patrick Mullican	pt. Patricks Plains	200	12
Wm. Mullican, guardian	pt. Timber Neck	55	—
for John Mullicans heirs	Mullicans Chance	180	
	Timber Neck Addition	50	
	York	105	
Robert Neal	pt. Mt. Hope (resurveyed	80	5
Solomon Neal	Hickory Ridge	137	8
Deborah Nicols	Richmond	41	3
	Richmonds Addition	282	
Robert Lloyd Nicols	pt. Jobs Content, pt. Fort Hazard		6
	pt. Sisters Lott, pt. Jennings Hope,		
	& pt. Buckingham	801 1/2	
Ann Oldham	pt. Hard Measure	7	2
	Otwell	81	
	Jenny Close	12	
Nicholas Pamphilion	2 lotts	——	4
" for Thos. Chamberlain	4 lotts	——	—
" for Sprole	1 lott	——	—
Aaron Parrott	Edmondsons Freshes	106 2/3	—
	Hickory Ridge	94 2/3	
	French Hazzare	27 1/3	
	Dennys Content	8	

1783 TAX LIST OF TALBOT COUNTY, MARYLAND
Brooke & Third Haven Hundreds

Name	Tract Name	# of acres	# of white inhabitants
Aaron Parrott(continued)	pt. Mt. Hope	33 1/3	—
Abner Parrott	pt. Suttons Grange	135	8
Henry Parrott	pt. Canterbury Mannor	233 1/4	6
James Parrott	pt. Lowes Rambles	25	6
	pt. White Phillips	1	
Benjamin Parvin	Boston Clifts	250	6
	Troths Fortune	400	
John Pemberton (Queen Anne's Co.) 2 lotts in Oxford			
William Perry	pt. Edmondsons Deficiency	350	3
Charles Pickering	Chance Neglect	100	13
	Cedar Point	13 1/2	
	3 lotts-1 at Talbot Courthouse	—	
Howell Powell	New Scotland	500	9
	Powells Misfortune	26	
Rachel Pritchard	pt. White Phillips	32 1/2	6
Walter Pritchard	pt. White Phillips	32	3
William Rakes	pt. Kings Sale	42	3
Peter Richardson	1 lott		5
John Robert for Mary Sharp-Reeds Point		180	6
David Robinson Sr.	Security	26	3
	Nether Foster	5	
Rev. Gurling Robinson	pt. Long Point	100	2
Handly Robinson	pt. Taylors Ridge	100	
	pt. Timber Neck Addition	89	—
John Robinson	pt. Long Point	150	6
	Robinsons Beginning	17	
Capt. Thomas Robinson	Moorefield Adventure	100	4
	Nether Foster	50	
James Sangston for Mary Bullen- pt. Marsh Lane		150	7
James Seth	1 lott Talbot Courthouse	—	7
Ann Sharp	Hier Dier Lloyd	100	—
Margaret Sharp	pt. Rattle Snake Point	150	9
	pt. Conjunction	25	
	Sharps Addition	24	
	pt. Inclosure, Easons Lott, Easons Neck & Fancy	250	
Mary Sharp	Herbutts Choice	16	—
	Little Creek	200	
	Ivens Point	300	
	pt. Salem	134	
	Hobsons Choice	129	
	Millers Hope	11	
	Mitchells Hermitage	125	
	Millers Chance	85	

1783 TAX LIST OF TALBOT COUNTY, MARYLAND
Brooke & Third Haven Hundreds

Name	Tract Name	# of acres	# of white inhabitants
Samuel Sharp	pt. Nomini	302	5
	Chance	46	
	pt. Napps Lot	50	
Alice Sherwood	pt. Anderton	100	8
	Wintersell	142	
Edward Mann Sherwood	pt. Pitts Range	200	5
Hugh Sherwood	Exchange	100	6
	pt. Canterbury Manor	36	
James Sherwood	pt. Exchange	100	7
	Allembeys Field	124	
	Allembys Field Addition	7	
Peter Sherwood	pt. Lords Gift	60	—
Robert Sherwood	pt. Pitts Range	200	—
Sarah Slack	pt. Davids Folly	50	—
James Smith for Eliza. Martin	pt. Hier Dier Lloyd	150	7
Edward Stevens	pt. Catlin Plains	240	4
John Stevens	Williams Lott	45	11
	Edmondsons Cove	163	
	Compton	70	
	Kingstown	400	
	pt. Mullicans Choice	25	
Peter Stevens	pt. Nomini	200	10
Samuel Stevens	Stevens Island	45	6
	pt. Little Bristol	199	
	pt. Catlin Plains	150	
	pt. Buckroe	50	
	Samuels Beginning	139 3/4	
Wm. Stevens, guardian for Thomas Culearth	Cornelius Garden	50	8
	Lowes Rambles	85	
William Stevens Sr.	pt. Alexanders Chance	8	—
	pt. Yorks Destruction	10	
	pt. Powicks Ridge	94	
	pt. Little Bristol	108	
	Millers Hope	121	
	pt. Lowes Rambles	30	
	pt. Hunting Hill	34	
	pt. Hatton	63	
Elizabeth Thomas	pt. Reedby	200	8
	Killingsworth	50	
	Sheds Point	100	
	Venture	90	

1783 TAX LIST OF TALBOT COUNTY, MARYLAND
Brooke & Third Haven Hundreds

Name	Tract Name	# of acres	# of white inhabitants
Elizabeth Thomas	Suttons Addition & Hardship	278	
(continued)	Thief Keep Out	38	
	Addition	100	
	Partnership	18	
Capt. James Thomas	pt. Anderton	150	5
James Thomas, guardian for James Goldsborough	pt. Hier Dier Lloyd	400	4
Samuel Thomas	Oldhams Discovery	115 1/2	7
William Thomas	pt. Anderton	359	—
	Thomas' Discovery	25	
	Judiths Garden	73	
Elizabeth Trippe	Turners Point	204	6
	Skillington Hope	20	
	Marshey Point	82	
Henry Troth	Edmondsons Freshes	36 2/3	3
	Hickory Ridge	47 1/2	
	pt. French Hazzard	13 1/3	
	pt. Edmondsons Freshes	16 2/3	
	Dennys Content	4	
	Mt. Hope	16 2/3	
William Tucker, guardian for Holonels heir	pt. Buckrow, pt. Sutton	140	6
John Van Dike	1 lott	—	4
James Walker Sr.	pt. Jamaca	92	3
Phillip Walker of Caroline Co.	Crooked Lane	100	—
Peter Webb	pt. Reedby	306	4
Thomas Welch	Suddon Borough	100	9
	Plainsby	100	
	pt. Powicks Ridge	100	
Thomas Willson	pt. Mt. Hope	222	3

END OF TALBOT COUNTY

THE HUNDREDS OF HARFORD COUNTY, MARYLAND
(Approximate Locations)

Map courtesy of John H. Livezey

1783 TAX LIST OF HARFORD COUNTY, MARYLAND
Bush River Upper & Eden Hundreds

Return of Property in Bush River Upper & Eden Hundreds by Daniel McComas, assessor, 1783

Name	# of white inhabitants	Tract Name	# acres
Stephen Airs	8		
John Almony	—	Mollys Delight	90
Elizabeth Amoss	4	Joshua's Forest	36 3/4
		Black Stone Ridge	29
George Amoss	4		
James Amoss Sr.	6	Jame's Care	135
		Brantons Ridge	95
		pt. Fox Hills	20
		Shaws Dependance	12
		Shaws Priviledge	71
(Jos)hua Amoss	3	Fox Hills	200
Mordecai Amoss, Esq.	6	Joshua's Forest	100
		Third Addition	72
		Mordecai's Addition	63
Nicholas Amoss	12	Good Will Purchased Again	228
Robert Amoss, Esq.	10	Good Hope	614
		Roberts Enlargment	77 1/4
		Spanish Oak Hill	37 1/2
		Spanish Bottom	3
		John's Refuse	38
		pt. Brantons Ridge & Poverty Inclosed	29
		pt. Amoss' Pursuit	101
		pt. Saplin Ridge	49 1/2
		pt. Amoss' Outlett	16
		White Glade	30
		name unknown	9
William Amoss	7	James' Lott	123
		John's Lott	120
Major William Amoss	7	Joshua's Forest	63 3/4
		Joshua's Meadows	51
		Joshua's Choice	41
		Addition to Joshua's Choice	40
Catherin Anderson	6	Fews Fortune	190
		Pikes Refuse	100
James Anderson	—	Nancy's Delight	22 1/2
		Cabbin Branch	22 1/2
		Punch	25
		Prines Folly	61
		Grist mill	—

1783 TAX LIST OF HARFORD COUNTY, MARYLAND
Bush River Upper & Eden Hundreds

Name	# of white inhabitants	Tract Name	# acres
William Armitage	1	house & lott	1 1/2
John Ashmead	5	Millford	87
		Jones' Desire	78
		Brotherhood	90
		Mt. Pleasant	50
		1 grist mill	
Capt. Charles Baker	9	Good Will Purchased Again	283 1/2
		Gunpowder Upper	
		pt. Antioch	100
William Baker	7		
Joseph Baldwin	4		
William Bankhead	2		
John Barrett	4	Lewis' Refuse	45
		_uncheon Cabbin	31
		Rogers Addition	78
		Johns Mistake	35
		name unknown	13
Ann Barton	7	Bartons Harbour	133
James Barton	11	Robinson's Chance	92
John Barton		pt. My Ladies Manor	80
Joshua Barton	3		
William Barton			
William Baty	8	Hays Habitation	100
David Bell	6	Hanlys Repose	125
		Hanlys Choice	30
		pt. McComas' Manor	100
John Bell	7	Bloods Adventure	57
		Bloods Choice	63
Joshua Bently	11	Quarrelsome Ridge	73
Edward Berry	3		
Richard Bevin			
Walter Billingsley Jr.	5	Bonds Last Shift	125
John Black	5	Roses Range	54
		Butlers Choice	33
		Blacks Range	31
Edward Blany	3	Ogg King of Basham	112
Thomas Blany	11	pt. 3 Sisters	100
		pt. Brooks Cross	70
		1 fulling mill	
		pt. Wheelers Outlett	70
Patience Bond	5	Isles Caperia	200

-80-

1783 TAX LIST OF HARFORD COUNTY, MARYLAND
Bush River & Eden Hundreds

Name	# of white inhabitants	Tract Name	# of acres
Thomas Bond Esq.	—	pt. Isle Caperia	130
		Gunpowder Upper	
		pt. Clegits Forest	206
		Bush Lower	
		pt. Prestons Luck	200
Elijah Bosly	—	Dorseys Plains	180
Ann Briarly	3	Hanlys Habitation	105
		Hamiltons Addition	50
		pt. Hughes Spott	45
George Briarly	3		
Henry Briarly	5	Second Addition	76
Hugh Briarly	6	Bonds Last Shift	220
Robert Briarly	1	Meadow Ground	75
		pt. James' Hope	16
		Hanlys Repose	15
John Brown	7	Whitakers Lott	62
Solomon Brown	7	Poteets Pleasure	90
Richard Burton	6		
John Bush	4		
Bennett Bussey	4	pt. Pearsons Outlett &	
		Wetheralls Addition	50
		pt. Cuning Furguson	50
		Talbotts Addition	50
Jesse Bussey	—	Hills Camp	250
Ruth Bussey	5	Colegates Last Shift	171
John Campbell	4	Double Purchase	93
James Carlong	4	Stoney Ridge	50
Hugh Carney	6		
John Carr	4	1 house & Lott	1/2
Peter Carroll	8	Simmons Exchange	100
		Clarks Delight	20
Josiah Carter	4	pt. My Ladies Manor	100
John Cary	4	Hills & Dales	8
George Chalk	9	pt. Ogg King of Basham	21
		Chalks Addition	25
		Amoss' Delight	92
John Chalk	6	pt. Amoss' Outlett & Delames Addition	112
		pt. Ogg King of Basham & Chalks Reserve	56
Sarah Chalk	—		

1783 TAX LIST OF HARFORD COUNTY, MARYLAND
Bush River & Eden Hundreds

Name	# of white inhabitants	Tract Name	# of acres
James Cherry	7	pt. Good Will Purchased Again	174
Robert Clark	11	Stones	86
		Jacobs Delight	84
George Coalman	6		
William Condron	4		
Don Connoly	10	James' Inlett	35
Michael Cook	11		
Matthew Cooly	6	Hitt or Miss	128
Richard Cooly	5		
Richard Coop	5		
John Corbett	5		
William Corbett	3	Valley Broad Run	58
		Briarlys Choice	29
		Ramseys Triangle	30
		name unknown	25
Edward Cowan	4		
John Cox	7	Whitakers Delight	100
		1 grist mill	20
Alexander Crawford	6	lott in Abington	
		1 house & lott	1 1/2
James Curry	7	Mount Atlass	30
		Elijahs Enlargement	80
		Elijahs Chance	30
		Fox Hills	37
		Stewarts Neglect	40
		Elijahs Addition	72
		pt. Clothworthys Harb.	9
		pt. Londonderry	35 1/2
David Davis	6		
Rev. John Davis	4	Arams Favour	95
		Alexanders Delight	10
		McComas' Delight	10
Thomas Davis	9	Fews Industry	30
		Daniels Lookout	26
John Demoss Jr.	5		
John Demoss Sr.	4	Ramseys Reserve	70
		pt. Prospect	61
		Obb Long	70
		Addition to Obb Long	38

1783 TAX LIST OF HARFORD COUNTY, MARYLAND
Bush River Upper & Eden Hundreds

Name	# of white inhabitants	Tract Name	# acres
John Denbow	9	Wilsons Choice	48
		Chesnut Ridge	30
		Sarah's Desire	36 1/2
		pt. Astons & Dales Chance	13 1/2
David Dick	7	house & lott	
Francis Dines	9	Dine's lott	20
William Ditto	7	pt. Good Will Purchased Again	210 1/2
Daniel Donahoo	—		
Thomas Dorsey	1		
William Dowland	6		
David Durham	8	Powells Choice	57 1/2
		pt. Wheelers Outlett	69 1/2
		Denbows Choice	24
Thomas Elliott	5	pt. My Ladies Manor	100
Elizabeth England	7	Hysoms Garden	80
David Evans	5	Addition to Deserted & lott	102
Evan Evans	3	Little John's Industry	86
Griffith Evans	3		
John Evans-B.S.(blacksmith)	10		
John Evans (nailor)	5		
James Farroll	3?		
James Finley	8	Armagh	100
		Savorys Refuse	39
John Finley	6	Abraham's Beginning	42
		Mollys Delight	17 1/2
		Abrahams Neglect	27
		Black Rock	25
Joshua Flearty	6		
James Fitzgerald	2	Rocks Delight	130
Benedict Foster	3		
Charles Galaspy	6	Miles Forest	125
Cornelius & Philip Garretson & John Deyoung	4	Isles Capiria pt.	200
Francis Gibson	2		
Richard Gill	7		
John Giving	6	pt. My Ladies Manor	30
		pt. Pitaspers Choice	60
Robert Glenn	9	Roberts & Davids Delight	99 1/2
		pt. Hughes Hope	34

1783 TAX LIST OF HARFORD COUNTY, MARYLAND
Bush River Upper & Eden Hundreds

Name	# of white inhabitants	Tract Name	# acres
John Gray	7	Grays Dairey	28
		pt. Eastops Hope	50
Bennett Green	9		
Abraham Guiton	8	Abrahams Inlett	33
John Guiton	1	Prospects Reserve	196
Joshua Guiton	5		
Thomas Gullifer	2		
John Hamby	1	pt. Manor	30
Hugh Hannah	3		
John Hannah	5		
Samuel Hannah	2		
William Hannah	8		
Joseph Hanover	5		
Samuel Harper	3		
William Harvey	7		
Thomas Hasking	4		
Thomas Hawkins	1	Pearsons Outlett & Wetheralls Addition	65
Arthur Heaps	3		
Robert Heaps	6	Browns Delight	40
Robert Heaps Jr.	3		
Francis Henderson	5	High Springs	208
William Hill	5	Bonds Gratuity	175
Asael Hitchcock Jr.	4	Hitchcock's Harbour	45
Asael Hitchcock Sr.	5	Nancy's Delight	80
		Bartons Harbour	50
		Bowans Addition	45
		The Axe	33 1/2
Josiah Hitchcock Jr.	6	Hitchcock's Mistake	31
Josiah Hitchcock Sr.	6	pt. Goodwill Purchased Again	285 1/2
Randal Hitchcock	5		
William Hitchcock	8	Williams Addition	37
		Better Luck by Browns lott	137
James Hobbs	6		
Richard Hope	9	Friendship	120
Thomas Hope	7	Miles Inheritance	27
		Richards Spott	2 1/4
		Horn Point	101
		Elizabeths lott	37
		Cuckhold's Makiers	57
		pt. Pleasant Vally	19

1783 TAX LIST OF HARFORD COUNTY, MARYLAND
Bush River Upper & Eden Hundreds

Name	# of white inhabitants	Tract Name	# acres
Thomas G. Howard	—	pt. Isles Caperia	410
		Gunpowder Upper	
		34 barrels flour at Amoss mill	
Aram Hughes	7	Addition to Beautiful Island	60
Charles Hughes	10	James' Forest	267
Isram Hughes	9	name unknown	38
Nasson Hughes	7	Hannah's Reserve	8
Thomas Hughes	10	Rock Ridge	61
Zenas Hughes	9	Beautiful Island	63
William Hunnell	5		
Thomas Huskins	4		
Alexander Huston	5		
Richard Hutchins	8	Tho. Slades lott-M.L. (My Ladies Manor)	170
John Ingram	3		
Elizabeth James	8	Savories Desire	10
		Thomas' Forecast	44
		The Willett	14
		Thomas' Desire	55
		James' Meadows	10
		James' String	23
Thomas James	8	Minster	80
		pt. Brothers lott	13
William James	7	pt. Manor	110
		Gunpowder Upper	
		10 barrels flour at Amoss mill	
Martha & Jesse Jarrett	6	Hobbs Neighbour	66
		Good Luck	33
		pt. Three Sisters	150
		pt. Isles Caperie	246
		John's Forest	125
		Rhoad Necessity	56
		pt. Daniel's land	60
		pt. Whitakers Delay	64
		Reserve land purchased of his Lordship Com.	623 1/2
		purchased from Wm. Robinson	134 1/2
		purchased from Alexander Allison-	66
		Bricks & Things	136
		Reserve Lane	200

1783 TAX LIST OF HARFORD COUNTY, MARYLAND
Bush River Upper & Eden Hundreds

Name	# of white inhabitants	Tract Name	# acres
Martha & Jesse Jarrett (continued)		Gunpowder Upper	
		Briarlys Refuse	3 3/4
		Dogwood Thickett	116
		Rockholds Chance	38
		Pattersons Regulation	345
		Nancy's Fancy	50
		Deer C(reek) Upper	
		Wild Cat Den	610
		George Deer Park?	300
		Jacobs Mount	40
		Deavers Good Will	60
		Pearsons lott	52
Mary Jarrett	1	Tates Neighbour	186
		Pattersons Trouble	100
Samuel Jenkins	4	Collins First Shift	100
		McComas' Desire	25
George Jewell	5	pt. James' Choice	60
John Johnson	3		
Joseph Johnson	2		
Moses Johnson	9	Goodwill Purchased Again	180 1/2
Joseph Jones	3	pt. James' Care & Foxe Hills	90
John Kean	—	Ramsays Choice	80
		Keans Addition	80
William Kerns	11		
James Kidd	4	Simmonds Hope	57
		Sure Bind Sure Find	50
		Kidds Addition	41
Robert Kirkwood	9	Guitons Prospect	65
		Prines Folly	64
		Cabbin Branch	60
William Kirkwood	1	Denny's Addition	54
		name unknown	68
Amoss Lacy	2		
Thomas Lacy	5		
William Lattimore	5		
George Lewis	6		
John Long Jr.	5	James' Forest	170
		pt. Addition to James' Forest	16
John Long Sr.	8	Maw Meadow	95 1/2
		pt. Leonards Triangle	15

1783 TAX LIST OF HARFORD COUNTY, MARYLAND
Bush River Upper & Eden Hundreds

Name	# of white inhabitants	Tract Name	# acres
Jonathan Lyon	14	Rattlesnake Den	60
		Pleasant Valley	62
James Lytle-B.C.(Balto.Co. ?)	_	Elizabeth's Delight	91
Roger McCandlass	7	pt. Manor	108
James McClasky	7	Minster	20
		Brothers lott	57
		pt. Brothers lott	28
John McClure	11	Barton's Folly	100
Joseph McClasky	7		
Daniel McComas (assessor)	5	Hills & Valleys	85
		Addition to Hills & Valleys	162
Daniel McComas of Wm.	1		
James McComas of Aquilla	6	Aquilas Forest	75
		Eleanors Delight	50
		pt. McComas' Manor	100
William McComas Esq.	3	Wards Purchase	191
		Lees Adventure	244
		Gunpowder Upper	
		200 barrels flour at Amoss mill	
Arthur McCord	6	Guitons Design	60
David McCullough	10		
Cornelius McDonald	2	North Hill	18
		Nicholas' Fancy	110
John McDonald	4	Apple Hill	17
		Rich Leval	33
Patrick McGill	7	Keans Adventure	48
		Guitons Addition	47
Daniel McGilton	11	house & lott	5
Mark McGovern	1	Bare Range	75
		Bare Lodge	28
		Harris' Delight	75
John McGuire	8		
Ann Maddin	1	house & lott	1 1/2
James Maddin	6	James' Delight	50
Philip Maddin	6		
William Marsh	5		
Isaac Marshall	2		
Samuel Marshall	2		
James Meads Jr.	7		
James Meads Sr.	3	Barnabys Delight	45

1783 TAX LIST OF HARFORD COUNTY, MARYLAND
Bush River Upper & Eden Hundreds

Name	# of white inhabitants	Tract Name	# acres
Margaret & Aquilla Miles	4	Addition to Chance	128
Isaac Montgomery	10	Alexanders Delight	50
Dr. James Moore	2		
John Morris	4		
Dr. Francis Neale	1	house & lott	1
Robert Nelson	4	Bishops lott	250
		pt. Manor	50
Joseph Newton	3		
John Norrington	7		
Mary Norrington	8	Lions Den	120
Alexander Norris	10	Hills & Valleys	47
Aquila Norris	8	Addition to James' Forest	92
		pt. Daniel's land	50
		pt. Whitakers Delay	40
James Norris-sadler	7	Margarets Best Way	49
		Randals Retirement	81
		Nutterfields lott	25
John Norris	7		
Thomas Norris	15	Turkey Range	54
William Norris Sr.	7	William's Trust	95
		Norris' Venture	64
George Palmer	3		
Aquila Parker	5		
Martin Parker	7	Brantons Ridge	50
		Amoss' Outlett	64
		Amoss' Desire	79
		pt. Saplin Ridge	9 3/4
James Parr	5	pt. Astons & Dales Chance, Ayres lott & Frinchs Bedford	100
Isaac Parsons	5	Daniel's Chance	73
		Parsons Addition	21
Samuel Patterson	5	Patterson Maidenhead	100
William Patterson	5	Necessity	30
		Kings Ridge	50
		Addition to Kings Ridge	15
George Patton	7		
Thomas Patton	5	pt. 3 Sisters	100
Daniel Pocock Jr.	2	pt. Manor	115
Daniel Pocock Sr.	8	pt. Manor	100
Thomas Poteet	10	Field of Blood	96
		Hills & Valley's	50

1783 TAX LIST OF HARFORD COUNTY, MARYLAND
Bush River Upper & Eden Hundred

Name	# of white inhabitants	Tract Name	# acres
Thomas Poteet Jr.	5	Frinch's Bedford	100
Thomas Poteet Sr.	4		
John Poulson	2	pt. Pattersons Chance	51
		Standiford's Meadows	19
John Price	5	Summers Deer Park	30
James Prine	7	Long Meadows	35
John Prine	2		
John Renshaw	5		
William Roberts	3		
William Robinson	7	Chesnut Ridge	185
		Mary's Delight	10 1/4
Patrick Rock	12	Patricks lott	27
		Demoss' Reserve	81
Thomas Rockhold	5	Pattersons Chance	100
William Roe	10	The Meadow-M.L. (My Lady's Manor)	70
		Reserve land	30
Simon Ruscorn	5		
John Russell	5		
Thomas Russell	5	pt. Nathans Choice	41
John Rutledge	4	Good Will Purchased Again	213
Henry Scarff	5	Henry's Outlett	100
John Scarff	4		
John Scarff of John	4		
James Sciffington	5	Larges Neglect	145
Nathan Scott	6	Friends Discovery	241
Henry Shane	4		
Thomas Sharp Sr.	5	Shaws Privelidge	100
Richard Shiply	7		
Jane Simms	3	Penny Grove	20
Archibald Simpson	6		
James Sinclair	9	pt. Claxons Forest	57
		Wallers Good Luck	50
		Jackmans Addition 20	20
		Addition to Bond's Gratuity	21
		Freemans Rest	100
John Sinclair	1	pt. Bonds Gratuity	50
Lester Sinclair	9	pt. Claxons Forest	47
		Wallers Good Luck	50
		Green's Good Luck	15

1783 TAX LIST OF HARFORD COUNTY, MARYLAND
Bush River Upper & Eden Hundreds

Name	# of white inhabitants	Tract Name	# acres
William Sinclair	1	pt. Bonds Gratuity	50
Ezekiel Slade	10	pt. Manor	55
Nicholas Slade	5		
Elizabeth Smith	—	Fews Enlargement	84
		Bonds Meadows	112
		Hanly's Repose	21
John Smith	7	Allisons Choice	22
		Whitakers Retirement	63
Peter Smith	3		
Winston Smith	1	Daniel's Inheritance	40
		Richards Hope	50
		Eagons Choice	15
		Charles Delight	42
David Smtihson	2	Averilla's Choice	175
William Standiford	8	pt. Manor	62 1/2
Alexander Stewart	4		
John Stewart Sr.	10		
Thomas Street Jr.	4	John's Chance	100
Thomas Street Sr.	8	Elliotts Tent	50
		Harpers Resolution	60
		Streets Dark Bottom	56
		Deer Creek	26
		Wards Folly	49
		Streets Fancy	34
		Hobbs Choice	100
		Garland	100
		Thomas Rocky Adventure	42
		pt. Bonds Gratuity	25
		Hitchcocks Hope	28
Frederick Swan	9		
Matthew Talbott	1	Ogg King of Basham, Pearsons Outlett & Wetheralls Addition	135
Philip Tarney	6	Good Luck	100
David Tate	8	Davids Hope	100
		Briarly's Delight	50
		David's Beginning	15
Alexander Thompson	6	pt. 3 Sisters & Wheeler Outlet	100
Aquila Thompson	16	Michael's Delight	52
		Aquila's Addition	39
		Hughes Habitation	125
		pt. Roberts & Davids Delight	10 1/2

1783 TAX LIST OF HARFORD COUNTY, MARYLAND
Bush River Upper & Eden Hundreds

Name	# of white inhabitants	Tract Name	# acres
Daniel Thompson	11	pt. Amoss Outlet, Wallus Hope- & Better Luck	100
James Thompson	6	pt. Brantons Ridge	50
		pt. Jones Addition	50
John Thompson	2	pt. Better Luck	60
Joshua Thompson	5		
Thomas Thompson	10	pt. Astons & Dales Chance	31 3/4
		Rachels Delight	4 1/2
		Chesnut Ridge	25
Daniel Tredway	8	Eastops Hope	112
		Tredways Meadows	13
Isaac Truelock	7		
Andrew Turner	3		
Samuel Turner	5		
Thomas Turner	5	Rock Stones	142
John Vance	5	Hugh's Cabbin	70
James Varnay	4		
George Vogan	3	Poteets Industry	58
James Vogan	6	Brown's Delight	60
		Brown's Lookout	25
		Rileys Long Meadows	24
		Addition to Rileys Long Meadows-18	
James Ward	5	Colegates Last Shift	171
Jane Ward	7	pt. Bond's Gratuity	100
Robert Watt	6	Decumples Choice	73
John Weir	4		
Thomas Weir Jr.	3		
Thomas Weir Sr.	10	Powells Choice	100
		Taylors Good Luck	100
		Luck Lease	61
John Welch	3	Sadlers Shooting Ground	68
William Wells	5	pt. Manor	178
David West	6	name unknown	50
John West	7		
Thomas West	5	Mary's Delight	100
Jacob Wheeler	6		
Rebeccah Wheeler	3	Wheelers Security	100
		Wheelers Outlett	136
Thomas Wheeler	6	pt. 3 Sisters	150

1783 TAX LIST OF HARFORD COUNTY, MARYLAND
Bush River Upper and Eden Hundreds

Name	# of white inhabitants	Tract Names	# acres
Abraham Whitaker Esq.	7	Begin	87
		Whitakers lott	160
		Leonards Triangle	145
		pt. Brothers lott	23
David Whiteford	4	Ogg King of Basham & Amoss' Industry	20
Matthew Wiley	6	Black Rock	100
		1 grist mill	
Abraham Williams	6		
David Williams	5	Summers Deer Park	70
Richard Williams	1	Franklin Chance	100
Hugh Wilson	3		
Robert Wilson	3		
Blois Wright	4	Reids Best Way	116

Paupers in Bush River Upper & Eden Hundreds, Harford County, Maryland.

Paupers	# of whites	Paupers	# of whites
John Baker	3	Richard Jordan	4
Barnay Clemons	3	William Jordan	5
Andrew Craven	2	Clement Leach	4
Christopher Dawson	8	Thomas McClung	3
Simon Draper	2	John McClure	4
William Ervin	2	John Mallack	2
William Greenfield	5	Barnay Murray	2
George Harper	2	John Willard	5

Securities	Single Men
George Amoss	Frederick Amoss
Mordecai Amoss Esq.	Aquila Amoss
Mordecai Amoss Esq.	Mordecai Amoss Jr.
Catherine Anderson	Hugh Anderson
James Barton	James Barton Jr.
Daniel Thompson	John Blany
Daniel Thompson	James Bertwhistle
Patience Bond	Thomas Scott Bond
Hugh Briarly	Eleasor Briarly
Solomon Brown	John Brown
James Cherry	Robert Cherry
Jesse Jarrett	James Condron

1783 TAX LIST OF HARFORD COUNTY, MARYLAND
Bush River Upper & Eden Hundreds

Securities

Matthew McClehany
Richard Cooly
Matthew McClehany
Richard Coop
Thomas Wheeler
James Curry Sr.
Ruth Bussey
Elizabeth England
Elizabeth England
Elizabeth England
Francis Gibson
David Tate
Robert Glenn
Charles Gillespy
Samuel Harper
Asael Hitchcock
Asael Hitchcock
Joseph Jones
Matthew Cooly
Matthew Cooly
Matthew Cooly
James Cherry
Matthew Cooley
John Long Sr.
John Long Sr.
John Long Jr.
Hugh Briarly
Thomas Poteet (Barrim)?
James Carlon
William Ditto
Philip Maddin
William Norris Sr.
William Norris Sr.
John Poulson
James Prine
William Bankhead
John Poulson
Daniel McComas
William Robinson
Charles Gillespy

Single Men

Thomas Connor
Richard Cooly Jr.
Barachia Coop
James Coop
James Corbett
James Curry Jr.
John Dearmott
George England
Robert England
Samuel England
John Gibson
Jacob Gladdin
William Glenn
John Goggings
James Harper
Henry Hitchcock
John Hitchcock
Thomas Hutson
Eli Kennard
Joseph Kennard
Levi Kennard
Patrick Kean
Ambrose Jones
Daniel Long
Luke Long
Peter Long
John Lattimore
Daniel Mc Donald
James McGaw
Daniel McGuire
James Maddin
James Norris
Thomas Norris
Asael Poulson
Peter Prine
John Reardon
Noah Reaves
John Slygar
Joseph Robinson
Michael Rock

1783 TAX LIST OF HARFORD COUNTY, MARYLAND
Bush River Upper & Eden Hundreds

Securities

Richard Hope
John Rutlidge
Moses Johnson
James Sinclair
Thomas G. Howard
Thomas Sharp
Thomas Ayres
Ezekiel Slade
Alexander Stewart
Thomas Street
Thomas Sharp
Robert Watt
John Long Jr.
Josiah Carter

Single Men

John Ross
Shadrack Rutlidge
William Rutlidge
Andrew Scott
Ruebin Sealy
Thomas Sharp Jr.
Richard Shores
Thomas Slade
William Steward
John Street
John Tilbrook
Josiah Watt
Casper Waver
John Worrick

LIST OF FREE MALES UNDER 21

Andrew Bigam
John Blany
Thomas Denbow
Jesse Everett
Abraham Kadel?
John Heaps
Archibald Henderson
William Huston
Abraham Jarritt
John Roste?

John Kirkwood
David Davis Jr.
Joseph McClasky
William McClasky
Alex. McComas
Jesse Norris
Nathaniel Norris
Jesse Pocock
John Rockhold
Peter Varnay

End of Bush River Upper & Eden Hundreds

1783 TAX LIST OF HARFORD COUNTY, MARYLAND
Bush River Lower Hundred

Return of Property in Bush River Lower Hundred made by William Bradford, assessor, 1783

Name	# of white inhabitants	Tract Name	# acres
William Ady, cooper	8	pt. Friends Discovery & Colegates Last Shift	181
Joseph Aston	11		
John Baker	3		
Jacob Baxtor	3		
John Baxtor	5		
Hugh Bay	—		
William Bay	7	Hopewell	60
		Busseys Adventure	22
Francis Billingsley	11	pt. Gibsons Park	200
		Paca's Search	33
Moses Byford	8		
Buckler Bond	6	pt. Poplar Neck & pt. Joshua's Meadow	300
		Mill Seat & Improvements	27
Dennis Bond	6	pt. Poplar Neck	500
		pt. Joshua's Meadow	20
		Clarksons Purchase	16
James Bond	2	pt. Poplar Neck & pt. Joshua's Meadow	250
		pt. Morgan's lott	66
Ralph Bond	—	pt. Osborns Lott	200
		pt. Harris' Trust	100
		pt. Abells Lott	150
		pt. My Lords Gift	18
		Websters Gift	12
Samuel Bond	5	pt. Burr	132
Thomas Bond Sr.	2	pt. Harris Trust	50
		pt. Gibsons Ridge	180
		pt. Prestons Luck	20
		pt. Abells Lott	150
		Kavis Misfortune	143
		Tower Hill	100
		Mile's Improvement	40
William Bradford, assessor	11	pt. Littleton	371
Mary Brownen	8		
John Brown, weaver	5		

1783 TAX LIST OF HARFORD COUNTY, MARYLAND
Bush River Lower Hundred

Name	# of white Inhabitants	Tract Name	# acres
William Bond, Esq.	2	pt. Poplar Neck & pt. Joshua's Meadow	250
		pt. Scotts Improvement Enlarged & pt. Addition to ditto	200 1/2
		pt. Morgan's lott	133 1/3
William Brown, quaker	2		
William Brown, carpenter	6	pt. My Lord's Gift	64
Edward Bull	5	pt. Bells Camp	100
Jacob Bull, Jr.	3	pt. Bolls Camp	60
Jacob Bull of John	5	pt. Hewitts Range	100
		pt. Cockens lott	39
		Rocky Point	20
		pt. Tricks in Things	4 1/2
Jacob Bull, Sr.	9	pt. Bells Camp	139 1/2
		pt. The Group	120
		Grist Mill	
William Bunting	2		
James Carroll Jr.	8	pt. Harris' Trust	100
James Coalman	2	Lott in Scotts Fields	1/2
Robert Collins	2	Pork Hill	100
		pt. Survivors Point	12
John Cook	3		
John Cooper	4		
John Creighton, carpenter	5		
Matthew Criswell	3		
John Cuddy (B.S.) blacksmith	4		
George Cuningham	5		
John Daugherty	4		
Hugh Deaver	3		
Joshua Dickinson	3		
Josiah Dier	—	pt. Websters lott	35
James Dobbins	5		
Eleanor Durham	5	pt. Edmunds Cap & pt. Bilbury Hole	155
Joshua Durham	11		
Samuel Durham	10	pt. Bilbury Hole, pt. Ewings Contrivance, pt. Friends Advise, pt. Durhams 1st & 3rd Add. to Bilbury Hole & 2nd Add. to Durhams Meadows	242

1783 TAX LIST OF HARFORD COUNTY, MARYLAND
Bush River Lower Hundred

Name	# of white inhabitants	Tract Name	# acres
James Everett, surveyer	2	pt. Wilson Choice	52
		pt. Astons & Dales Chance-6	
		pt. Wheelers Purchase &	
		pt. Bulls Care	48
John Fulton	10	pt. Bush Grove	10
		The Meadows	44
Nathan Gallion	7	pt. Everly Hills &	
		Gibsons Ridge	234
William Godwin	6		
John Green	6	pt. Bells Camp	100
		pt. Gibson's Camp	246
Nicholas Groceman	5		
William Hall of Aquilla	1	pt. Constant Friendship	400
		Hickory Ridge	30
		pt. Haha Indeed	525
		Harford Upper Hundred	
		Mill & Improvements	5
		pt. Come by Chance	30
Edward Hamilton	3		
Michael Hamnor	8		
Patrick Haney	7		
Patrick Hanlin	6		
John Hathorn	13		
John Hays Jr.	0	pt. My Lords Gift	54
		pt. Gillingham	135
Lemuel Howard	11	pt. Andersons lott & pt.	
		of luck	264
		pt. Giffins Camp	138
		Poor Mans Purchase	50
Benjamin Howard's heirs	_	pt. Andersons lott	264
Robert Hunt	4		
James Jarvis	7	House & Lott in Scott's Field	2
John Jarvis	6		
Gilbert Jones	3	House & Lott in Scott's Fields	
Hannah Jones (widow)	8		
William Jones	11	pt. Gillingham	150
		pt. My Lords Gift	25
		Websters Lott	5
		Gunpowder Lower (abington lott)	

1783 TAX LIST OF HARFORD COUNTY, MARYLAND
Bush River Lower Hundred

Name	# of white inhabitants	Tract Name	# acres
William Jones, Jr.	1		
Christopher Kent	1		
Hannah Kitely	6	Gunpowder Lower	
		Abington Lott Improved	
		Prestons Deceit	50
		pt. William's Fortune	30
		Name unknown	80
John Kitely	8		
Thomas Knight	5		
John Lewis	6		
Joseph Lewis	0	pt. Ewings Contrivance,	
		pt. Durham's 1st & 3rd	
		Addition & Bulbury Hole	229
Aaron McComas	1	pt. Littleton	57
Aaron McComas Jr.	0	pt. Ann's Dower	50
Alexander McComas	6	Horse Range	200
Alexander McComas, Jr.	0		
Edward McComas	5	Edinburgh	100
		Gunpowder Lower	
		Abington lott	
James McComas, Esq.	11	pt. Greshams College	305
		pt. Littleton	73 1/2
		pt. Osborn's lott	65
		Gunpowder Lower	
		Abington lott Improved	
John McComas of Daniel	7	pt. Osborn's lott	200
		Gunpowder Lower	
		Abington lott	
John McComas of William	8	pt. Ann's Dower	100
		pt. Littleton	19
Martha McComas	2		
William McComas of Solomon	5	pt. Ann's Dower	50
Daniel McPhail	6		
John Maddox	9		
David Malsby	5		
James Mather	7	pt. Come by Chance	20
		pt. Whitakers Enlargement	69
		Bradford's Barrens	100
Michael Mather	0		
James Matthews	0	pt. Majors Choice	535
James Moore, Jr.	4		

1783 TAX LIST OF HARFORD COUNTY, MARYLAND
Bush River Lower Hundred

Name	# of white inhabitants	Tract Name	# acres
Israel Morris (Refused to render an account of his property)			
	6	pt. Gibsons Ridge	200
		Grist & Saw Mills	
Joseph Morrison	5		
Alexander Norris	1		
Benjamin B. Norris	7	pt. Burr	264
Daniel Norris	3		
Jane Nugeant, (widow)			
John Norris of John	1	pt. Burr	72
		pt. Gibsons Ridge	50
Richard Norris	6		
Sarah Norris	4	pt. Everly Hills	178
William Osborne	3	pt. Burr	112
William Paca, Esq.	—	Paca's Meadows	202
		Island	48
		Harford Upper Hundred	
		Pearsons Park & Bond's Purchase	275
Barnard Preston	5	Prestons Conquest	75
Benjamin Preston	1	Scotts Range	180
		Scotts Spott	61
Joseph Renshaw	—	pt. Rachels Delight	100
		pt. Wheelers Purchase	8
Philip Renshaw	—	pt. Wheelers Purchase Enlarged	33
Thomas Renshaw	1	pt. Wheelers Purchase Enlarged	45 1/2
Benjamin Rhoads	—	pt. Pleasant Hill	50
Mary Rhoads	4	pt. Pleasant Hill	17
		Good Neighbour	14
George Riley (Virginia)	—	pt. 3 Brothers	50
Edward Robinson	5		
Richard Robinson	7	pt. Poverty Inclosed	29
		pt. Surveyors Point	69
		Wilson's Retreat	100
		Averillas Garden	11
		pt. Cocken's lott	25
William Robinson, (cooper)	5		
Robert Rogers	9		
James Roney	3		
John Roney	7		

1783 TAX LIST OF HARFORD COUNTY, MARYLAND
Buxh River Lower Hundred

Name	# of white inhabitants	Tract Name	# acres
James Saunders	8		
James Scott (Coroner)	7	pt. Ewings Contrivance-194	
Aquila Scott of Aquilla	8	pt. Bulls Camp & pt. Trust	256
Aquila Scott of James	3	pt. Scott's Improvement Enlarged	200
		pt. Burr	30
		as Ex. of Ann Scott deceased	
Daniel Scott	1	pt. Bells Camp	60
		House & Lott in Scotts Fields	
Joseph Saunders	—		
Thomas Saunders	3	pt. Gibsons Ridge	50
John Smith (fuller)	9	Land name unknown with improvements	20
		Grist Mill	
		Fulling Mill	
John Smith Jr.	—		
Nathaniel Smithson	—	pt. Bells Camp	100
Thomas Smithson	7	pt. Bells Camp	100
William Smithson, Esq.	5	Meritons Lott	500
		pt. Burr	100
Abel Spencer	5	pt. Pleasant Hill	50
		pt. Partnership	17
		pt. Kerseys Lodge	120
		Jenny's Delight	55
		Rachels Delight	28
Aquilla Standiford	11	pt. Homer Resurvey	271
John Stockdail	9		
William Stokesbury Jr.	10		
Andrew Thompson	10	pt. Hewits Range	100
Thomas Tredway	6		
Samuel Vance	6		
Richard Waldrum	4		
Robert Watters	7		
John Weaks	9		
Enoch West	5		
Michael West	6		
Nathaniel West Sr.	4		
Isaac Whitaker	8	pt. Prestons Luck	70
		pt. Gibsons Ridge & Add. to Gibsons Ridge	200

1783 TAX LIST OF HARFORD COUNTY, MARYLAND
Bush River Lower Hundred

Name	# of white inhabitants	Tract Name	# acres
Isaac Whitaker (continued)		House & lott in Scotts Field	1
		House & lott in Abington	1
Joshua Whitaker	4	Chesnut Ridge	242
		pt St. Albans	250
		pt. Bonds Discovery	110
Stephen White	6		
Francis Williams	5		
Henry Wilson	—	Bush Grove	460
		pt. Walnut	30
		Addition to Bush Grove	146
Rachel Wilson	—	pt. Gibsons Park	200
William Wilson, Esq.	1	pt. Gibson's Park	400
		Gunpowder Lower	
		Abington lott	1/2
Edward York	3		

Paupers	# whites	Paupers	# whites
Isaac Akeright	5	negro Tom Howard	—
John Battensly	2	James Jolly	1
William Baxtor	4	Catherine Malone	3
John Blev ?	4	Elizabeth Mitchell	9
Robert Calender	—	Thomas Monohon	5
Charles Coalman	4	John Reise	3
Elizabeth Crosby	4	William Roles	2
Mary Deamon	2	Paul Shields	5
Alexander Duncan	3	William Stokesbury Sr.	
Alexander Harvy	5	John Thorn	3

Securities

Andrew Thompson
Moses Byford
Joseph Aston
John McComas of Daniel
Daniel Norris

John McComas of Daniel
John McComas of Daniel

Single Men

Edward Brown
William Byford
William Chinworth
Daniel Cuningham
James Cuningham
Thomas Cuningham
Joshua Day
Robert Day

1783 TAX LIST OF HARFORD COUNTY, MARYLAND
Bush River Lower Hundred

Securities	Single Men
John Stockdail	Jacob Dimmett
	Aquila Durham
Joshua Durham	Daniel Durham
Joshua Durham	John Durham
John Fulton	William Fulton
	Alexius Fulton
John Green	Henry Green
John Green	John Green Jr.
Patrick Hanlin	Thomas Hanlin
Joseph Rose	Richard Harper
Hugh Bay	Arthur McCann (weaver)
Patrick Hamlin	John Moore (weaver)
William Bradford	John Norris of Benjamin
B. B. Norris	Thomas Norris of John
Aquila Durham	James Rattican
Edward Robinson	Richard Robinson of Edward
John Roney	Roger Roney
John Smith Jr.	Thomas Stockdail
Alexander Norris	George Taylor (shoemaker)
Gilbert Jones	John Thompson (joiner)
Robert Collins	Esau Turk
Robert Collins	John Weaklin

GUNPOWDER UPPER AND LOWER HUNDREDS

Name	# of white inhabitants	Tract Name	# acres
Jacob Adams	5		
Jonathan Ady	5	pt. Bonds Pleasant Hills-102	
John Allen	7		
Ann Allinder	2		
Jane Allinder	7		
John Allinder	8	Goldsmiths Neck & Wolfs Harbour & Arthurs Delay & Og King of Basham	350
		Peirsons Outlett & pt. Wetheralls Addition	300
Benjamin Amoss of Benj.	1	pt. Amoss'Care	106
John Amoss	1?	Wilsons Neighbour	39
		pt. Saplin Ridge	16
		Addition to Carkles Park-39	

1783 TAX LIST OF HARFORD COUNTY, MARYLAND
Gunpowder Upper & Lower Hundreds

Name	# of white inhabitants	Tract Name	# acres
Benjamin Amoss of James	6	George & Joseph's Farm	25
		Abrahams Pleasure	140
		Land with Mill	10
		Eden Hundred	
		Chestnut Ridge	38
		pt. Fox Hills	63 1/2
		Bowan's Addition	59
		pt. Londonderry	10 1/2
		pt. Clothwortheys Harbour	10
		Grist Mill	
		ditto ditto	
		pt. Powells Choice	46 3/4
		Wheelers Outlett	20
James Amoss, Jr.	7	Pt. the Grove	100
		Harford Upper Hundred	
		pt. My Lords Gift	208
		Eden Hundred	
		Brantons Ridge & Sons Add.	310
		Roaches Choice	40
Maldon Amoss	8	pt. The Grove	133
Mordecai Amoss	2	pt. The Grove	100
		Land purchased of Benedict Wheeler	80
Robert Amoss	—	Name unknown	50
Thomas Amoss	—	pt. Robinson's Venture	100
		Timber Swamp	30
William Amoss Jr.	9	pt. The Grove	75
		pt. Bond's Forest	139
William Amoss Sr.	8	pt. Clarksons Purchase	200
William Andrews heirs	—	7 1/4 lotts in Joppa	
		Land name unknown	50
Shepherd Armstrong	9	pt. Charles' Bounty	100
Joseph Aston	1	pt. Charles' Neighbour	138
Charles Baker	6	Preston's Receipt	50
		Center	30
		Hills Hill	50
Theophiles Baker	4		
William Baker	5		
William Baldwin	4	pt. Brooks' Cross	200
John Barnes	3		
Hugh Barthlay	4		
Hugh Bay	3	pt. Charles' Bounty	100

1783 TAX LIST OF HARFORD COUNTY, MARYLAND
Gunpowder Upper & Lower Hundreds

Name	# of white inhabitants	Tract Name	# acres
Elizabeth Berry	5		
Samuel Birkhead	7	Colerain	403
Elijah Blackstone	4		
Charles Blagdon	3		
Henry Both	4		
Jacob Bond	5	pt. American's Inheritance For Ever	344
John Bond Sr.	2	pt. Bond's Forest	87
John Bond of John	—	Add. To Bond's Tanyard	100
		pt. Bond's Forest	98 1/2
		Bond's Sylvania	123
Peter Bond	—	pt. Cleggets Forest	252
		pt. Bond's Forest	478
William Bond of John	6	pt. Bond's Forest	125
John B. Bordley	—	Pools Island	246
Robert Brazeir	6		
Arthur Brownly	4		
John Brooks	—	pt. Brook's Cross	100
Joshua Brown	6	Bond's Inheritance	249
		Hog Point	40
		pt. Elk Neck	15 3/4
		Hucklebury Hill	7
William Bull Sr.	10	Partners Hill	69
		Robertsons OUtlett	170
		pt. Cecils Adventure	120
		Beaver Dam Cleared	25
		Robinson's Add. to Outlett	32
William Bull of Abraham	6	pt. Cecils Adventure	139
David Calwell	6		
Samuel Calwell, assessor	10	pt. The Grove	111
		pt. Bond's Forest	133 1/2
Lancelot Carlile	5	Carliles Range	44
		Carliles Park	50
		Carliles Park	10
Robert Carlile	1		
Elizabeth Carroll	1		
James Carroll, Sr.	2	pt. Expectation	134
		pt. Barton's Chance	15
Christopher Cashman	5	lott in Abington	
William Chambers	3		
David Chelson	7		

1783 TAX LIST OF HARFORD COUNTY, MARYLAND
Gunpowder Upper & Lower Hundreds

Name	# of white inhabitants	Tract Name	# acres
Richard Chesny	6		
John Clark	5	pt. Paca's Park	566
Abnur Cloud	—	Envilles Chaise	175
		pt. Home & Resurvey	176
		Little Brittain	116
Isaac Cochron	7		
Robert Conn	10	Rangers Range	100
		pt. Morgans Lott	62
Edward Connard	6		
Calvin Cooper	9		
John Corbin	1	pt. Charle's Bounty	100
Nathan Corbin	9	pt. Charle's Bounty	100
Alexander Cowan	5	Preston's Deceit	50
		Preservation	340
Elizabeth Cox	3		
John H. Cromwell	1	Joppa Lott	
Edward Cuningham	6		
William Daily	6		
Dr. Dales heirs	—	Joppa lotts improved	
Henry Darnall of Baltimore	—	property at Amoss Mill	
Isaac Daws	7	pt. Clarksons Purchase	50
John Day Jr.	8	pt. Maxwells Conclusion	200
		pt. Days Priv. elidge	10
John Day Sr.	10	pt. Maxwells Conclusion	314
		Days Double Purchase	73
		pt. Homewood	84
		Gays Meadows	30
		Locust Neck	100
		Hansons Neglect	60
Amelia Debruler	4		
George Debruler	10		
James Debruler	6	White Oak Swamp	4 1/2
William Debruler	1	pt. Gods Providence	50
		Sarah's Delight	80
		Hills Double Purchase	23
John Denning	7		
John Devins	8		
Thomas Downs	—		
John Domey	12		
Thomas Domey	7	pt. Warrington	128
		Days Privelidge	6 3/4

1783 TAX LIST OF HARFORD COUNTY, MARYLAND
Gun Powder Upper & Lower Hundreds

Name	# of white inhabitants	Tract Name	# acres
John Dorsey (Joppa)	2	Savories Farm	290
		Thompsons Fortune	140
		Joppa Lott	2
John H. Dorsey	4		
William Doterage	5		
Joseph Dulre	4		
Abel Dungan	6		
Thomas Durbin	7	pt. Smith's Chance	50
John Durham	9	Eyruks Garrison	150
		Richardson's Right	69
		Websters Otto Point	11 1/2
Robert Dutton	1	pt. Bonds Forest	50
Joseph Dyer	9	pt. Bonds Forest	304
William Eaton	7		
James Elliott	3	pt. Bonds Forest	164
John Elliott	7		
James Erven	8		
Isaac Everett	5	pt. Bonds Forest	75
James Everett	4		
James Everett	7	pt. Charles Bounty	100
Samuel Everett	4		
Patrick Finnagan	0	lott in Abington Improved	1 1/2
Negroe Fip (set free by Jo Presbury)	0		
John Flanagan	9		
Benjamin Ford	5		
John Ford	6		
Moses Ford	1		
William Ford	0	Bednal Green	100
		pt. Bonds Pleasant Hills	61 1/2
Joshua France	4	Swathmore	170
George Garretson	3	pt. Jerusalem	159
James Garretson	1		
John Garretson	2	pt. Bonds Gift	170
Thomas Garritson	1		
John Lee Gibson	0	(Flour at Otto Point 41 barr. condemned)	
Richard Gorthorp, blacksmith	9		
Henry Gough	0	pt. Masseys Addition	200
		Halls Ridge	218
		Websters Landing	10
		Lock	64
		Leval	26

1783 TAX LIST OF HARFORD COUNTY, MARYLAND
Gunpowder Upper and Lower Hundreds

Name	# of white inhabitants	Tract Name	# acres
Henry Gough (continued)		pt. Masseys Ridge	50
		Websters Meadows	54
		pt. Warrington	50
Copeland Gouldsmith	0	property at Onion's Mill	
Richard Graves	0	pt. Warrington	300
		Legals Chance & Trouble	50
		Chelbury Hall	122
		pt. Hathonays Trust	82
		pt. Williams Fortune	16
		pt. Outlett	8
James Green	7		
Richard Gregory	8		
William Groves (Joppa)	0		
William Gurn	0	pt. BondsWater Mills & Mill	30
Christopher Hanover	5		
David Harry	7	pt. Bonds Forest	12
William Hassett	4	1/2 lott in Abington Improved	
James Hayhurst Jr.	5		
James Hayhurst	3	Harford & Carliles Park	160
		Leased land	40
James Hicks	10		
James Hill	0	Diverses Chance	58
Martha Hill	1	pt. Warrington	140
		pt. Days Priveledge	7 3/4
Sarah Hill	6		
Thomas Hill	0		
Holland & Cowan (Otto Point)	0	Lotts, wharf, house, shipyard, & 1 small vessall on the stocks	
Francis Holland	7	Spesutias Lower Hundred	
		Primrose Hill	304
Jane Horner	8	Williams Ridge	170
Henry Houching	0	pt. Bonds Forest	8
		land on winters Run	30
James Huggans	7		
John Hughes	6		
William Hughes	3		
John Hughston	14	Lott in Joppa	
		American Inheritance Forever	344
William Rightston	3		

1783 TAX LIST OF HARFORD COUNTY, MARYLAND
Gunpowder·Upper and Lower Hundreds

Name	# of White inhabitants	Tract Name	# acres
Joseph Hunter	5		
Thomas Hutchins	3		
John Hambleton Jones	2		
Levan Ingram	0	Joppa lott improved	
Rachel Irons	4		
Cordelia James	1		
Francis Jenkens	4	lott in Abington	
Jonathan Jenkins	9		
William Jenkens	5	pt. The Grove	150
Lewis Jiner	4		
Michael Jenkins (B.C) Balto. County?	0	pt. Brooks Cross	200
Hugh Karnay	6		
Thomas Kell	10	Williams Delight	50
		Bonds 2nd Thought	125
William Kerr	5		
Rachel Kitely	1		
Thomas Lacy	6		
Benjamin Lancaster	4	pt. Bonds Forest	75
Joseph Lancaster	5		
Jesse Lancaster	7?	pt. Charles' Bounty	100
David Lee	10	pt. Bonds W. Mills Mill thereon	50
William Lee	6		
Benedict Legoe	7		
Mary Legoe	0		
Ann Lewin	5		
Clement Lewis	12	pt. Cleggets Forest	198
Elizabeth Lusby	2		
Joseph Lusby	1		
Susanna Lusby	1		
Matthias Lynch	4	Abington Lott improved	
Elizabeth Lytle	2	pt. Agaway	106 3/4
James Lytle	3	pt. Agaway	212 1/2
Nathan Lytle	1	Lott at Otto Point	
Daniel McComas of Wm.	10	Gresoms Colledge	100
		pt. Clagets Forest	200
Nicholas McComas	0	Lott at Abington	
Moses McComas	7	pt. Gresoms Colledge	95
Moses Magnus	5		

1783 TAX LIST OF HARFORD COUNTY, MARYLAND
Gunpowder Upper and Lower Hundreds

Name	# of white inhabitants	Tract Name	# acres
Wheeler Malsby	5	pt. Charles' Bounty	100
Thomas Marford	0	Oxford Resurvey	111
		Edward Loyd (Joppa Lotts)	
Thomas Marford (Forest)	6	Nancy's Gift leased	43
Robert Martin	2	pt. Charles' Bounty	100
James Mason	7	pt. Grooms Chance	150
John Mason	8	pt. Grooms Chance	150
Thomas Maul	3	1/4 lott in Abington Improved	
Benjamin Meads	5		
Robert & A. McKim	0	720 Busshels wheat & 100 barrels of flour	
Thomas Mills	6		
Enoch Mitchell	8	pt. Bonds Pleasant Hills	50
Richard Monk	7	Matthews Double Purchase	120
Kidd Morsall	4	Lott in Abington Improved	
George Mulherren	4	Smiths Fortune	100
Henry Murphy	2	2 lotts in Abington Improved	
David Nelson	5		
James Nichols	2	Bartons Chance	25
		Anything	9
Francis Norrington	8		
Aquila Norris of Edward	5	pt. Prospect	52 1/2
		pt. Betseys Anaiety	73 1/2
Edward Norris of Edward	7	pt. Prospect	111
		Addition to the End	40
		pt. Betsys Anaiety	42
Edward Norris of Joseph	6		
Hannah Norris	2		
James Norris Jr.	3		
James Norris Sr.	6	Norris' Adventure	50
		pt. Expectation	50
Rebecca Norris (wife to Abraham)	3		
Thomas Norris of Edward	6	pt. Prospect	51
William Norris of John	8	pt. Cleggets Forest	122
William Norris of Joseph	5	Pt. Macedon	50
Joseph Nubraugh	4		
Henry Oldham	0	pt. Bonds Gift	69
Thomas Onion	0	Sweaty Banks	206

1783 TAX LIST OF HARFORD COUNTY, MARYLAND
Gunpowder Upper and Lower Hundreds

Name	# of white inhabitants	Tract Name	# acres
Hannah & Stephen Onion	14	Onion's Inheritance	804
		3 lotts in Joppa	
		2 mills & improvements	
		pt. Jerusalam	149
		Turky Hills	160
		pt. Home Resurvey	1121
		Add. to Onions Pasture Ground	310
		White Hall	300
		Onion's Gravilly Hills	254
		Addition to Hopewell	310
		Coopers Paradise	100
		Onion's Pasture Ground	226
		pt. The Dock Resurveyed	100
		Ishams Addition	27
		Rebecca's Lott	100
Samuel G. Osborne	8	pt. Colerain	252
		Gunpowder Lower Hundred	
		Greenfields Double Purchase	105
Edward Parker	4	pt. Brooks Cross	117 1/2
		James' Range	90
		Stewards Desire	84
		Temperance's Lott	20
		Land & Oil Mill	3
Daniel Parsons	3	1/5 of a lott in Abington	
John Parsons	7		
George Patrick	6		
Aquila Paca Sr.	0	Lott & Wharf House at Otto Point	
		White Hall	10
		Addition to Water Mills	210
Joseph Phipps	5		
Nathan Phipps (Joppa)	3		
John Pierce	11	Addition to Poverty Inclosed	115
		pt. Bonds Forest	60
James Poteet	3		
George Pouge	7		
Joseph Presbury Jr.	4	Cotteth Neglect	228 1/2
		Presburys Discovery	10
George Presbury	7	Hopewell	123
		New London	162
		Elk Neck	410
		pt. Little Brittain	32

1783 TAX LIST OF HARFORD COUNTY, MARYLAND
Gunpowder Upper and Lower Hundreds

Name	# of white inhabitants	Tract Name	# acres
Mary Presbury (wife to Joseph)-0			
Mary Presbury	0		
Benjamin Preston	0	Whitely	50
		Martin's Adventure	92
		pt. Hog Neck	20
James Price	3		
Nathaniel Ramsey	0	pt. Jone's Inheritance	56
James Reace	4		
Thomas Richardson	3	Timber Hills	175
		Bonds Pleasant Hills	56
William Richardson	9	Stony Batter	150
		Jarretts Discovery	36
		pt. Antioch	114
		pt. Macedon	50
		pt. Charles' Bounty	40
Samuel Richmond	8		
Samuel Ricketts	4		
Billingsley Roberts	6		
John Roberts	1	Pitch Craft & Pole Cat	146
Archibald Robinson	5	Betseys Hope	100
Edward Robinson	0	Little Worth & Wards Adventure	100
Elizabeth Robinson	1		
Temperence Robinson	2	pt. Carliles Part	46
William Robinson	7	pt. Bonds Gift	40
		Reserved land	65
Aquila Rose	2		
Joseph Rose	8	pt. Wood Yard	22
		2 lotts in Abington	
Daniel Ruff	8	lott in Abington	
Benjamin Rumsey	8	Westminster	260
		Hall's Pasture Ground	23
		Richardsons Reserve	118 3/4
		Good Endeavour	142
		Anns Delight	200
		Risteaus Security	40
		Joppa lotts as guardian for Maxwell heirs	
		Fathers Last Will	925
		Maxwells Addition	70
		Yorks Hope	190

1783 TAX LIST OF HARFORD COUNTY, MARYLAND
Gunpowder Upper and Lower Hundreds

Name	# of white inhabitants	Tract Name	# acres
Benjamin Rumsey (continued)		Briarton's Troubles	70
		pt. Bridewell Dock	50
		Cabbin Neck	124
		for Phebe Maxwell	
Jacob Rush	8	pt. Bonds Forrest	160
John Saunders	9		
Robert Saunders	9	Jone's Inheritance	396
		Smith's Discovery	77
Thomas Saunders, miller	3	pt. Expectation	10
		Susquehanna Hundred	
		Scottland	100
William Saunders	1	lott in Abington	
Henry Scarff	8	pt. Friendship	78
John Scarff	8	pt. Bonds Gift	100
Robert Scott	5	Coot Hill	135 1/2
John Sewell	9	pt. Cleggets Forrest	150
		Archibald Rolers Addition &	
		Turkey Hills	100
		Joppa lott, lott & shipyard	
John Skinner	0	Joppa Lotts improved	
Averilla Smith	4	pt. Foxes Refuse	100
Basil Smith	4		
James Smith	0	Buckinghamshire	150
John Smith	1	Aarons Spring Neck	23
		Websters Enlargement	106
		Abington lott	
Josias Smith	5	pt. Fools Refuse	30
Thomas R. Smith	1		
William Smith	6	Bonds Forest pt.	200
Daniel Smithson	3	pt. The Grove	50
Enoch Spencer	5	pt. Carliles Park	20
		Carliles Range	100
		Addition to Carliles Park	65
James Spencer	6		
Ann Standiford	4	land name unknown	9 1/2
Bathia Standiford	1		
James Standiford	1		
John Standiford	7	pt. Bonds Forest	60
Dixon Stansbury	0	pt. Abrahams Pleasure	75
Edmund Stansbury	0	pt. Bonds Gift	218

1783 TAX LIST OF HARFORD COUNTY, MARYLAND
Gunpowder Upper and Lower Hundreds

Name	# of white inhabitants	Tract Name	# acres
John Stewart	2		
Sarah Stewart	2	pt. Brantons Ridge	100
Thomas Strong	9	pt. Maxwells Conclusion	200
Benjamin Talbott	5		
Edmund Talbott	5	pt. Bonds Gift	100
Andrew Tate	6		
Charles Taylor	4	pt. Charles' Neighbour	190
John Taylor Esq.	0	pt. Clarksons Purchase	294
		pt. Cleggetts Forest	196
		Bonds Good Will	20
Rachel Taylor	0		
Thomas Taylor	7	lott in Joppa Improved	
John Thomas	7		
Mary Thomas	11		
Thomas Thomas	5		
Edward Thompson	3	lott improved at Otto Point	
Thomas A. Thompson	4	pt. Charles' Neighbour	166
James Thrift	5		
John Timmons	5	pt. Friendship	150
Joseph Townsend, school Master	0		
Joseph Toy	8	Abington lott improved	
James Trapnall	3	pt. Dunkeil	475
Robert Travis	11		
Thomas Turner	8	pt. Envilles Chance	55
Daniel Tyson	0	pt. Prospect	190
Richard Vanhorn	5		
Charlton Waltham	6	pt. Maxwells Conclusion	635
Charles Watters	1	Dallam's Self Preservation	200
Isaac Watters	4		
Stephen Watters	6	Hopewell	204
		pt. Seneko Ridge	84
		Seniko Ridge	50
		Talbotts Care	80
		James 2nd Addition	100
Walter Watters	0	Abington lott	
Michael Webster	5		
Henry Wetherall	0	Linnen Manufactory	167
James Wetherall	0	Lewis' Purchased Improved	205
		Samuels Hill	45
Robert Whiteford	9	pt. Bonds Gift	158

1783 TAX LIST OF HARFORD COUNTY, MARYLAND
Gunpowder Upper and Lower Hundred

Name	# of white inhabitants	Tract Name	# acres
Hugh Wiley	4		
Enoch Williams	8		
Lambert Wilmer	10	pt. Bonds Forrest	65
Benjamin Wilson	1	pt. Maxwells Conclusion	200
		Mirino	600
		Taylors Chance	57
James Wilson	0		
John Wilson	1		
John Wilson, miller	8	Smalls	18
		pt. Dunkeil mills	25
John Wilson	8	Timber Hall	100
		pt. Bonds Forrest	50
Margaret Wilson	1		
Martha Wilson	1		
Thomas Wilson	0	pt. Bonds Forest	87 1/2
William Wilson	9	pt. Smith's Chance	100
Edward Wise	4		
Henry Wise	5		
John Weston	0	1/2 lott in Joppa	
Richard Woollen	7		
Jonathan Woodland	0	Masseys Addition	200
George Yates	8		
Edward York	4		
Edward York Sr.	2	pt. Yorks Chance	43 1/2
George York Jr.	4	pt. Bridewell	25
		pt. Yorks Chance	60
George York Sr.	7	pt. Gods Providence	160
Oliver York	0	pt. Bridewell	25
		pt. Yorks Chance	60
Samuel Young's heirs	0	pt. Bonds Forest	47

Securities

Jonathan Ady Sr.
Jonathan Ady Sr.
Jonathan Ady Sr.
Jonathan Ady Sr.

Single Men

James Ady
John Armstrong
Benjamin Bateman (at W. Amoss)
Abraham Bull
James Cahall
John Calder, joiner
Benjamin Carroll
John Carson

1783 TAX LIST OF HARFORD COUNTY, MARYLAND
Gunpowder Upper and Lower Hundreds

Securities

John Trap
Isaac Everitt

Joshua France
Hugh Wiley

William Ford
John Garretson

Charlton Waltham
Charlton Waltham

Patrick Finnagan
James Trapnall

Benjamin Lancaster
Edward Parker
James Poteet
John Parsons
William Baldwin

David Lee
Samuel Ricketts

John Sewell

John Stewart

John Day

William Hughston

Single Men

Darby Carty
Joseph Colling
John Conn
Thomas Conn
Alexander Cook
Nicholas Cratts
James Crinstone
Thomas Cuningham
Benjamin Daws
Thomas Ford
Samuel Garretson
John Garritt
Charles Gillespy, cooper
Thomas Hill, mariner
John Holland
Richard Holloway, school master
Jacob Hutchins
William Jefferys, school master
Amoss Jones at Wilsons Mill
William Jones
Charles Kelly
Anthony Knowlman
Benjamin Lancaster, Jr.
WilliamLobe
Joshua Norrington
John Parsons, Jr.
John Pruitt
John Evans Reese
James Renshaw
Edward Ricketts
John Roberts of Billingsley
James Robinson
L. Smith
Nicholas Spencer
Edward Taylor
John Taylor of Charles
Joshua Taylor
John Thrap at B. Wilsons
William Trus
Daniel Weaks
John Weaks

-115-

1783 TAX LIST OF HARFORD COUNTY, MARYLAND
Gunpowder Upper and Lower Hundreds

Securities

Robert Whiteford

Jane Homer or Horner

Charles Watters

Single Men

John Whiteford
Robert Whiteford, weaver
Matthew Wigfield
William Wigfield
James Witherall, sadler
John Wollon
John Wood at Moses Dillions

Paupers in Gunpowder Upper & Lower Hundreds

Name	# Whites	Name	# Whites
Prudence Arnold	5	Samuel Oaks	2
Edward Apleton (infirm)	—	Richard Ogan	
John Aston (infirm)		John Phips	3
Perry Brown	2	Thomas Richardson Jr.	10
William Cammell	4	Thomas Sampson	2
Samuel Day	2	John Silva	3
Charles Divine	4	Elizabeth Smith	4
John Durham	2	John Strickland	2
Sarah Fory & Eliza. Morrow	—	Matthew Swany	
Thomas Freeman	3	Toby Toogood	1
John G. Howard	5	Richard Tue	2
James Huston	3	James Underhill	
Patrick McCue	4	Martha Vanhorn	3
Sarah Marrett	2	Thomas Weaks	6
William Meads (infirm)	—	Jacob Wear	6

End of Gunpowder Upper and Lower Hundreds

1783 TAX LIST OF HARFORD COUNTY, MARYLAND

A return of Property in Deer Creek Upper Hundred by John Barclay, assessor 1783.

Name	# of white inhabitants	Tract Name	# acres
Humphry Andrews	4	Warners Meadows	31
		Addition to Warners Meadows	45
Thomas Arlett	2		
Hugh Bankhead	6	Greers Neighbour	61
John Bean	6		
Vincent Bosly	4	name unknown	263
John Bullock	2		
Thomas Burk	7	Frazers Garden	29
		Wilsons Chance	22
William Cnnon	3		
Daniel Carter	8	Kellys Neglect	350
Josiah Carter	—	land, mill & seat	20
Bartholomew Connell	7		
James Crighton	7		
James Danny	3		
William Dawson	4		
Aquila Deaver	1	Paca's Pleasure	110
Richard Deaver	3		
James Deaver	3	Chesnut Spring	125
		John sons 3rd Addition	72
Sarah Deaver	1	Deavers Fancy	61
John Dewberry	4		
Margaret Doran	9	Foxes Pit?	18
		Knavery Disappointed	25
		Moxons Cabbin	50
		Lewis Town	50
		Fowlers Refuse	50
		Newport	50
		Richardsons Wilderness	109
Joshua Durham	—	Deavers Park	125
William Ea.skins	6		
John Flatt	7		
Samuel Foster	7		
Henry Fullard	5	Jones' Meadows	50
William Gibson	4		
James Gordon	7	McSwain's Purchase	147
Jeremiah Hawkins	3	Deavers Retirement	30
		pt. Deavers Project	50
		Mount	20
Robert Hawkins	8	Ducks Delight	15
William Hutson	7		

1783 TAX LIST OF HARFORD COUNTY, MARYLAND
Deer Creek Upper Hundred

Name	# of white inhabitants	Tract Name	# acres
Elizabeth Jones	1	Jones' Beginning	30
		Jones' Inheritance	47
Isaac Jones	6	Hawks Nest	85
		Richardsons Retirement	15
William Jones	8	Andrews Inheritance	32
Robert Kenedy	6	Hogs Hole	77
		pt. Legs & Arms	40
		Kenedys Beginning	38
Jesse Kent	5	pt. Briarly's Beginning	41
Edward Leonard	2	Elizabeth's Delight	20
		Mt. Pleasant	16
Benjamin Lukins	10	Dry Glade Thickett	54
Jacob Lukins	2		
John McClave	4		
Benjamin McCreary	1	pt. Miles Beginning	8
Robert McCreary	5		
Miles McGaugh	6	Miles Adventure	75
		The Valley	33
Jane Miles	5	Miles Beginning	22
Thomas Montgomery	3	Brazers Endeavour	200
Samuel Morgan	5	Jones Defence	22
John Neill	7	Chance	30
		Hawkins Valley	43
		Speirs Adventure	87
Mary Norris	7	Salbury Plains	1838
Benjamin Price	5		
James Ramply	10	Morgans Mount	11
		pt. Richardsons Mount	80
		Whitakers Desire	50
Benjamin Richardson	5	Richardsons Outlett	80
Henry Richardson	3	Isaac's Lott	111
Samuel Richardson	9	Richardsons Outlet	80
Benjamin Rigdon	1		
Stephen Rigdon	2	pt. Rock Quarter	115
		pt. Crooked Ridge	52
		Fathers Gift	50
Thomas B. Rigdon	3	pt. Rock Quarter	41
		pt. Crooked Ridge	68
		Bakers Chance	88
		Fathers Safeguard	54
		Rigdons Lookout	90
		pt. Roberts Venture	24

1783 TAX LIST OF HARFORD COUNTY, MARYLAND
Deer Creek Upper Hundred

Name	# of white inhabitants	Tract Name	# acres
Alexander Rigdon	6	Leggs & Arms	115
		Reserve of my ____?	205
		Jones' Reserve	13
		Jones' Meadows	3
		Long Alley	67
		pt. Crooked Ridge	28
		Brazers Beginning	40
		Johnsons Choice	314
		Bishops Last Shift	19
		pt. Rock Quarter	44
		Morgans Grove	50
		Walkers Desire	23
		Spesutia Upper Hundred	
		pt. Turky Forest	150
		pt. Nobles Wonder	50
		Johnsons Lott	9
		Pittsburg	50
Jacob Ruth	10		
Joseph Smith	4		
Robert Smith	7		
William Smith	1	Rigdons Range	150
		Briarlys Grove	80
Zachariah Spencer	3	Batchelors Beginning	100
John Taylor	6	pt. Deavers Retirement	17
		Deavers Inheritance	61
		Fox Hole	14
John Ward	10	Sherry's Bottom	22
		Gallions Delight	50
Elizabeth Watkins	5	Watkins Right	68
		Miles Garden	27
James Watkins	2		
John Watkins	3		
John Watt	2	McRory's Prospect	85
James Webb (Y County)	—	_____ Webb	47
John Webb	4		
John Whiteford	6	Whitefords Request	42
		Watts Purchase	39
		Hawkins Purchase	127
		Littons Request	50
		Watts Folly	63
		Now Design	257

1783 TAX LIST OF HARFORD COUNTY, MARYLAND
Deer Creek Upper Hundred

Name	# of white inhabitants	Tract Name	# acres
John Wilson (Scotch)	7		
John Wilson	7	Ann's Lott	85
		Wilson's Range	34
		Cobbs Knavery	34
		Wilson's Addition	32
John Wilson - Hd. Glade?	3		
Archibald Wilson	8	Whitten Beginning	55
		Brasers Beginning	26
William Wilson	1	Pogues Prospect	76
		Pogues Fancy	18

Paupers	# whites	Paupers	# whites
James Allen	7	William Allum	4
Thomas Ammons	4	George Badthers	4
Edward Callaghan	4	James Cook	4
Philip Creal	6	William Cromwell	3
Henry Dickson	8	Samuel Elliott	5
Samuel Forsythe	4	Jesse Foster	6
William Frasher	2		
Lawrence Gest	6	John Griffith	3
William Harkly	3	Daniel Haley	3
William Hall	7	John Hays	6
John James	2	Charles Johnson	5
Simon Jordan	6	John Lansly	2
James Larkin	7	Henry McCart	
John Shields	3	William Smith	4
John Tardy	3	Thomas West	2

Securities

Robert Kenedy
Miles McGaw
Robert Smith
Stephen Rigdon
John Wilson

Single Men

Benjamin Duberry
William Gash
John McGaw
William Smith
William West
John Yeldon

End of Deer Creek Upper Hundred in Harford County, Maryland

1783 TAX LIST OF HARFORD COUNTY, MARYLAND
Harford Upper Hundred

Name	# of Whites	Tract Name	# acres
John Antill	10		
James Armstrong	8	Pt. Stoney Ridge	107
Mary Bennett	5	land	10
Ruth Billingsley	5	pt. My Lords Gift	236
John Blackburn	5		
Robert Blackburn	3		
Thomas Blany	0		
Ann Bond	0		
George Bradford	11	pt. Turky & Strawberry Hills	131
		Gunpowder Lower	
		Abington Lott	
William Bradford Jr.	5	pt. Abbets Forest	85
		Turky Pen Glades	121
John Brooks	7		
Edward Brown	3		
John Bull	6	House & Lott	1
		shop at Daniel Campbells	
John Calwell	9	pt. Brooms Bloom	214
Daniel Campbell	7		
Matthew Conelin	5	pt. Wilsons____	100
Nicholas Connoly	5		
John Copeland	5	pt. My Lords Gift	116
Sarah Curry	8		
Jeremiah Dailey	5		
Frances Davis	0	pt. Comeby Chance	3
Jesse Dawson	4		
William Divas	4	pt. Stony Ridge & Paca's Enlargement	100
Jane Dixon	4		
John Drimer	2		
John Ellis	8	pt. My Lords Gift	208
		pt. Brooms Bloom	40
William Ensor	10		
Isaac Fryer	10		
Joseph Gallion	7		
David Glenn	9	pt. Brooms Bloom	189
James Gray	2	land	10
Aquila Hall (B.C.)Balto. Co.	0	pt. Turky & Strawbury Hills	90
		Gunpowder Upper	
		40 bus. wheat at Guins Mill	
Alexander Hannah	8		
William Hannah	3		

1783 TAX LIST OF HARFORD COUNTY, MARYLAND
Harford Upper Hundred

Name	# of whites	Tract Name	# acres
Edward Hanson	7	pt. Abels Forest	300
Richard Harbert	7		
Andrew Harriott	8		
Aughtry Hart	0	pt. Stony Ridge & Paca's Enlargement	40
James Holmes	0	pt. Stony Ridge & Paca's Enlargement	21
James Huston	4		
Elizabeth Jeffery	6	pt. Stony Ridge	125
Hugh Jeffery	7	pt. Best Endeavour	250
Thomas Jeffery	1		
James Kenedy	8	pt. Stony Ridge & Paca's Enlargement	119
Thomas Kenedy	2	pt. Stony Ridge & Paca's Enlargement	119
Hugh Kirkpatrick	3	pt. Brooms Bloom	300
William Lacky	0	pt. Stony Ridge & Paca's Enlargement	106
Elizabeth Lusby	0		
Jacob Lytle	0	pt. Island Hills	133
John McAdon	6	pt. Christophers Camp	250
James McCandless	0	pt. Brooms Bloom	400
		pt. George's Neighbour	40
Jane McGay	6		
Matthew McClintock	2	pt. Paca's Enlargement	10
George McGlaughlin	6	pt. Paca's Enlargement house & lott	8
Bennett Matthews	0	pt. Bonds Purchase	30
Roger Matthews	2		
John Mitchell	12	pt. Stony Ridge	150
John Morris	7		
James Morrison	11		
Roland Murnahon	6		
James Nower	8		
Daniel Nutterwell	0	Farmers Delight	100
John Parker	4		
John Perryman	7	Stony Ridge	100
James Philips (Inn Keeper)	8	pt. Stony Ridge	100
		house & lott in Harford	4
Hutching Pike	5		
Jacob Potts	3		

1783 TAX LIST OF HARFORD COUNTY, MARYLAND
Harford Upper Hundred

Securities

John Perryman
John Shinton
James Amoss
Hugh Kirkpatrick
William Ensor
Barnard Thompson
John Bull
Robert Blackburn
William Wilson, silversmith
Sarah Curry
Gabriel Manhorn
Joseph Gallion
Ruth Billingsley
John Ellis
Thomas Jeffery

Ruth Billingsley
Alexander Hanna
Hugh Kirkpatrick
John McAdon
John Brook
Jane McGay
Jane McGay
Richard Ruff
John Perryman
Ruth Billingsley
Samuel Smith
George Young
Gabriel Vanhorn
Ann Stephenson
John Perryman

Thomas Hall
Barnard Thompson
Barnard Thompson

Single Men

Nicholas Allender
John Andrews
John Beaver
Andrew Bronn
Negro Ben
Samuel Bing
Richard Bull
Bryson Blackburn
Edward Bradly
James Curry
Elihu Davis
Grigory Gallion
Jarvice Gilbert
Thomas Hinks
Robert Jeffery
Alexander Jeffery
Nathaniel Kenedy
Nathaniel McClure
Arthur Murnohon
Andrew McAndon
William Morris
James McGay
John McGay
Peter Nuburk
Isaac Perryman
Robert Smith
Jonathan Smith
Negro Jim Sly
Thomas Smith
Edward Stephenson
Richard Spencer, sadler
John Thornton, mulatto
Mulatto Toney
negroe Waping
Aaron Vanhorn

End of Harford Upper Hundred, Harford County, Maryland

1783 TAX LIST OF HARFORD COUNTY, MARYLAND
A return of property in Harford Lower Hundred made by Richard Ruff, assessor.

Name	# of Whites	Tract Name	# acres
John Armstrong	6		
Archibald Beaty	4		
Thomas Brown	8		
Benjamin Chancy	1		
George Chancy	2	pt. Hollis Refuse	100
		pt. Hollis Chance	40
		Parkers Lott	176
George Chancy Jr.	7		
George Copeland	5	Stepney Improved	200
		pt. Sophias Dairy	28
		Come by Chance	26
		pt. Addition	194
James Deaver	5		
Morris Dixon	6		
Anthony Drew	5		
Drews Enlargement	338		
George Drew	9		
John Dwire	3		
Rachel Gallion	5		
Garret Garretson	8	Fox's Harbour	205
		pt. Clarks Town	17
		pt. Taylors Hall	100
Edward Giles	0	Minorca	2
		Rummy Marsh	770
		Mate Island	90
		Hog Neck	50
		Shepherds Choice	147
		Shepherds Adventure	28
		Atkinsons Purchase	314
James Giles	6	pt. Benjamins Choice & James' Park	500
		Come by Chance	91
		Cranbury Meadows	28
Charles Gilmore	7		
Bathia Hall	6	pt. Cranbury Hall	255
Edward Hall	1	pt. Cranbury Hall	510
John Hanson Sr.	4	Narrow Neck	100
		Hansons Begruged Neck	24
		Hollis' Refuse	90
John Hanson Jr.	1		
Hollis Hanson of John	0		

1783 TAX LIST OF HARFORD COUNTY, MARYLAND
Harford Lower Hundred

Name	# of whites	Tract Name	# acres
Sophia Hall	6	pt. Sophias Dairey	673
		Dairy Inlarged	168
		pt. Friendship	200
		Harford Upper Hundred	
		Abels Forest	238
		Montreall	1675
		Susquehanna Hundred	
		Monserado	275
		Littleworth	8
		Bush Lower Hundred	
		pt. Constant Friendship	160
		Pt. Hathaways Trust	228
		Neighbours Affinty	235
		Harrisons Resolution	135
		pt. Haha Indeed	300
Mary Hanson	1		
Elizabeth Henderson	6		
Dr. Philip Henderson	0	**Gunpowder Lower**	
		Abington lott improved	
Amoss Hollis	10	pt. Hollis Refuse	83
		pt. Holly Hill	22
William Hollis Sr.	3	pt. Ellinge	50
		pt. Islington	12
		pt. North Union	48
Jonathan Hudson	0	mill in Harford Town	
		pt. Come by Chance	50
		Spesutia Lower	
		Swan Harbour	565
		Paca's Bit	10
		pt. Cohairs lott	556 1/4
		Great Like Hill	24 1/2
Joseph Johnson	7		
James Kelly	7		
William Knight	4		
George Little	8	Jeffrys Neck	130
		pt. Swampy Point	49
		pt. South Union	89
Joseph Lusby (Kent Co.)	0	pt. Drews Enlargement	288
John McComas	3	pt. Deavers Addition	17
		pt. Novascotia	25
		pt. Strawbury Hills	15

1783 TAX LIST OF HARFORD COUNTY, MARYLAND
Harford Lower Hundred

Name	# of whites	Tract Name	# acres
Lloyd Marsh	7		
John Marshall	4		
James Osborne	6	pt. Common Garden	110
		pt. Planters Neglect	50
		Pt. Howletts Nest	50
		pt. Hollis' Chance	50
		Shepherds Good Friendship	104
William Osborne of James	8	pt. Common Garden	90
George Patterson	1		
James Philips Esq.	11	pt. Benjamins Choice &	
		James' Park	1850
		Hunting North	150
		Mates Angle	100
		Chelsea	125
		Lambert Marsh	100
		pt. Convent Garden	100
		James' Addition	630
		Brown's Chance	190
		Fraternity	152
		pt. Leaf Junior	90
		Crab Hill	100
		Colliers Meadows	143
		Upper Ellinge	100
		Chilbury Neck	1350
		pt. Arkins Hope &	
		Middlemans Defence	66 2/3
		Shipping Dock	35
		Gunpowder Lower	
		Abington lotts	
James Redman	3		
John Reed	6		
Col. John Rogers	0	pt. Runney Marsh	375
		pt. South Union	60
John Ruff	5	Hunting Neck	300
William Smith (ship Captain)	6		
Zachariah Smith	7		
Oswin Sutton	9		
Jonathan Woodland	8		

1783 TAX LIST OF HARFORD COUNTY, MARYLAND
Harford Lower Hundred

Name	# of whites	Tract Name	# acres
James Webster	0	Millon James Run	___
		Friends Addition	20
		Friendship	300
		Littleworth	7
		Addition to Littleworth	3
		pt. Novascotia	43
		pt. Turky Hills	10
		Harford Upper	
		pt. Come by Chance	33 1/4
		pt. Turky Hills	7
		Creids Beginning	106
		Stoney Ridge	100
		Bell Grade	75

Securities	Single Men
	Dr. William Annen
	William Bolster
	Leven Bennett
	Francis Deavor
James Phelps Esq.	John Everie
	William Gawly
William Hollis Sr.	Clark Hollis
James Osbourne	Robert Jones
William Lester	John Johnson
Alexander McComas, James' Run	Nicholas Jones
	Alexander McComas, James Run
Samuel Hanson	Francis Pitt
	Mitchell Stewart
Charles Gilmore	Moses Trulock
James Osborn	Peter Vanhorn
James Osborn	William Williamson

Paupers	# whites	Paupers	# whites
Michael Adkerson	7	John Buckly	3
Henry Collingham	7	William Jones	3
Dennis Lundrogon	2	Joseph Mabbitt	4
James Oliver	4	James Osborne	1
William Robinson	4	James Shepherd	3
John Thomas	5	Assa Taylor	3
James Brown	1		

1783 TAX LIST OF HARFORD COUNTY, MARYLAND
Spesutia Lower Hundred
A return of property by Richard Ruff, assessor, 1783.

Name	# whites	Tract Name	# acres
John Adams	7		
George Budd	6	Hollands lott	400
Mary Brucebanks	8	Adventure	30 1/2
John Brown (B Side)	5	pt. Oakington	703 1/2
Garrett Brown	1		
Amoss Barnes	4	house in Haverde grass	
William Bowyer	1	1/2 skooner boat	
John Brown of Sadler	3		
John Chancy	3	Good Toddy	256
Jacob Combest	6	pt. Middleborough	46 3/4
Amoss Cord	8		
John Casseldine	2		
Thomas Chaney	5		
John Collins	6		
Sarah Collins	3		
Ashbury Cord	4		
Moses Collins	6		
Utie Combest	0		
Gabriel Christie	5	Palmers Point	480
		Palmers Neglect	35
Christie & Stokes	0	wharf house in Haverde grass	
Richard Dallam	0	Spries Inheritance	640
		pt. Palmers Point	225
		Gunpowder Lower	
		land on Winters Run	187 1/2
		Askens, Hope & Middle &	
		Simmons Defence	66 2/3
		Abington lotts	5
		Bush River Lower	
Josias William Dallas	10	Fanny's Inheritance	893
		Union	100
		pt. Palmers Forest	375
Francis Dallam	4		
Jacob Durant	3		
John Durant	10		
George Daugherty	3	Roberts Choice	69
		Daughertys Angles	19
Matthew Dorsey	5	pt. Expectation	18
		pt. No name	8
Frisby Dorsey	1		
Micajah Deaver	5		

1783 TAX LIST OF HARFORD COUNTY, MARYLAND
Spesutia Lower Hundred

Name	# whites	Tract Name	# acres
David Deaver	0		
John Dunn	5	House in Haverde grass	
Greenbury Dorsey	12	Clarks Rest	330
		Dorseys Fancy	16
		Dorseys Advantage	4
		Dorseys Conveniency	2 1/4
		Dorseys Choice	4
		Clarks Meadows	50
		Dorseys Meadows	7
		Dorseys Marsh	21
Daniel Donavin Jr.	5	House in Haverde grass	
		Susquehanna	
		Montreall	50
Thomas Dorsey	1		
Joseph Everett	9		
Thomas Everett	6		
John Everett	2		
James Ford	7		
Paltus Fie	9		
Samuel Fowler	9		
Joseph Field	6		
Jacob Forwood	10		
Thomas Garretson	0		
Aaron Grace	6		
James Garretson	3	pt. New Park	75
		pt. Matthews Chance	25
Aquila Garrettson	5	pt. Rummey Royal	80
		pt. Dispatch	20
Freeborn Garretson	1	pt. Dispatch	134 3/4
		Timber Swamp	30
		Matthew Chance	53 1/2
		Watkins Inlett	18 1/2
		Great Like Hill	1
		Little Like Hill	3
Luke Griffith	0	Williamsons Hope	39
		Hopes Addition	50
		pt. Rummey Royal	100
		Contrivance	200
		Harford Upper	
		pt. Abbets Forest	163
Elizabeth Gallion	8	Smiths Folly Resurvey	129

1783 TAX LIST OF HARFORD COUNTY, MARYLAND
Spesutia Lower Hundred

Name	# white	Tract Name	# acres
Samuel Griffith	13	Leaf Junifer	68
		Philips Swamp	100
		pt. Rummey Royal	234
		Gunpowder Lower	
		Taylors Neck	400
		for heirs Garretson	
		pt. Oakington	300
		Grove	250
Frances Garretson	0		
Thomas Giles	7	pt. Brothers Lott	500
James Gordon	4	Eden Addition	100
Amoss Garrett	0	pt. Hazard Enlarged &	
		Cooks Double Purchase	522 1/2
		pt. Smith Folly Resurved	23
		Fishery	17 1/2
		Bare Neck	96
Samuel Hanson	5		
James Hollingsworth	5		
Mary Hynson	4	pt. Penny Come Quickly &	
		Matthews Addition	208
		pt. Matthews Enlarged	64
William Hall	4	Harmans Swan Town &Resurvey-240 1/2	
		pt. Gouldsmiths Rest	11
		Ives Town	26
		pt. Fishery & Cooks Double	
		Purchase Resurveyed	19 1/2
		Hollis' Discovery	2 1/2
		pt. Coheirs lott	597 1/2
Parker Hall	1		
Hughes & Hall	0		
James Hall	0		
William Horton	8	House in Haverde grass	
		Susquehannah Hundred	
		Pritchards Security	100
		Halls Plains	218
		Horton's Fancy	19 3/4
Christian Hoopman	3	House in Haver de grass	
William Lester	1	Garden of Eden	150
		Spring Garden	127
Thomas Lancaster	3		
Norris Lester	1	1 sailing boat	

1783 TAX LIST OF HARFORD COUNTY, MARYLAND
Harford Upper Hundred

Name	# of whites	Tract Name	# acres	
Rinard Potts	4			
Robert Price	5			
Daniel Richardson	5	Wilsons Range	100	
		pt. Friendship	150	
		pt. Abels Forest	85	
Barnard Riley	8	pt. Novascotia	280	
Daniel Robertson	8	pt. Rangers Lodge	25	
		pt. Novascotia	175	
Charles Robinson	0	pt. Paca's Enlargement	153	
Roland Rogers	7			
Henry Ruff	9	pt. Turky Hills & Improvements-1 1/2		
Richard Ruff, assessor	3	pt. Strawbury Hills	18	
		pt. Comeby Chance	80	
		Daniel's lott Resurvey	570	
		Bonds Adventure Resurveyed		123
		Ruffs Addition	7	
		pt. Turky Hills	14	
James Sheredine	10			
William Sherewood	7			
John Shinton	3			
Samuel Smith, cooper	5			
Major Samuel Smith	8	pt. Stony Ridge & Paca's Enlargement	221	
Kent Stallion	8			
John Standly	7			
Ann Stephenson	5	pt. Stony Ridge & Paca's Enlargement	72	
John Stephenson	1	pt. Stony Ridge & Paca's Enlargement	144	
Joseph Stiles	5	house & Lott	2	
		pt. Turky & Strawbury Hills	50	
Andrew Tease	4			
Barnard Thompson	5			
George Tollinger	7			
John Tornsly	4	house & lott		
		pt. Paca's Enlargement	6 1/2	
Garbiel Vanhorn	7	house & lotts Harford		
		pt. Wilson's Range	44	
David Waldrum	3			
Archibald Watson	9			
Godfrey Watters	1	pt. My Lords Gift	100	

1783 TAX LIST OF HARFORD COUNTY, MARYLAND
Harford Upper Hundred

Name	# of whites	Tract Name	# acres
Stephen Watters	0	pt. Montreall	135
		pt. Stony Ridge	29
Thomas Watters	10		
Isaac Webater	10	pt. Rangers Lodge	445
		pt. Sedgely & Best Endeavour	185
		pt. Wilson's Range	6
		pt. Novascotia & Improvements	-56
James Webster of John	0	pt. Best Endeavour	250
Michael Webster	7	pt. Howards Forest	50
Richard Webster	10	pt. Stony Ridge	202
		pt. Howard's Forest	50
Samuel Webster of Isaac	8	pt. Sedgly	150
		pt. Brooms Bloom	100
		pt. St. George's	188
Samuel Webster Sr.	1	pt. Howard's Forest	60
Samuel Webster of Samuel	7	pt. Webster's Forest	50
John Wild	5		
Richard Wilmott	4	pt. Christophers Camp	500
		Wilmott's Discovery	30
William Wilson, silversmith	4	pt. Rangers Lodge &	
		Websters Contrivance	173
		Winters Mill Seat	13
William Wilson of John	8	Abington lotts	
		pt. Hall's Plains	200
		Margaret's Mount	140
Joseph Woolsy	6		
Alexander Young	1	pt. St. Georges	188
George Young	2	house	

Paupers	# of whites	Paupers	# of whites
Charles Penny	7	George Roby	3
Tayman Byfott	2	Morris Collins	2
William Catrel	3	John Crosby	3
Margaret Cowan	2	Mary Campbell	3
Benjamin Dickson	4	John Debruler	3
Anthony Debruler	3	Francis Debruler	—
Mary Duncan	3	Samuel Evans	5
Henry Ellis	5	William Evans	4
Ann Gaines	3	John Giffen	2
Ann Jewitt	4	James Lawrence	3
Reese McIntire	3	Edward Martin	4
Elizabeth Shea	5	Joseph Wootton	1

1783 TAX LIST OF HARFORD COUNTY, MARYLAND
Spesutia Lower Hundred

Name	# whites	Tract Name	# acres
Benedict Edward Hall	6	Shandy Hall	381
		Halls Purchase	887
		Halls Addition	42
		Sheriffs Hall	214
		Middle Borough	216
		Dismal Swamp	55
		Halls Angles	18
		Smiths Folly Resurveyed	81 1/2
		Parkenton	100
		pt. no name	17
		Kimbles Hazard	54
		Hall & Bonds Discovery	200
John Hall Jr.	1	Halls Meadows	101
		Georges Hall	11
		Smith Folly Resurveyed	153
		Kimbles Chance	86
Moses Loney	4		
Mary Loney	3		
William Loney	7	Proctors Hall & the Enlargement-234	
		Planters Delight	200
		pt. Coheirs lott	50
		Collets Point	320
		Frisbys Convenience	100
		Black Island & Surplus	200
		pt. Middle Borough	6
		pt. Smiths Folly Resurveyed	18 3/4
Griffith Jones	6		
Stephen Kimble	5	pt. Jacksons Outlett	30
		pt. no name	24
Samuel Kimble	6	pt. Kimbles Double Purchase	146
John Kimble	5	pt. Kimbles Double Purchase	34
Giles Kimble	3	pt. Kimbles Double Purchase	62
Michael Kennard	9		
Thomas Knight	5		
Edward Morris	0		
John Matthews	8	Matthews Enlargement	567
		Shipping dock	22
		pt. Penny Come Quickly	20
		pt. Covent Garden	60
Sarah McGay	6		
Sarah McCarty	0	Jacksons Hazard	100

1783 TAX LIST OF HARFORD COUNTY, MARYLAND
Spesutia Lower Hundred

Name	# whites	Tract Name	# acres
John Moore	5		
Timothy Murphy	7		
William Monk	3		
William Murphy, cooper	5		
Samuel Miller	4		
William Mooberry	4		
John McNabb	2		
Benjamin Osborne	2		
Aquila Paca Jr.	1	Delph	600
		pt. Gouldsmiths Hall	100
		pt. Palmers Point	23
		pt. MoalsSuccess	298
		Newsoms Meadows	38 3/4
		Paca's Convenience	17
		Gunpowder Lower	
		pt. Paca's Park	630
		White Hall	10
		Add. to Water Mills	210
Mark Pringle	0	Wilton	450
		pt. Swan's Harbour	120
James Reardon	8		
John Riddle	7	Riddles Riddle	10
		pt. Mary's & Thomas Repose-50	
Abraham Robinson	7		
Richard Rutter	6	House in Haverde grass	
Robert Stokes	6	lott on ground rent in Haverde grass to amount of 285 pounds	
		pt. Harmans Swan Town	400
Elizabeth Stewart	4		
Elizabeth Smith	0		
Samuel Sutton	8		
Jonas Stephenson for Garretson	6	pt. New Park	75
Rueben Sutton	11		
John Steel	6		
Frances Taylor	4	pt. Perkington	60
		pt. Kembles Double Purchase-70	
		pt. Taylor Hall	100
Robert Taylor	6	Jacksons Outlett	70
Abraham Taylor	6		
Edward C. Tolley	5	Betseys Choice	573

1783 TAX LIST OF HARFORD COUNTY, MARYLAND
Spesutia Lower Hundred

Name	# whites	Tract Name	# acres
Stephen Taylor	8	pt. Good Speed	100
		pt. Taylors Outlett	11
		pt. Hazard Enlarged & Cooks Double Purchase	20
James Taylor	8	pt. Carters Rest	68
		pt. no name	10
Henry Vansickle	7		
John Wood	9	pt. Greenfields Double Purchase	148
		pt. Gouldsmiths Rest	28
		pt. Primrose Hill	10
		pt. Woods Adventure	13
Col Thomas Whites heirs	0	pt. Rummey Royal	1036
		Delph Island	375
John Lee Webster	6	Gouldsmiths Rest	847
		Clarks Town	110
		Harford Upper	
		pt. Christophers Camp	250
		pt. Best Endeavour	210
		pt. Abbets Forest	120
		Miles Forest	300
		pt. Novascotia & Strawbury Hills	20
Henry Warfield	6	pt. Covent Garden	65
Purify Watkins	7		
James Wiggins	6		
John Walker	4		
Rev. James Wilmer	3		
John Williams	0	House in Haverde grass	

Securities

John Brown
Gabriel Christie
Joseph Everitt
William Loney
Christian Hoopman
Jonias Dallam & Wm. Murphy
Frances Taylor
Greenbury Dorsey
Samuel Griffith

Single Men

Augustus Brown
Augustine Bailey
James Bond (alias Kimly)
John Brown
William Carbire
John Carty
Abraham Cord
Jacob Collins
John Bartholomew Clear
Edward Dooly

1783 TAX LIST OF HARFORD COUNTY, MARYLAND
Spesutia Lower Hundred

Securities

John Duran
Josias Wm. Dallam

James Oliver
Benedict Hall
Joseph Everett

John Kimble
Samuel Kimble

Sarah McGay
Sarah McGay
Sarah McCarty
John Matthews
William Monk
Benjamin Body
Jonias Dallam

Jonas Dallam
Benjamin Osborne
Robert Stoke
Mary Hynson
Asbury Cord

Single Men

Alexander Duran
negroe Dick
William Ellis, Quaker
James Fitzgerrald
Peter Fontain
Michael Fitzpatrick
Capt. Michael Gilbert
Adam Johnson
James Kimble
James Milburn (mollotto)
George McGay
John McGay
Jacob McCarty
Bennett Matthews
Richard Monk
Charles Oglesby
negroe Peter
Richard Reason
negroe Tower
Philemon Thomas
James Watkins
Isaac Whitaker
Hezekiah Whitaker

Pauper	# whites	Pauper	# whites	Pauper	# whites
Solomen Armstrong	2	John Deaver	5	Jesse Morgan	2
Thomas Ashy	3	William Evans	2	Andrew Martin	5
Nicholas Brady	5	Perry Fowler	4	Jane Major	2
Benjamin Body	6	Harman Hill	4	James Oliver Jr.	5
James Brown	4	Elizabeth Hamby	3	Oscar Reardon	7
Joseph Bignell	2	William Hill	5	John Reese	4
John Beck	7	David Hampton	2	Abraham Steel	7
Edward Cotty	4	John Lovit	2	John St. Clair	4
Thomas Cowley	6	Luke Jones	2	John Sullivan	6
Jacob Collins	5	William Judd	4	Michael Truelove	4
Ephraim Collins	4	Daniel Judd	8	Isaac Tolson	
John Catty	4	William Jeffery	1	alias Grant	4
William Colb	2	William Murphy	4	James Welch	2
Margaret Dixon	5	Thomas Morris	6	Jonathan White	4
Samuel Daugherty	2	John Morris	3	Benj. Wellingsford	3
James Drew	5	Patrick McLean	5	John Wright	3
		Wm. Morgan, Quaker	1	John Wimley	4

1783 TAX LIST OF HARFORD COUNTY, MARYLAND
Susquehanna Hundred

A return of property made by John Dallam, assessor 1783.

Name	# of whites	Tract Name	# acres
Joshua Armstrong	11	pt. Montreall	50
Daniel Anderson	7	Carpenters Plains	100
		Sawan Hunting Ground	66
Solomon Allen	0		
William Arnold	7		
Ephraim Arnold	4	pt. Montreall	52
		pt. Paradise	48
Ephraim Andrews	2	pt. Westwood	385
Agnus Baker	5	Lows Lott	100
		Durbins Beginning	58
James Byards	3	Culverts Chance	3
William Borly	13		
James Barnes	3	Culverts Entrance	100
James Barnes	7		
Richard Barnes	2		
Josiah Bailey	6		
William Barnes	6	pt. Montreall	100
Gregory Barnes	11	Middletons Angles	195
		pt. Cooks Rest	50
		pt. St. Martins Ludgate	50
		Scotchmans Generosity	50
		Beals Reserve	50
Job Barnes	5		
Nehemiah Bailey	5		
Catherine Boardman	3		
Daniel Bailis	3	pt. Good Neighbourhood	1/4
Jane Burton	6	pt. Whitakers Ridge	62
Thomas Brown	9		
Isaac Blake	4		
Michael Belcher	11		
Bennett Barnes	5	Repultic	228
Ruth Barnes	0		
Thomas Bowlis	9	pt. Rich Leval	45
George Botts	12	Wests Favor	100
Patrick Bowman	7		
Henry Bowman	8		
Nathaniel Bailes	7	pt. Mary's Lott	90
William Brannon	4		
Joseph Bailey	5		
Jacob Botts	3		

1783 TAX LIST OF HARFORD COUNTY, MARYLAND
Susquehanna Hundred

Name	# of whites	Tract Name	# acres
John Botts	9	pt. Eightrap	53
James Bonar	2		
William Barrett	4		
Jonathan Benjamin	8		
Samuel Bailes	12	Margaret's lott	200
John Buckleigh	8		
James Bevard (Bevaid?)	3		
Freeborn Brown	5	pt. Jerico	234
		pt. Margarets Mount	120
William Colhoun	7		
Paul Cummins	7		
Ephraim Coale	7	pt. Paradise	40
Hugh Carmichael	8		
Robert Culver	7	Culvers Entrance	100
Benjamin Culver	2	Culverts (sic) Entrance	202
Thomas Courtney	10	Hammonds Hope	100
		pt. Contest	50
Nathaniel Carr	6	Royal Exchange	200
Benjamin Cowan	7	Woods Close	50
Nicholas Cruse	2		
John Cruse	7	pt. Aquilas Inheritance	230
John Casly ?	4		
Richard Cruse	4	pt. Aquilas Inheritance	150
John Carmichael	4		
Elizabeth Cowan	0		
Robert Creswell	1		
John Cooly	4	____ines ____tents ?	211
William Creswell	5	Green Spring Forest	200
William Carson	3		
William Cowan	5		
George Close	7		
William Carroll	2		
Patrick Cretin	4	Good Neighborhood	260
John Corry	6		
James Coale	9	pt. Montreall	80
		Royal Exchange	70
Jane Coale	5	pt. Montreall	100
		pt. Paradise	100
William Cox	14	pt. Westwood & Wests Beginning	143
		Margarets Mount	

-138-

1783 TAX LIST OF HARFORD COUNTY, MARYLAND
Susquehanna Hundred

Name	# of whites	Tract Name	# acres
Israel Cox	0	Murdocks Chance	134
George Dillion	8		
Daniel Donavin Sr.	4	pt. Montreall	70
Philip Donavin	9	pt. Paradise	80
Hugh Daugherty	3		
William Donavin	7		
Daniel Durbin	10		
Philip Darnall	0	Convenience	400
		Rich Leval	579
Thomas Durbin	1	Eightrap	24 1/2
Margaret Durbin	1	Eightrap	24 1/2
Mary Durbin	4		
Francis Dallam	0	Culverts Entrance	167
Benjamin Everett	8	pt. Paradise	120
		pt. Paradise	40
		Cooks Rest	50
		Gravilly Hills	50
		pt. Royal Exchange	90
James Edwards	4		
Alexander Ewing	5		
William Evitt	?		
Andrew Evitt	4		
Patrick Fowler	8	Cowans Addition	50
John Farmer	2		
Andrew Ferguson	10	Trible Union	50
Francis Foster	6		
Benjamin Fleetwood	6	Eightrap	2
Frederick Ford	2		
George Ford	7		
John Goutz	3		
Aquila Gilbert	5		
Michael Gilbert	2		
Parker Gilbert	9	Gilberts Pipe	100
John Gordon	3		
Micah Gilbert	8	Gilberts Pipe	100
Charles Gilbert	4	Westwood	210
		Obediahs Venture	50
		Improved Venture	
		Jacks Purchase	75
		Clarks Tobacco	40
		The Union	33 1/2
		Gilberts Pipe	50

1783 TAX LIST OF HARFORD COUNTY, MARYLAND
Susquehanna Hundred

Name	# of whites	Tract Name	# of acres
Philip Gilbert	3	Gilberts Pipe	50
Samuel Gilbert	1	pt. The Union	31
Martin T. Gilbert	8	Gilberts Pipe	75
		Clarks Tobacco	25
Thomas Gilbert	5	Royal Exchange	61 1/4
Charles Gilbert	6	Gilberts Pipe	100
George Goodwin	0	Royal Exchange 313	
Richard Greenland	4		
Michael Gilbert	4	Gilberts Pipe	87
		Union	9
		Gilberts Chance	25
		Clarks Tobacco	25
		Michaels Begining	10
John Gallion	5	pt. Agreement	50
Thomas Gisom	4		
William Gulbraugh	6	Mary's Lott	458
Philip Gover	11	pt. Republic or Repultic	150
William Gorrell	4	pt. Cordwood Grove	15
Ambrose Gehogan	4		
Samuel Gallion	7	Cairns Addition	44
John Gorrell	8	pt. Woods Choice	65
		Penny Made Reserved	106
Jacob Giles	8.	Gilberts Pipe	666
		Rich Bottom Corrected	89
		Friendship	200
		pt. Eightrap	99
		Harford Upper	
		pt. Novascotia	214
Nathaniel Giles' heirs	0	Land of Promise	712
		pt. Eightrap	202
Abraham Huff	5	Whitakers Ridge	50
John B. Hall	6	pt. Cranbury Hall	400
John B. Howard	0	pt. Cranbury Hall	400
		Gunpowder Lower, Joppa lotts	
Samuel Howell	4	Johnsons Rest	50
		Johnsons Bed	100
Richard Haddaway	3		
James Hannah	8		
Richard Hawkins	6	pt. Westwood	80
		pt. Margarets Mounty	72

1783 TAX LIST OF HARFORD COUNTY, MARYLAND
Susquehanna Hundred

Name	# of whites	Tract Name	# acres
Robert Hawkins	4	pt. Margarets Mount	73
William Horner	4	Nonamy	50
Hollis Hanson	7	pt. Good Neighbourhood	250
Richard Hargrove	9	Halls Plains	100
Benjamin Harbert	4	pt. Agreement	100
John Hanson	3		
John Hughes	9		
Joseph Hall	1	pt. Montreal	269
		pt. Halls Plains	64
Thomas Hawkins	0		
William Husband	7		
James Horner	9	Harmans Addition	196 1/4
	5	pt. Paradise	7 1/4
		pt. Royal Exchange	119 1/2
		Williams Chance	100
		Horner's Fishery	9
Dr. Carvill Hall	5	Halls Chance	196
		Halls Park	1102
		Halls Addition	53
		pt. Contest	50
		Spesutia Lower	
Joseph Husbands	10	Bachelors Good Luck	350
Thomas Hall	?	Thomas & Mary's Repose	50
		name unknown	157 1/2
		pt. Jerico	150
		Windmill Hill 106	
		Simons Neglect	135
		Halls Rich Neck	652
		Aquilla's Inheritance	56
		Harford Upper Hundred	
		House in Harford Town	
		pt. Friendship	160
		Spesutia Upper	
		Leight of Leighton?	630
Samuel Hughes Esq.	3	Gears? Angles	67
		McCurders? Neighbours	8 1/4
		Addition to Brothers Lott	22
		St. Martins Ludgate	87 1/4
		Brothers Lott	825
		Spesutia Lower	
		Spesutia Island	2154

1783 TAX LIST OF HARFORD COUNTY, MARYLAND
Susquehanna Hundred

Name	# of whites	Tract Name	# acres
Robert Hoops	0	pt. Good Neighbourhood	60
Thomas Harrison heirs	0	Browns Discovery	434
		Cowans Neighbour	265
William Judd	7		
Sarah Ingram	3	land	3 1/4
Nathaniel Johns	10	Rich Bottom	87 1/2
Aquila Kean	6	Woods Meadows	60
Ann Kean	4		
Robert Kelly	3		
Alexander Kelly	6	Hughes Increase	50
David Knight	7		
Jonathan Knight	5		
Light Knight	0		
David Knight	0		
John Laurence	6		
Robert B. Landrum	3		
William Lucky	8	Stony Ridge	156
William Laughlin	9		
Samuel Litton	12		
Micajah Mitchell	7	pt. Eightrap	38
		Hugh's Choice	100
John Mahon	11	Woods Meadows	60
Hannah Mitchell	4	Gilberts Addition	100
		Gilberts Outlett	50
		Gilberts Lott	100
Martha Martin	3	Cowans Settlement	100
Thomas Mitchell	10	St. Martins Ludgate	100
Kent Mitchell	2	Division ?	100
		Robin Hoods Forest	50
		pt. Division	62
		Royal Exchange	134
		Hammonds Addition	50
William Mitchell	9		
James Mitchell	7	Mitchells Reputation	156
		Lowells Dream	73
		land	50
		land	12
		Hughes Hazard & Venture	100
William Martin	2	pt. Aquilla's Inheritance	124?
John Monohon	5		
William Magill	6	Whitakers Ridge	75

1783 TAX LIST OF HARFORD COUNTY, MARYLAND
Susquehanna Hundred

Name	# of whites	Tract Name	# acres
James Mitchell	7		
William Mahon	8		
Archibald McCurdy	4		
Samuel M. Faddin	9		
Negroe Jehu	0	West's Long Acre	50
Negroe Joshua	0	West's Long Acre	50
John Orr	5		
Ann Osborne	7	Robin Hood's Forest	50
		Disdales Inheritance	50
Nicholas Poor	3		
Jacob Ponock	2		
Obediah Pritchard	3	Hughes Choice	50
John Patterson	5	Whitakers Ridge	75
		Addition	5 1/4
		pt. Montreal	82
		Miles End	100
James Pritchard	5	Hughes Enlargement	145
Samuel Pritchard	1	Hughes Choice	50
George Plaxico	6		
William Perkins	1	Eightrap	100
Charles Rigdon	6		
George Ray	8		
Joseph Reese	6	Wests Favour	50
Joseph Roles	7	Cowans Meadows	100
Joseph Reese	6		
William Ramsey	6	Greenspring Forest	200
Abraham Reese	4		
John Rumsey	8	Greenspring Forest	965
		Spesutia Upper	
		Rough Stone	170
		Isaac's Delight	80
		Gunpowder Lower-property in Joppa	
Peter Strepeck	8	White's Entrance	61
Richard Spencer	5		
Robert Smith	9		
James Seale	1		
Samuel Sage	0		
John Smith	5	Mary's Lott	10
Millison Silvers	6		
Benjamin Silvers	8	Mary's Lott	200
Thomas Smith Jr.	5		

1783 TAX LIST OF HARFORD COUNTY, MARYLAND
Susquehanna Hundred

Name	# of whites	Tract Name	# acres
William Smith	7	Johnson's Bed	90
		Nonserado	475
		Royal Exchange	48
		Stephenson's heirs	
		pt. Coheirs lott	556 1/2
Rowland Spencer	5	pt. Trible Union	50
William Stephenson	0	pt. Line Tents ?	300
Henry Stump	8	pt. Limestones	236
		pt. Eightrap	50
		Stumps Chance	25 1/4
		Betty's lott	97 1/2
		Trible Union	13 1/4
Henry Stump Jr.	1	Durbins Chance	150
Hugh Smith	5	pt. Cordwood Grove	40
Thomas Smith	7	Cordwood Grove	82
		Wests Favour	70 1/4
		Conestents ?	147 1/4
Joshua Stapleton	6		
Benjamin Smith	7		
George Shannon	4		
Elizabeth Stewart	1	pt. Agreement	200
John Trago	8		
Edward Thompson	?		
John Tipton	4		
Jabes Murray Tipton	3		
Mary Thompson	4		
Walter Taylor	5		
Samuel Thomas	0	Friendship	400
		Treble Union	130
George Vandergreif	6	pt. Good Neighborhood	10
William Venkworth	3	Bircks Feilds Venture	50
		Howell's Contrivance	52
		Garritson's Neglect	5
		Johnsons Rest	33
Grafton White	2		
James Walker	8	Aquila's Inheritance	12
Moses Wood	3		
Andrew Wilson	6	Culverts Entrance	61 1/2
James West	8		
Enoch West	6	pt. Woods Close	108

1783 TAX LIST OF HARFORD COUNTY, MARYLAND
Susquehanna Hundred

Name	# of whites	Tract Name	# acres
John Williams	4		
William Worthington	9		
Thomas West	8		
Phelix Welch	4		
James West	0		
James Wells	4		
John Woolly	11		
William Williams	9		
Moses Williams	3		
Samuel Wells	2		
Richard White	7	Eightrap	24 1/4
Andrew Wallis	3		
Samuel Wilson	5	Aquila's Inheritance	300
		pt. Good Neighbourhood	189
		Daugharty's Choice	50
		Deer C (Creek?) Plantation	60
Elizabeth Wood	1	Wood's Meadows	125
		Chestnut Ridge	78
William Wood	11		
Rachel Wilson	1		
Cassandra Wilson	1		
William White	0	Hammonds Hope	215
		Paradise	101
		Swansbury	295
		Eaton	437
		Addition to Hammonds Hopes	17
Sarah McCarty	0	Robin Hoods Forest	170

Paupers & # whites	Paupers & # whites	Paupers & # Whites
Elizabeth Bonar-1	Hannah Griffith-3	Samuel Richardson-4
John Condron-6	Isabella Gorrell?-1	John Rich-4
James Chandly-3	James Brewer-7	James Reese-3
Elizabeth Cord-3	Thomas Knight-1	John Reese-3
William Canker-8	Hannah Knight-2	Jones? Taylor-3
John Donavin-4	Sarah Knight-3	John Wilson-4
Thomas Donavin-4	Jonathan Mardon-2	Simon Leet-2
James Ellis-8	James McCota-3	Ann Wood-3
William Frull-4	Jane McDowell-3	Rachel Mitchell-3
Margaret Goodin-4	Ruth Evitt?-?	William Hobbs-5
	William Perry-1	

1783 TAX LIST OF HARFORD COUNTY, MARYLAND
Susquehanna Hundred

Securities
Thomas Smith
James Barnes
Gregory Barnes
Michael Belcher
Bennett Barnes
Mary Thompson
William Cultraugh
Henry Bowman
Thomas Smith
Joseph Bailey
William Williams
Joseph Bailey
Philip Gover
William Creswell
George Ford
William Cox
Alexander Kelly
Benjamin Harbert Sr.
Ann Kean
James Horner
Abraham Huff
William Worthington
John Monohon
Sarah Ingram
Enoch West
Richard Cruson
Isaac Blake
Robert B. Londrum
Thomas Bontis
John Cosly
Benjamin Harbert
James Hannah
Samuel McFaddin
Thomas Smith Jr.
Enoch West
Thomas West
William Evitt
Mary Thompson
James Mitchell
Samuel Litton
Charles Rigdon
Matthew Molton

Single Men
John Beaty
Benjamin Barnes
Ford Barnes
John Belcher
Ford Barnes
Peter Boler
Henry Bowman
John Bowman
John Beaty
Charles Bailey
Benedict Bailey
Aquila Bailey
Thomas Clark
Robert Creswell
Alexander Ford
Michael Carroll
Andrew Kelly
Benjamin Harbert
Timothy Kean
Thomas Knight
Thomas McCleary
Edward Mahon
Barnard Monohon
John McVay
Matthew Motton
Alexander Jamison
Alexander Long
Hosea Renshaw
Henry Smith
Thomas Smith & George Smith
Matthew Snody
Thomas Hannah
Wm. Williams & John Porter
John Williams
Thomas West
James West
John Williams
James Thompson
William Price
Peter Donavin
Mark Noble
James Martin

1783 TAX LIST OF HARFORD COUNTY, MARYLAND
Susquehanna Hundred

Securities

Dr. Carvill Hall
Dr. Carvill Hall
Dr. Carvill Hall
Aquila Kean
John Stump
Samuel Wilson
Andrew Wallis
Robert Smith
Manumitted by William Cox
Manumitted by Nathaniel Rigbie
Manumitted by Richard Johns
Manumitted by Jeremiah Sheredine

Single Men

John Hufman
John Adams
William Gawly
John Spence
Robert Johnson
James Donavin
William Smith
Thomas Smith
Negroe Bob & Jacob
Parraway
Pollidox, Will, & George
Aaron

End of Susquehanna Hundred

A return of property in Broad Creek Hundred made by John Barclay, assessor.

Name	# of whites	Tract Name	# acres
George Anderson	7	Wests Angle	111
William Ammons	9		
Henry Benington	10	Morgans Addition	75
		Morgans Delight	52
Robert Bodkin	16	Collins Park	150
		Troublesome Hill	15
Cooper Boyd	2	Coopers Addition	50
John Boyd	0	Poppo Bottom	10
Matthew Curry	4		
William Casky	2		
Thomas Cooper	0	Nobles Craft	50
		Coopers Prospect	3
		Rumages Add On	8
		pt. Cromics Instruction	40
William Duncan	4	James' Chance	15
		Millers Point	13
James Dags	7		
Richard Downing	3		
Francis Downing	6	pt. Aribia Patria	200
Samuel Eakin	6		
Alexander Ewing	0	pt. Maidens Mount	150
John Flowers	4		
Peter Fourt	8		

-147-

1783 TAX LIST OF HARFORD COUNTY, MARYLAND
Broad Creek Hundred

Name	# of whites	Tract Names	# acres
Andrew Howlett	6	Howletts Triangle	15
		pt. Ambition	60
		Packharts Purchase	78
		Lynch's North Tract	14
Samuel Henry	8	Pilgrims Grove	100
		Pilgrims Rest	60
		Pilgrims Neighbor	57
		Land of Canan	99
Francis Harper	5	Collens Old Fields	35
William Howe	5		
Jonathan Hamilton	11	Bishops Folly	18
		name unknown	39
Aquila Jones Jr.	3		
Aquila Jones Sr.	6		
Thomas Johnson	11	Prospect	42
		Lewis' Chance	40
		Wells Grorr?	17
Thomas Johnson Jr.	0	Robinsons Inheritance &	
		C:<mies Instruction	145
Stephen Jay	8	Barnes Neglect	163
		name unknown	25
		Littons Improvement	25
		Spo____ Neighbour	75
Joseph Karr	1		
John Litton	3	pt. Maidens Mount	104
		Partnership	21
		Littons Vein	30
John Montgomery	4	Patricks Purchase	50
		Williams Lott	30
		Montgomerys Meadow	16
		John's Purchase	30
		St. Patrick	25
William Montgomery	2	Patricks Purchase	50
		James' Portion	60
		St. Patrick	25
Agnus Morrison	3	Hawkins Purchase	25
James McCandless	0	McCandless' Change	230
James McNabb	8	Prospect	89
Joseph Miller	0	Guffeys Romantick Prospect-140	
		Guffeys Romantick Delight- 100	
		Guffeys Romantick Meadows-124	
		Afhonoyes Retirement	100

1783 TAX LIST OF HARFORD COUNTY, MARYLAND
Broad Creek Hundred

Name	# of whites	Tract Name	# acres
Daniel McAnnick	7		
Samuel McKisson	8		
negroe Pompy	0		
negroe Ruth	0		
James Parks	5		
William Porter	2		
James Philips	7	Beaver Pain	5
		Doolys Beginning	45
William Reese	4	Prospect	45
		Reeses Chance	42
		Littleworth	10
		Reeses Range	17
Walter Robinson	0	Robinsons Purchase	100
James Reed	0	Montgomery	25
Capt. James Steel	3	Thomas' Knole	87
		Steels Rest	87
Thomas Steel Esq.	1		
Benjamin Smith	1		
John Stewart	4	Maxfields Range	62
David Steel	6		
Francis Stones	7		
James Simms	3		
David Sweeny	11	F__once?	90
		Dear Bought & Nothing Got	25
		Morgans Addition	25
		Morgans Neglect	25
John Thomas	6	name unknown	13
James Visage	4		
Nathaniel Wiley	7	Bachelors Delight	63
Hugh Whiteford Jr.	3	Whitefords Adventure	175
William Williams	10	Tho. & Wm.	72
		Allens Desire	14
John Windman	1	Dallams Fancy	64
John Wilson Sr.	3	Famers Neighbour	131
John Wilson Jr.	4		
John Barclay, assessor	7	The Grove	210

No paupers are listed in Broad Creek Hundred

1783 TAX LIST OF HARFORD COUNTY, MARYLAND
Broad Creek Hundred

Securities	Single Men
Nathaniel Wiley	James Wiley
Henry Benington	Nehemiah Benington
Samuel Eakin	Joseph Eakin
Francis Donning	John Donning
Thomas Johnson	Elijah Johnson
James McNabb	Abraham Holmon
Robert Bodkin	John Bodkin
Robert Bodkin	James Wilson
Samuel McKesson	William Benington
David Sweeny	Thomas Brasher
	Barnett Williams
John Barclay	Barnard Frazeir
Samuel McKisson	John Benington

A return of property in <u>Deer Creek Lower Hundred</u> by John Dallam, assessor.

Name	# of whites	Tract Name	# acres
John Bruce	7	Brothers Discovery	100
Job Barnes Jr.	5		
Job Barnes Sr.	7	Maidens Mount	50
		Brothers Discovery	50
		Paradise	75
Charles Bevard	4	Aribia Patria	100
Thomas Brown	0		
Samuel Carter	4		
Robert Cook	8	Maidens Mount	76
		pt. Paradise	125
		Cooks Island	5
		Renshaws lott	50
John Cook	1	pt. Paradise	65
Vinicia Cromwell	1	pt. Neighbourhood	50
Mordecai Crawford	5	Aribia Patria	211
James Crawford	4	Aribia Patria	2
William Coale Sr.	3	Aribia Patria	135
William Coale of Wm.	1	Aribia Patria	125
Thomas Chew	0	Bachelors Good Luck	100
Skipwith Coale	4	Stone Hall	352
William Coale	6	Bachelors Good Luck	107
Philip Coale	11	Ariba Patria	150
Richard Dallam	1	pt. Neighbourhood	84
		Miles Improvement	100

1783 TAX LIST OF HARFORD COUNTY, MARYLAND
Deer Creek Hundred

Name	# of whites	Tract Name	# acres
John Dallam, assessor	7	pt. Neighbourhood	103
William Downing	5		
Joseph Davis	8	Newstead	50
Hugh Deaver	6		
Margaret Dallam	4		
Thomas Ely	4	Brothers Discovery	215
Hugh Ely	3	Paradise	50
Thomas Ely	5	Paradise	100
Mahlon Ely	4	Paradise	100
Sarah Fisher	2	Aribia Patria	100
James Fisher	9	Aribia Patria	100
William Gardner	4		
Robert Gover	1	pt. Elberton	125
Ephraim Gittings Gover	1	pt. Elberton	125
Samuel Gover	4	pt. Elberton	237
Aquila Giles	0	pt. Elberton	500
		Rigbies Hope	230
		Giles Addition	33
		Rich Bottom Corrected	150
Elizabeth Gover	4		
Thomas Gorrell	4		
Joseph Hopkins	9	pt. Philips Purchase	600
Joseph Harris	1		
Samuel Harris	8		
John Hawkins	1		
William Hopkins	5	Bachelors Good Luck & Jones Venture	438
		Aribia Patria	93
Elizabeth Husband	?	Aribia Patria & Neighborhood	364
		Clay Hill	300
		Elberton	13
		Parkers Chance	100
Gerrard Hopkins	8		
Edward Jolly	2	Dooly's Beginning	100
		pt. Aribia Patria	88
		Stapleton's Lott	40
Elizabeth Jolly	7	pt. Aribia Patria	200
		Wallis Beginning	50
		Wallis Addition	50
Skipwith Johns	0	Rigbies Hope	230
Thomas James	2		
Rueben Jones	7	Aribia Patria	58

1783 TAX LIST OF HARFORD COUNTY, MARYLAND
Deer Creek Hundred

Name	# whites	Tract Name	# acres
Richard Kenly	3		
Daniel Kenly	0	Aribia Patria	4
Elizabeth Lee	3	Freeland Mount	160
Alexander Murray	7	Aribia Patria	247 1/2
John Murray	2		
Daniel McComas	2		
George McKenny	5		
Isaac Massey	1 ?	pt. Philip's Purchase	350
Stephen Norton	5	pt. Neighbourhood	100
John Patrick	11	Aribia Patria	105
		Limestones ? & Addition	209
John Peacock	4	New Stead	150
James Rigbie	4	Philips Purchase	500
Nathan Rigbie	2	Rigbies Chance	400
		Husbands Angles	4
		Parkers Chance	75
John Rogers	10	Ten Acre Field	10 1/2
		other land	13 1/2
Guideon Purvail	8		
Samuel Rogers	6	Aribia Patria	95 1/2
Joseph Rogers	5	Aribia Patria	100
Jacob Slack	3	pt. Philips Purchase	1
Henry Spence	11		
Martha Smith	8	Newstead	150
		2nd Venture	39 1/4
		Mill Seat	25
Samuel Salelay	7		
John Stump	4	pt. Lines tents ?	150
William Taylor	6		
Thomas Varley	2		
Edward Ward	3	Aribia Patria	280
Charles Worthington	9	Philips Purchase	300
		Wills Lott	100
Crosdal Warner	11	Paradise	150
Richard Ward	5		
Cuthbert Warner	9		
Richard Wells	4	Aribia Patria	306
Richard Wells Jr.	3		
Thomas Wallis	6	Aribia Patria	92
		Coobs ? Delight	100
Joseph Wallis	6		

1783 TAX LIST OF HARFORD COUNTY, MARYLAND
Deer Creek Hundred

Name	# of whites	Tract Name	# acres
John Worthington	10	Worthingtons Dividend	354
		Wills Lott	100
Joshua Wood	3		
Samuel Wilson's heirs	0	pt. Neighbourhood	25
Joseph Wilson Jr.	1?	Aribia Patria	50
Joseph Wilson Sr.	3	pt. Neighbourhood	96
		Aribia Patria	50
		Daughertys Chance	84
		Deer Creek Upper	
		Wilson's Choice	37
Benjamin Wilson	9	Aribia Patria	123
Daniel Sheredine	1	Cumberland Forge	40
Worthington & Amoss	0	Aquila's Inheritance	836
		West Wood	60
		Wilburns Venture	86
		Aquila's Beginning	18
Philip Warnock	3		
John West	6	John Pipe	4 1/4
John Jenkins	0		
Joseph Warner	7	Aribia Patria	230

Securities

Job Barnes
Charles Bevard
Gerrard Hopkins
Thomas Ely
Thomas Ely
William Hopkins
John Stump
Gittings Gover
Joseph Hopkins
James Fisher
Skip Coale
Aquila Gilse
John Dallam
John Stump
Martha Smith
William Morgan
Edward Jolly
Edward Jolly

Single Men

Ezekiel Barns
James Bevard
Skipwith Coale
Joseph Ely
William Ely
William, John, & Charles Hopkins
John Handy
John Harris
Samuel Harris
Christopher Hall
Jacob Hall
Joseph Ford
James Rigbie Jr.
___man Stump
Rolph Smith
Michael Sivars
Joseph Gorrell
John McCracken

1783 TAX LIST OF HARFORD COUNTY, MARYLAND
Deer Creek Lower Hundred

Securities	Single Men
Moredcai Crawford	James Lemmon
William Coale	Negroe Tom
Charles Worthington	Negroe Harry
William Hopkins	Negroe Benn
Levin Hopkins	Negroe Jack
Elisabeth Husband	Negroes George & James
John Worthington	Negroe David & Pompy
Joseph Hopkins	Negroe Luke
James Rigbie	Negroe Jacob
Jeremiah Sheredine	Negroe Jacob
Susanna Chew	Negroe Holiday
Joseph Wilson	Negroe Tom
James Rigbie	Negroe Tower
Elizabeth Husbands	Negroes Jeffery & Sam

Paupers & # whites	Paupers & # whites
Michael Divan-3	Thomas Stephenson-2
William Strode-5	James Tasker Sr.-4
James Tasker Jr.-3	Joseph Wiggins-9
William Knott-7	James Cuddy-5
Roger _____-7	James Budgis-9
John Pinock-9	Thomas Wilson-3
John Clark-5	James Spence-5

Return of property in Spesutia Upper Hundred made by William Bradford, assessor 1783.

Name	# whites	Tract Name	# acres
Rebecca Allen	5	Henry's Neighbour	30
		Folly of Gout? Bottle	30
John Archer, Esq.	10	pt. Out Quarter	200
		pt. Uncles Good Will	250
Christian Baker	3	pt. Bedmore	9
		Graftons Entrance	10
		pt. Frenchmans Repose	60
Grafton Baker	3		
John Baker of Maurice	3		
John Barnes	0	pt. Edmunds Delight	44
Joseph Barnes	11	pt. Edmunds Delight	44
William Barnes	0	pt. Edmunds Delight	44
John Barnhouse	4		

1783 TAX LIST OF HARFORD COUNTY, MARYLAND
Spesutia Upper Hundred

Name	# whites	Tract Name	# acres
Walter Billingsley	3	Rigdon's Escape & Redm(an)	102
		Bonds Lott	225
		Dallams Deer Purchase	153
		Friendship	40
		Billingsleys Lott	23
		Pulsons Priveledge	98
		pt. Loves Addition	15
Robert Briarly	2	Bonds Last Shift	200
George Brown	3		
Joseph Brownly	8	pt. Out Quarter	200
Francis Bull	11	Ruffs Chance	130
		Howards Harbour	21
Jacob Bull of Edmun;	3		
Susanna Bull	3	Whitakers Chance	50
		Land of Promise	200
		Roberton	42
		Stephens Hope	12
		Bulls Care	29
		Bulls Ford	54
James Cain	8		
William Carlon, taylor	3		
David Clark	11	pt. Roberts Chance	39
		Wheelers Union Refused	206
		pt. Good Neighbourhood	122
		pt. Great Brittain	29 1/2
Lawrence Clark	5	Add. to John & Isaacs Lott	80
William Clark	8	John's Lott	156
		Roberts Adventure Enlarged	237
Christopher Clement	0	pt. Southhampton	75
James Clendening	9	pt. Desired Lott	221
		Sarlon's ? Contrivance	144
		pt. James' Lott	90
Henry Cooper	10	Coopers Chance Improved	150
		pt. Howards Invitation	100
Nathaniel Cooper	1		
James Creaton	2	Jacob's Chance	70
		Hardens Delight	45
		Hardens Last Shift	22
		Whites Beginning	100
John Creaton	2	pt. Uncles Good Will	155

1783 TAX LIST OF HARFORD COUNTY, MARYLAND
Spesutia Upper Hundred

Name	# of whites	Tract Name	# acres
Robert Creswell	4	pt. Out Quarter	190
John Cummins	3		
Philip Cummins	6		
Samuel Daugherty	2	pt. Jerico	100
Michael Denny	3		
William Downs	7	Smithsons Delight	69
Simon Denny	3	pt. Southampton	125
		Simons Friend	25
James Erwin	8		
Edward Flanagan	6	Prospect	403
Mary Flanagan	3	pt. Out Quarter	200
Jacob Forwood of Samuel	3		
John Forwood of Samuel	9		
John Forwood	3	pt. Maidens Meadows	91
		John's Friend	4
		Forwoods Purchase	32
		John's Addition	25
		pt. St. Homer	20
		John's Adventure	49
		pt. Colegates Addition	7
		part in Grist Mill	
Samuel Forwood	8	George's Fancy	94
		Henry's Pleasure	50
		Colegates Contrivance	100
		Roberts Chance	60
		pt. Webbs Discovery	11 3/4
		part in Grist Mill	
Frederick Fraily	6		
John Gibb	5	pt. Out Quarter	200
Jacob Gates	6		
John Lee Gibson	5	pt. Maidens Bower? &	
		Paca's Enlargement resurvey-476	
		Hopewell & Scotts Add. to	
		Trust	425
James Gilbert	3		
Aquila Grafton	3	Brazers Desire	100
Daniel Grafton	3	Thompsons Addition	40
		Fatherly Care	18 3/4
		Graftons Endeavour	52
Nathaniel Grafton	0	pt. Graftons Entrance	63
		Billingsleys Lott	82

1783 TAX LIST OF HARFORD COUNTY, MARYLAND
Spesutia Upper Hundred

Name	# of whites	Tract Name	# acres
Samuel Grafton	4	pt. Bedmont	100
Sarah Grafton	3	pt. Grafton's Entrance	130
William Grafton	8	Graftons Lott	188
Benjamin Green	9	pt. Bonds Beginning	9
		pt. Francis Delight &	
		Good Neighbourhood	205
Henry Green	3	John & Isaacs Lott	142
		pt. Uncles Good Will	20
		pt. Francis Delight,	
		pt. Good Neighbourhood,	
		pt. Bond's Choice and	
		pt. Bonds Beginning	397
Leonard Green	7		
Thomas Gash	7	pt. Persons Park	60
		pt. Matthews Neighbour	89
Henry Hagan	3		
John Hannah	9	pt. Uncles Good Will	125
Archer Hays	7	pt. John & Isaacs Lott	200
John Hays Sr.	4	pt. Uncles Good Will	361
		pt. John & Isaacs Lott	100
		Flanagans Vexation	13
		Howards Forest	100
Elizabeth Harris	6	pt. Good Neighbourhood	
		with improvements	25
John Hart	5	pt. Out Quarter Improved	8 3/4
		Widows Care	100
Stephen Hill	7		
George Hollinger, sadler	7		
Samuel Hopkins	10		
Thomas Hudson	5		
James Hughes	9		
Joshua Jervis	6	Johnson's Range	62 1/2
William Jervis	2		
Bernard Johnson of Barnard	0	pt. Turky Forest	150
Bernard Johnson of Thomas	1	pt. Turky Forest	150
Hester Johnson	7	pt. Nobles Wonder	50
		Johnsons Range	20
		Andrews Struggle	2
Rachel Johnson	5	pt. Bonds Lott	210
		Billingsleys Bitt	10

1783 TAX LIST OF HARFORD COUNTY, MARYLAND
Spesutia Upper Hundred

Name	# of whites	Tract Name	# acres
Thomas Johnson, Esq.	5	pt. Bonds Lott	83
		Bond's Addition	150
		Johnson's Strife	35 1/2
		pt. Johnson's Range	62 1/4
James Lee	10	pt. Isaacs Inheritance	200
Parker Lee	4		
Samuel Lee	8	pt. Jerico	500
		pt. Isaacs Inheritance	200
		Preston's Conquest	123
Negroe London.	0	H. Wilson's	
John Love, Esq.	11	Loves Addition Improved	219
		Waxford	100
		Great Brittain	296
		Roberts Lott	100
		Bonds Fortune	22
		Bonds Lott	5
		Hazard	40
		Kidminster	40
		pt. Rigdon's Escape	21
David McCasland	6		
Matthew McClintock	0	pt. Good Neighbourhood Improved	1
Matthew McClintock, Jr.	0	pt. Good Neighbourhood	7/8
Andrew McCoy	6		
Matthew McIlhaney	7		
Ann Preston	1	pt. Grafton's Gift	70
		Preston's Choice	100
Thomas P. Presbury	2	pt. Edmunds Camp	100
		pt. Delight	85
Barnard Preston	5	pt. Ruff's Chance	150
Barnard Preston of James	6	pt. Vineyard	100
		pt. Andrews Addition	25
		pt. Young's Neighbour	25
		different tracts name unknown	100
Grafton Preston	0	Prestons Conquest	108
James Preston	6	pt. Prestons Lott	100
		Second? Lease	50
Martin Preston	7	Prestons Conquest	250
Ralph Pyles	10	Webbs Discovery	272 1/4
		Pyles Addition	50

1783 TAX LIST OF HARFORD COUNTY, MARYLAND
Spesutia Upper Hundred

Name	# of whites	Tract Name	# acres
Ralph Pyles Jr.	0	pt. St. Homer	200
Philip Quinlin	11		
negroe Rachel	0	pt. Good Neighbourhood with improvements	1
Martin Renshaw	0	pt. Friends Discovery	100 1/2
Robert Renshaw	3	pt. Friends Discovery	100 1/2
James Rigdon	3		
Charles Robinson	0	pt. United Lott	16 3/4
Joseph Robinson	6		
Thomas Rogers	5	pt. Matthews Neighbour	20
Henry Ruff	4	Ruffs Chance	200
James Sparrow	3		
Thomas Stroud	4		
Thomas Stroud Jr.	4		
Henry Thomas	9	Henrys Patch	45
		Henrys Inspection	26 1/2
		Henrys Hope	40
		Henrys Inspection Resurvey	189
John Thomas	8	Braziers Troubles	100
		Gladdins Beginning	20
		Donovins Choice	20
Aquila Thompson	4		
James Thompson	12	Pearsons Lodge	100
		Andrews Addition	25
		Thompsons Chance	12
John Thompson	10	Neighbours Good Will	120
Daniel Turner	7		
Mary Vaneleaf	4	Rigdons Escape	50
James Watson	4	Hickory Ridge	40
		pt. Deserted lott	60
Samuel Wilmoth	3		
Henry Watters	4	pt. Howards Harbour & Mary's Chance	146
Jonathan West	3	Miles Desire	103
		Jonathan West Jr.	5
Benedict Wheeler	1	Fatherly Care	100
Ignatius Wheeler Esq	3	Wheelers & Clarks Contrivance	1000
		Peirsons Range	230
		Benjamins Camp	150
		Childrens Roaling?	5

1783 TAX LIST OF HARFORD COUNTY, MARYLAND
Spesutia Upper Hundred

Name	# of whites	Tract Name	# acres
Benjamin Wheeler	8	Wheelers First Add.	19
		Wheelers Second Add.	10 3/4
		Green Spring	30
		pt. Clarks Park	94 1/4
		Wheelers Beginning	13
		Success	70 3/4
		Mt. Pleasant	21
		Rough Borough	111
		St. Homer	80
		Thomas' Biging	180
		Wheelers Third Add.	23
Thomas Wheeler of Benj.	0	Roses Green	162
John Whitaker	4	Howard's Chance	200
		pt. of Albano	250
Ann Wright	4	pt. Southampton	75

Securities
Rebecca Allen
Sarah Grafton (widow)
John Lee Gibson
John Cummins
Michael Denny

James Clendening
Benjamin Johnson of Barnet
Andrew McCoy
Samuel Webb Sr.
John Forwood
John Forwood
Henry Thomas
Joseph Brownly
Philip Quinlan
Samuel Forwood
Mary Vancleaf
Samuel Webb Jr.
Henry Ruff Sr.
Henry Thomas
Daniel Turner
Joseph Toy

Single Men
Moses Allen
Horatio Coop
David Cooty
Samuel Cummins
William Holloway
William Hughes
Jacob Johnson
William McClay
Robert & Andrew McCoy Jr.
James McDaniel
Samuel Martin
Matthew Moratto
John Piles
Thomas Pritchard
James Quinlin
James Richardson
William Rigdon
George Rollins
Henry Ruff Jr.
David Thomas
Samuel Turner
negroe Charles (H. Watters)

1783 TAX LIST OF HARFORD COUNTY, MARYLAND
Spesutia Upper Hundred

List of Paupers & number of whites

Charles Burkin-5
Catherine Humble-5
Mary Logue-3
Roderick McKinsey-7
Thomas Reese-2
John Slack-9

Joseph Conely-4
Thomas Jackson-2
John Lowry-6
Arthur Monaghon-2
Benjamin Reso-3
Henry Toutchstone-6
negroe Dick (James Bond)

Daniel Douglas-3
James Lee Sham-1
Alley McDaniel-8
James Quinlin Sr.-1
William Shepherd-8
John Whitaker-4

Deer Creek Middle Hundred by John Barclay, assessor

Name	# of whites	Tract Name	# acres
Jacob Albert	7	Bachelors Abode	40
		Bachelors Beginning	50
Philip Albert	3	Bonds Hope	68
James Alexander	2	Jones' Abode	50
William Allender	8	pt. Fruland Mount	50
James Anderson	6	pt. Abrahams Inheritance	100
William Ashmore	4	Ashmores Adventure	109
		Brothers Discovery	49
		Ashmores Choice	434
		pt. Giles & Websters Discovery	25
		James' Gift	150
		pt. Aribia Patrea	400
Isaiah Balderson	7	pt. Aribia Patrea	40
Jacob Balderson	4	pt. Aribia Patrea	86
James Barnett	3	pt. Abrahams Inheritance	100
James Barnett Jr.	4		
Mark Barnett	9	Hills Hall	25
Charles Beaver	1	pt. Aribia Patria	100
Stophell Benshaft	6	pt. Aribia Patria	
Sias Billingsley	9	Sias Range	166
John Boshong	2		
Elizabeth Brice	3	Brice's Purchase	153
		Ups and Downs	42
James Calley	6		
James Camble	2	Swords Defence	63
George Cartlon	5		
James Clark	5	Ross' Rich Neck	35
		Hickory Hollow	30

1783 TAX LIST OF HARFORD COUNTY, MARYLAND
Deer Creek Middle Hundred

Name	# of whites	Tract Name	# acres
Robert Clark	11	Robert's Garden	120
		Roberts Addition	30
		Cain's Chance	30
		Knavery Prevents	36
Mary Connelly	2	Pinny Valley	84
Joseph Davis	0	Bachelors Beginning	63
Edward Diggins	7		
Andrew Dunsmore	2		
Kerron Elliott	4		
Thomas Elliott	0		
		pt. Giles & Websters Discovery	75
		Renshaws Last Purchase	50
Mary Fisher	8	Aribia Patria	150
Thomas Foster	2	pt. Aibia Patria	174
John Lee Gibson	0	Jonathans Inheritance	100
		Rich Point	200
		Bennetts Prospect	25
Jarvis Gilbert	0	pt. Jenkins Range	100
		Fair Cross	100
		pt. Billingsleys Lott	153
Aaron Gordon	6		
John Halbert	3		
John Haley	6		
John Haley Jr.	3		
James Howlett	4	Minors Adventure	200
Jane Hutchason	7	Clarks Discovery	108
		Hills Providence	40
James Jackson	3	Second Edition	55
John Jackson	0	Clarks Dunmurrgin	150
John James	1	Bargins Folly	22
		Ross Gray	25
		Fools Inspection	40
Sedgwick James	6	John's Beginning	200
Rachel Jenkins	0	pt. Aribia Patria	55
Richard Jewells	3		
Joseph Johnson	5		
Benjamin Jones	5	Benjamins Beginning	41
Stephen Jones	4		
Daniel Kinly	7		
Samuel Kinly	4		
James Lewis	5		

1783 TAX LIST OF HARFORD COUNTY, MARYLAND
Deer Creek Middle Hundred

Name	# of whites	Tract Name	# acres
Josiah Lee	8	pt. Maidens Bower	6
		Planters Paradise	200
		pt. Freeland Mount	10
		Gunpowder Lower Hundred	
		pt. Hog Neck	80
		Plum Point	50
		James' Fortune	100
		Abington Lott	
Andrew Linsay	9	pt. Giles & Websters Discovery	98
		pt. Brothers Discovery	35
Samuel Lockard	3	Abrahams Inheritance	93
James Lynch	4		
George McAtee	10	Isaacs Enlargement	127
		David's Enlargement	8
		Donavins Choice	88
John McCullough	2		
John McFaddin	7	Ohio	248
		Jones Reserve	109
John McFaddin Jr.	2		
John McLaughlin	6		
Joseph McNamarra	5		
John Majors	0	McCalls Delight	80
William Majors	9		
Robert Morgan	5	Fathers Request	190
		pt. Brothers Purchase	70
		pt. William's Discovery	47
		Morgan's Angle	7
		Broad Creek H.(Hundred) land	60
		Deer Creek Lower Paradise	300
William Morgan	8	Johnson's Chance	142
		Meadow Land	46
		Ashmore's Retirement	70
		Mountain	100
		pt. Aribia Patria	110
		Trellec	36
		Deer Creek Lower Freeland Mount	90
		Simmons Choice	184

1783 TAX LIST OF HARFORD COUNTY, MARYLAND
Deer Creek Middle Hundred

Name	# of whites	Tract Name	# acres
John Morgan	6	pt. Aribia Patria	320
John Munn	2		
John Murray	0	pt. Aribia Patria	368
Thomas Nail	0	The Addition	74
Simon Navill	5		
Samuel Palmer	8		
John Peacock for heirs Jenkins	0	pt. Freeland Mount	45
Luke Peacock	9	Andrews Choice	113
		Jame's' Meadows	43
Richard Perkins	2		
William Perry	3		
Edward Prigg	2		
William Prigg	5	Sheppard Paradice	45
		Morgans Paradice	11
		Morgans Paradice	18
		Mort. Cost	11
		Harry Mans Folly	35
William Prigg Jr.	2	Sias Range	50
Andrew Ralston	8	Wills Lott	36
		Patricks Ventrue	40
Thomas Renshaw	9	Thomas' Desire	82
John Richards	5		
Baker Rigdon	6	Jenkins Range	147
Benjamin Rogers	3		
Thomas Rutman	2		
Euclidus Scarborough Jr.	2		
John Scarborough	9	pt. Rutman's Enlargement	45
		pt. Giles & Websters Discovery	115
		pt. Center	50
Joseph Scarborough	6	pt. Giles & Websters Discovery	70
Thomas Scarborough	5		
William Scarborough	3		
John Scofeild	4		
Jane Slone	2	Fishers Delight	45
John Smith	4		
Nathan Smith	8		
Robert Smith	3	Frankford	54
		Garden Spott	10
		Williams Discovery	282

1783 TAX LIST OF HARFORD COUNTY, MARYLAND
Deer Creek Middle Hundred

Name	# of whites	Tract Name	# acres
William Smith	4		
Joseph Stokes	11	pt. Clarks Dunmurry in	
James Taylor	6	Antrim	51
Benjamin Warner	5	pt. Clarks Dunmurry in	
		Antrim	100
		Peace Proclaimed	40
Joseph Warner	0	pt. Abrahams Inheritance	100
Samuel Webb Jr.	5		
Samuel Webb Sr.	2	Spittle Craft	469
		pt. Brothers Discovery	37
		pt. Webbs Neglect	68
		pt. Giles & Websters	
		Discovery	11
		Webbs Spott	18
		Webbs Neglect	342
Joseph West	2	pt. Aribia Patria	25
Ignatius Wheeler Jr.		Maidens Neighbour	200
		pt. Center	190
		Johnsons Neighbour	32
		Websters Inspection	265
		Websters Intention	50
		The Enlargement	90
		pt. Giles & Websters	
		Discovery	200
		Spittle Craft	250
		Fathers Request	350
Joseph Wheeler	0	Rigdon's Adventure	78
		Wheelers Range	137
Hugh Whiteford Jr.	11	Bachelors Delight	49
		Intent	117
William Whiteford	2	Whitefords Delight	27
		Whitefords Level	52
		Whitefords Range	93
		Whitefords Choice	82
Godfrey Wilmore	3		
John Wright	4		

1783 TAX LIST OF HARFORD COUNTY, MARYLAND
Deer Creek Middle Hundred

Securities	Single Men
James Anderson, Sr.	James Anderson
Robert Clark Sr.	William Clark
Robert Clark Sr.	Samuel Clark
Robert Clark Sr.	George Clark
Robert Clark	David Clark
Samuel Webb Jr.	Samuel Crockett
William Ashmore	Alexander Cummins
Elizabeth Brice	Joseph Ewing
Sias Billingsley	William Ewing
William Ashmore	Barnett Forter
	William Gallion
John Barclay	Archibald McNair
James Kelly	John Marford
John Holbert	Matthew Morrison
Luke Peacock	Samuel Peacock
William Prigg Sr.	John Prigg
	Richard Proctor
John Holbert	Joseph Rogers
James Lewis	William Taylor
John McFaddin Sr.	John Wilson

No paupers were listed in Deer Creek Middle Hundred.

1783 TAX LIST OF CALVERT COUNTY, MARYLAND
First District Return by Francis King, assessor

Name	# of whites	Tract Name	# acres
Chania Allnutt	5	pt. Truman's Chance	153
James Allnutt	8	pt. Truman's Chance	150
Susanna Austin	4	pt. Cox's Choice	80
James Austin	7	pt. Cox's Choice	80
John Addington	5		
Henry Addinton	5		
William Askew	10	pt. Lowries Chance	39
Abram Askew	1		
Edmund Allnutt	1		
John Allsop	0		
Issabella Barton	2	pt. Upper Bennett	50
John Barker	7	pt. Illingworth's Fortune	200
John Brassaw Jr.	7		
Issabella Barton Jr.	1		
Jeremiah Baden	5	pt. Parkers Clifts	150
Joseph Blake	3	pt. Upper Bennett	375
		pt. Lordships Favor	97
Joseph Blake Jr.	1		
Richard Blake	1		
Thomas Blake	5	pt. St. Edmunds	200
		pt. Upper Bennett	200
		pt. Lordships Favor	95
		pt. Neglect	50
Charles Busey Jr.	7	pt. Gover & Griffiths Pasture,	
		pt. Skinners Chance &	
		pt. Turners Place	98
Charles Busey	5		
Thomas Blake Jr.	3	pt. Halls Craft	500
Margaret Connant	6		
James Cranford	4		
John Chambers	5		
Elizabeth Cox	4		
Samuel Chew	8	pt. Upper Bennett	456
		Bennetts Refuge	33
		pt. Setchworth's Chance	550
		Gore & Sane	51 1/2
		pt. Upper Bennett	25
Peter Clark	5	pt. Dunkirk & pt. Hornisham-	150
Samuel Chew (A.A.Co.)	0	Poppingay	486
Seaborn Carr	8		

1783 TAX LIST OF CALVERT COUNTY, MARYLAND
First District

Name	# of whites	Tract Name	# acres
Josias Crosby	8	pt. Turners Place & pt. Archer Hays	90
William Chew	8	pt. Halls Hills	736
David Carcand	4	pt. Johnsons Farm, pt. Turners Place & pt. Govers & Griffiths Pasture	236
Thomas Crutchley	5	pt. High Land	50
Sampson Crane	6		
Thomas Charlton	7		
Gabriel Childes	7	pt. Letchworth's Chance	336
Ann Childes	2		
Thomas Chaney Jr.	7		
Thomas Chaney	10	pt. Halls Hills	112
Joseph Cambden	7	pt. Halls Hills	112
Alexander Chesley	1		
Elizabeth Chesley	0	pt. Bachelor's Quarter	420
Michael Catterton	7	pt. Aldermaion, pt. Addition, pt. Lingans Purchase	330
Sabrit Card	9		
Margaret Cox	5	pt. Fuller, pt. Trumans Chance, pt. Deer Quarters, pt. Dosseys Folly	570
Francis Dossey	4	pt. Bennetts Desire	4
Elizabeth Dossey	3		
Benjamin Dossey	1		
William Denney	5		
Thomas Cloverly Dare	3	pt. Agreements	150
		pt. Parkers Clifts	21
		Bite The Biter	112
		Neglect	50
		Darby	46
		Sampions Divident	150
		pt. Warring	25
		pt. Device	76
John Dossey	8	pt. Robinsons Rest	143
		pt. Deer Quarter	62 1/2
		pt. Bennetts Desire	10
		pt. Mary Green	63
Philip Dossey	1	pt. Robinsons Rest	76
James Dossey	1	pt. Robinsons Rest	100
		pt. Garden	63

1783 TAX LIST OF CALVERT COUNTY, MARYLAND
First District

Name	# of whites	Tract Name	# acres
Samuel Dossey	1		
William Dare	6	pt. Swinsons Rest	250
		pt. Lowsies	26
William Deale	7	pt. Upper Bennett	50
John Dicks	5	pt. Johnsons Farm &	
		pt. Turners Place	157
John Dew	11		
Jacob Deale	1	pt. Upper Bennett	25
		pt. Devan	125
Benjamin Dotson	1		
John David	0	pt. Defence	64
Daniel Dossey	4	pt. Garden	60
John Dorvele	5	pt. Lingans Purchase	125
Gideon Dare Jr.	6		
John Elisha	6		
William Edmunds	7	pt. Agreement	100
Thomas Eads	7		
Robert Freeland	3	pt. Neglect	125
Dinah Freeland	5	pt. Letchworth's Chance &	
		pt. Fuller	279
Ann French	5		
John Frazier	1		
Alexander Frazier	0	pt. Sterlings Chance &	
		pt. Sterlings Perch	740
Kinsey Freeman Jr.	1		
Mary Gray	5	pt. Expectation	100
Ann Griffith	4	pt. Welch Poole &	
		pt. Skinners Chance	233
Ann Griffith	2	pt. Welch Poole &	
		pt. Cooper	315
Thomas Gantt	2	pt. Halls Craft, pt. Ordinary,	
		pt. Kingsbury Marsh	893
Robert Gover	2	pt. Archer Hays, pt. Goughs	
		Pasture, pt. Turners Place	189
Asenoth Graham	0	pt. Halls Craft &	
		pt. Howards Branch	300
John Graham	0	pt. Halls Craft &	
		pt. Howards Branch	263
Charles Graham	0		
Ann Griffin	2	pt. Robinsons Rest	60

1783 TAX LIST OF CALVERT COUNTY, MARYLAND
First District

Name	# of whites	Tract Name	# acres
Richard Harris	3	pt. Warring Town	150
		pt. Agreement	50
		Warrings Chance	56
Martha Hatfield	8		
Richard Hollandshead	1		
Thomas Hollandshead	2	Hemps Freehold	250
Thomas Hardesty	1		
Thomas Holland	5	pt. St. James Enlarged	1138
		pt. Alexanders Hope	38
James Hemmingway's heirs	0	pt. St. James Enlarged	1138
		pt. Alexanders Hope	38
John Hutchings	4	pt. Cork Hill	113
Francis Hollandshead	7		
Roger Hooper	5		
Philip Hunt	5	pt. Lordships Favour	50
Thomas Hardesty Jr.	7		
Joseph Hardesty	7		
William Hardesty	4		
John Hollyday	4		
Newman Harvey	5	pt. Turners Place	84
Thomas Hinton	7		
Benjamin Harris	7	pt. Expectation	160
		pt. Whittles Rest & pt. Parkers Clifts	160
Joseph Hutchens	4		
Elisha Hall	6		
Henry Hardesty	10	pt. Nicholas Chance, &	
Richard Howard	9	pt. The Denn	90
Richard Hinton	11		
Elisha Hall Jr.	3		
John Harrison	6		
John Howard	9		
Joseph Hardesty Jr.	10	pt. Nichols Chance & pt. The Den, pt. Nelsons Research	150
Benjamin Hance Jr.	0	pt. Parkers Clifts	128
William Hunter	3	pt. Busseys Orchard	100
		pt. Security	87
		pt. Brians Tree Water Mill	10
Richard Hance	2		
James Heighe Jr.	1		

1783 TAX LIST OF CALVERT COUNTY, MARYLAND
First District

Name	# of whites	Tract Name	# acres
James Heighe	5	pt. Beakley	97
		pt. Roberts Chance	34
		pt. Troster	150
		pt. James Chance	40
		Samuel's Addition	15
		pt. Chalk Hill	19
		Little Sound	11
		Hughe's Addition	15
		James' Addition	21
Betty Heighe	3	pt. Beakley	203
Priscilla Hardesty	3	pt. Lorships Favour	25
Richard Harrison	1	pt. Swinsons Rest	100
John Hunt	6	pt. Lordship's Favour	100
Henry Hunt	5	pt. Upper Bennett	200
George Ireland	4		
Thomas Isaac	3	pt. Lordship's Favour	205
Lewis Jones	9	pt. Smith's Lott	50
William Johnson of Jesse	3	pt. Exchange	150
Gilbert Ireland	7	pt. Lyon Creek & Dunkirk	562
William Ireland	10	pt. Halls Hills Water Mill	320
Thomas Ireland	1	pt. Halls Hills	200
William Johnson of George	3	pt. Red Hole & Halls Hills	-100
William Jonnsey	9		
Richard Isacke	2	Plumb Point	350
		Purchase	60
Benjamin King	3		
John King	2		
James Kendale	2	pt. Halls Hills	40
John Laveille	5	pt. Whittles Rest	304
John Landsdale	5	pt. Swinsons Rest	75
Samuel Lyles	6	Lowries Chance	50
Abraham Lore	1		
Samuel Lane	6	pt. Hornisham	251
William Lonnberth	9	pt. Smith's Lott	50
James Leach	4	pt. Exchange & Archer Hays	-409
		pt. Hornisham, & Dunkirk	150
William Lyles of Robert	4	pt. Red Hole & All Point	62
Catharine Lyles	7	pt. Red Hole & All Point	62
Henry Lyles	2		
Mary Lewis	1	pt. Lordship's Favour	50

1783 TAX LIST OF CALVERT COUNTY, MARYLAND
First District

Name	# of whites	Tract Name	# acres
William Lyles	6	pt. Red Hole & The S ? , pt. Turners Pasture & Long Lane	359
James Marr	1		
Elizabeth Marr	2		
Thomas McKenzie	5	pt. Newington, pt. Jones' Neglect & Ellingsworths Fortune	192
James Marcus	9	pt. Lordships Favour	100
Thomas Marr	5		
Susanna Mules	7	pt. Lowries Chance	148
James Mules	1		
John Marshall	9		
George McKoy	7		
Benjamin Mackall	0	pt. Majors Choice	346
Benjamin Mackall	0	pt. Corn Hill	2
Mark Nusence	3		
Martin Norris	4	pt. Dunkirk	150
Richard Norvell	5	pt. Halls Hills	37
Samuel Owens	4	pt. Angeliea & pt. Addition	159
Betty Owens	5	pt. Angeliea & pt. Addition	79
Charles Owens	1		
Mary Parker	3		
Fielder Parker Jr.	1		
George Parker Jr.	4		
Robert Peters	2	pt. Devan & Clares Hundred	142
James Pybus	4		
Richard Poole	6		
Thomas Poole	6		
Thomas Panan	2		
Elizabeth Prindowell	3	pt. Parkers Clifts	100
		pt. Roberts Addition	15
		pt. Roberts Chance	16
		pt. Beakley	250
		pt. Device	79
James Pattison	1	pt. Swinsons Rest	88
Arthur Prout	6		
John Pybus	5	pt. Cox's Choice	114
Daniel Prout	2		
Fielder Parker	8		
William Parker	4		
George Parker	9		

-172-

1783 TAX LIST OF CALVERT COUNTY, MARYLAND
First District

Name	# of whites	Tract Name	# acres
Daniel Ross	12	pt. Robinsons Rest	200
James Ruff	3	pt. Parkers Clifts	50
Job Roughton	4		
John Randall	8		
Elizabeth Robertson	2	pt. Defence & Halls Hills	150
Daniel Ross Jr.	1	pt. Coxes Choice	134
Edward Reynolds	7	pt. Lordship's Favour	385
		Sterling Perch	110
		pt. Robinson	191
		pt. St. Edmunds	150
		pt. Robinsons Rest	518
		pt. Good Luck	100
		Joynder or a Adjunction	10
		Rich Bet	5 1/2
		Neglect	44
		Troublesome	150
		pt. Hopewell	35
		The Angles Lane	37
		The Bite	5
Sarah Reynolds	1		
Rebecca Reynolds	1		
Richard Roberts	6	pt. Durin	200
		pt. Ellingworths Fortune	100
Ann Skinner	5		
Richard Skinner	8	pt. Millers Folly	145
Clement Skinner	1	pt. Millers Folly & Whittlers Rest-160	
John Smith	2		
John Davis Scarf	7	pt. Robinsons Rest	50
Thomas Sedwick	4		
Rezin Sunderland	6	pt. Lowries Chance	100
John Shears Jr.	4	pt. Lowries Chance	39
Susanna Sunderland	9	pt. Upper Bennett	50
Jonias Sunderland	1		
Elizabeth Sunderland	7	pt. Simmons Rest	62 1/4
Thomas Sunderland	4	pt. Simmons Rest	62 1/4
James Seivele	0	pt. Good Luck	150
Joseph Smith	12	pt Mordike	50
Verlinda Stamp	3	pt. Red Hole, Land & Turners Pl.	206
Henerietta Skinner	6	pt. Smiths Farm, Good Prospect & Lands Land	362

1783 TAX LIST OF CALVERT COUNTY, MARYLAND
First District

Name	# of whites	Tract Name	# acres
Abraham Sansbury	3	pt. Gover & Griffiths Pasture, pt. Skinners Chance & pt. Turners Place	98
Thomas Stamp	8	pt. Turners Place	111
George Smith	4	pt. Turners Place & pt. Smith's Chance	150
Thomas Simpson	6		
William Sansbury	8	pt. Archer Hays	40
John .Smith of Joseph	3	pt. Archer Hays	30
Daniel Smith	8	pt. High Land & Welch Poole	250
James Stone	1		
Mordecai Smith	9	pt. Smith's Chance, pt. High Land, pt. Turners Place	426
Betty Smith	4	Soldiers Fortune & pt. Ordinary	273
Alexander Hamilton Smith	10	pt. Bachelors Quarter Sneaking Point, Halls Revenge, & Halls Neglect	436 50
Leonard Specknall	4	pt. Hunts Chance, pt. Broaden Ashley, pt. Hamiltons Park	205
Patrick Smith Sr.	10	pt. Halls Craft	256
Clement Smith	4	pt. Halls Craft	230
Gregory Smithers	0		
Gavin Hamilton Smith	10	pt. Grantham Hole, Hazard, pt. Grantham, James Addition	483
Gideon Shoemaker	1		
Nathan Smith	8	pt. Smith's Chance, Pt. Mordike, pt. Turners Place	150
Absalom Stallings	3		
Elizabeth Stallings	4		
Henry Shears	4		
Richard Stallings	10	pt. Foxes Horns & Lingans Purchase	180
William Sullivant	4		
John Sunderland	5		
Isaac Simmons	0	pt. Chance & Millers Folly	222
Frederick Skinner	0	pt. Angelua, Mears & Addition	493
Samuel Trott (lawyer)	8	pt. Smiths Lott	127
Samuel Trott	7		
Abraham Tanquary	9		
Richard Turner	2		

1783 TAX LIST OF CALVERT COUNTY, MARYLAND
First District

Name	# of whites	Tract Name	# acres
John Taneyhill	13	pt. Welch Poole, pt. Cooper pt. Kalender, & Friendship	351
James Taneyhill	3	pt. Cooper	86
Leonard Taneyhill	5	pt. Cooper	86
Philip Talbott	9	pt. Expectation	94
Daniel Talbott	8	pt. Bachelors Fortune & pt. Trumans Chance	363
James Weems of David	7	pt. Regan, Green House, Chews Purchase, Grantham, Fall Short, Coxes Folly, The Farm, & pt. Coxes Choice	666
Mary Watson	6		
Hilleary Wilson	5	pt. Robinson	236
		Black Robin	38
		pt. Lordships Favour	129
		pt. Upper Robinson	
James Ward	5		
Richard Winfield	5	pt. Johnsons Farm	74
Daniel Wash	6		
Walter Watson	10		
Alexander Williamson	3		
Mary Williamson	4	pt. Bachelors Quarter	65
James Williamson	2	pt. Bachelors Quarter	131
Charles Williamson	1	pt. Den, Nettle, Lingans Purchase	493
Francis Whittington	10	pt. Halls Hills	125
Francis Whittington Jr.	6		
John Whittington	4		
William Whittington	5		
Henry Watson Jr.			
Richard Ward	6	pt. Devan, Clares Hundred & pt. Swinsons Rest	279
Benjamin Ward	1		
Elizabeth Wilson	8	pt. St. Edmunds & Neglect	180
Henry Wilson (Baltimore)	0	pt. Letchworths Chance	275
Basel Williamson	10	pt. Lingans Purchase	397
Robert Wilson	1	pt. Froster	150
Joseph Wilson	1	pt. James	300
		pt. Robinsons Rest	50
		pt. Deer Quarter	25
James Wilson	3	pt. Newington, Millers Folly & Williams Purchase	276
Henry Watson	10		

1783 TAX LIST OF CALVERT COUNTY, MARYLAND
Second District

Name	# of whites	Tract Name	# acres
Zacheus Allnutt	10	pt. Brooks Partition	236
		pt. Henry Chew	21
		pt. Hoggs Down	7
Rebecca Arnold	0	pt. Henry Chew	290
		Hardesty's Chance	130
		pt. Henry Chew	110 1/2
William Allein	0	pt. Henry Chew & Newington	159
		Cox Comb	150
		Coxes Head	50
		Smiths Conveyance	60
		Buck Chance	150
		Second Thought	92
Mary Allton	3	pt. Hardesty	22
Benjamin Bradey	13	pt. Preston	30
Levin Ballard	0	pt. Newington	133 1/2
Elizabeth Bond	7	Small Land	6 1/2
		Spittle	274
Richard Bond	0	Small Reward	54
		pt. Hogs Down	75
		Mitcham	243
		pt. Brooks Partition	4
Abraham Bowen	7	pt. Dividing Branch	169
		pt. Dividing Branch	177
		pt. Billingleys Farm	62 3/4
Jacob Bowen	5		
Francis Bowen	3		
Thomas M. Bowen	7	pt. Dividing Branch	105
Charles Bowen	3		
Parker Bowen	10		
Young Bowen	6		
Jesse Bowen	12	pt. Dividing Branch	32
		pt. Brooks Adventure	66
		Lamboth	75
John Bowen	6		
James Bowen	9	pt. Dividing Branch	105
David Bowen	8	pt. Dividing Branch	181
Isaac Bowen	10		
James K. Byrne	7	Adventure	116
John Beden	2		
Edward Burkett	4		
Sarah Bourne	0		

1783 TAX LIST OF CALVERT COUNTY, MARYLAND
Second District

Name	# of whites	Tract Name	# acres
John Beckett	0	pt. Gunterton	250
		pt. Hardesty	50
		Popy	40
John Bowen Jr.	1	pt. Smith's Forge	33
John Brooke, heirs	4	pt. Adventure	266
		pt. Cedar Branch	25
		pt. Bowen	230
		pt. Arnolds Purchase	200
Margaret Cox	0	pt. Bucks Chance	50
		pt. Refuge	50
		Hatchett	25
Jeremiah Cox	5	pt. Newington	218
John Cox	7		
Jeremiah Cox Jr.	7		
Samuel Chew	0	5 lotts Lower Marlboro	
Cook heirs	0	1 lott Lower Marlboro	
Mary Camblett	3		
Lewis China	4		
Denmund Cramphin	0	1 lott Lower Marlboro	
Thomas John Clagett	0	1 lott Lower Marlboro	
Thomas Cullember	7		
William Cullember	10		
Ann Crompton	4	Parkers Chance	263
		Jerusalem	124
		Simmons Adventure	25
		Bigger	1055
		Cattertons Lot & Barbers Delight	294
		pt. Godsgrace	100
John Cullember 3rd.	5		
William Conwill	6		
Cowman & Dawson	0		
Charles Doren	7		
James Deale	2		
Henry Deale	1		
Richard Deale	8	pt. Timberwell	74
John Dockett	3		
John David	0	2 lotts in Lower Marlboro	
James Dossey	7	Youngs Mount	159
		Youngs Fortune	40
		(Continued)	

1783 TAX LIST OF CALVERT COUNTY, MARYLAND
Second District

Name	# of whites	Tract Name	# acres
James Dossey (continued)	7	pt. Bowen	70
		pt. Brooks Adventure	124
		Taney's Addition	159
John Denton	9		
Thomas Denton Jr.	2		
Thomas Dixson	0		
John Dotson	6		
Joseph Essex	9		
Isaac Essex	11	pt. Woolfs Trap	55
		pt. Scrap	38
		pt. Reserve	14
William Edmondson	6		
William Everest	6		
Richard Evans	8		
Peregrine Freeland	6	pt. Mackalls Force	323 1/2
Mary Freeland	1	pt. Young Coxes Land	193
Frisby Freeland	8	pt. Mackalls Force	323 1/2
		Rich Bit & Bar___	166
		Lowreys Rest	442
		pt. Lott at Hunting Town	
		3 lotts Lower Marlboro	
Col. William Fitzhugh	0		
Benjamin Fowler	6		
Jesse Fowler	6		
Sarah Fowler	5		
Ezra Freeman	9	pt. Smiths Forge	17
Robert Freeland	0	lott at Hunting Town	
John Gibson	11	pt. Spittle & Add. to Spittle	231
John Gibson of Peter	3	pt. Brooks Partition	100
Priscilla Galloway	7	pt. Spittle & Add. to Spittle	29
Richard Gibson	8	pt. Islington	75
James Gibson	7	pt. Spittle	62 1/2
		pt. Addition to Spittle	88
		pt. Newington	22
Asenath Graham	5	Black Wall	38
		Bell	68
		pt. Hardestys Choice	180
		pt. Spittle & Add. to Spittle	59
		2 lotts Lower Marlboro	
John Gardner of William	5		
Absalom Games	9		

1783 TAX LIST OF CALVERT COUNTY, MARYLAND
Second District

Name	# of whites	Tract Name	# Acres
William Gray of John	5	pt. Reserve	45
		pt. Stinnetts Ramble	20
James Gray Jr.	0	pt. Brookes Adventure	100
Robert Gardner	8		
John Gardner	0		
John Griffith	2		
George Gray	4	Marsh Land & Burhead	345
		Hentel	100
		Hazard	42
Dr. James Gray	0	pt. Tillington	247
Thomas T. Greenfield	2		
William Harmon of James	8		
William Harmon of William	2		
William Howse	8	pt. Lowreys Point & Rest	50
Howerton Mary	3		
Joseph Hardesty 3rd	8		
John Hance	6		
Joseph Hance	7		
Benjamin Hance	10	pt. Marble Stone	181
William Harrison 4th	4	pt. Abbington	100
Samuel Harrison	5		
William Harrison	4	pt. Brooks Discovery	326
		pt. Lowreys Reserve	75
		pt. Coxes Freehold	128
		Turkey Thickett	200
Robert Harrison	6		
William Harrison of William	2		
William H. Harris	0	pt. Abbington	150
Joseph Harris (adm.)	10		
William Harris of William	6	Addition	140
Francis Holt	6		
Hugh Hemmingsworth	8		
Thomas Harwood	4	2 lotts Lower Marlboro	
Joseph Hance	7		
Thomas Hutchens	4	pt. Blind Tom	32
		pt. Fannys Delight	70
		pt. Taney's Right	29
Richard Hudson	5		
Ignatius Hutchens	7	pt. Magruder	61 1/2
Benjamin Harris 3rd	0		
Joseph Hardacre	6		
Joseph Hall	6		

1783 TAX LIST OF CALVERT COUNTY, MARYLAND
Second District

Name	# of whites	Tract Name	# acres
Arthur Harris	3	pt. Tillington	254
		pt. Hardesty	33
Elijah Hance	5		
Benjamin Hance of John	0		
Benjamin Hance of Samuel	6	Overton	250
Kenny Hance	2	pt. Stoakley	97
		pt. Taney's Ease	123
Samuel Hance	5	Purchase	150
		Busseys Garden	175
		pt. Taney's Ease	60
		Hances Lane	20
		pt. Borden Enlarged	59
Clement Hutchens	7	pt. Magruder	50
Francis Hutchens	8	pt. Magruder	61 1/2
Stephen Hutchens	0		
John Hudson	6	pt. Moroco	100
		pt. Arnolds Purchase	100
Leonard Hollyday Jr.	0	Buzzard Island	700
		pt. Arnolds Purchase	48 1/2
		Addition	51
Samuel Hance (adm.)	0		
Richard Hellen of Richard	0		
Benjamin Jones	7		
James Jones	2		
John Jones	5		
Thomas Jones	7		
William Ireland Jr.	6	pt. Ridge	94 1/2
		Georges Desire	44 1/2
		Addition	43
		Angle	81
		Ireland's Plains	32
John Ireland	6	pt. Tillington	189
		pt. Wolf Trap	45
Dr. Edward Johnson	0	Spott	4
		pt. Preston	270
		Moffetts Mount	200
		Turners Chance	50
		Woods Venture	50
		Add. to Woods Venture	33
		pt. Poor Land	134
		Muschitto Point	51
		Lott Lower Marlbro & pt. Henry Chew-66	

1783 TAX LIST OF CALVERT COUNTY, MARYLAND
Second District

Name	# of whites	Tract Name	# acres
Thomas Jenkins	3		
Henry Jefferson	4		
Basil Jefferson	8		
John Jefferson	4		
Benjamin Jefferson	6		
Elizabeth Johns	3	Copartnership	150
Benjamin Johns of Abraham	3		
Margaret Ireland	2	pt. Angle	40
		Leaches Freehold	125
		pt. Peakens Nest	75
		Lott at Hunting Town	
Francis King	0		
James King	6		
John King	3		
Henry King	0		
Daniel Kent	6	Timberwile	366
		Smiths Conveyance	29
		Bucks Chance	150
		pt. Wood's Adventure	97
Robert Lee	6		
Anabel Leach	7		
John Laurenee	11	pt. Islington	177
		Small Reward	57
		pt. Lowrey's Addition	145
Joshua Leach	3		
Jane Leach	3		
Jeremiah Leach	6		
Thomas Leach	0		
James Lyon	6		
James Mackale of James John	5	Lowreys Chance	130
Benjamin Mackale of John	10	Lowreys Point & Lowreys Rest	50
James Mackale of John	0	Taneys Reserve	312
		pt. Taneys Addition	132
John Mackale (St. Mary's)	0	Horse Range	162
		St. James	190
Thomas Mackale	0	pt. Sewells Purchase	30
		Exchange	350
		pt. Cedar Branch	240
John Miller	9		
John Miller Jr.	7		
Isaac Miller	0		
Rousby Miller	7	pt. Busseys Orchard	253

1783 TAX LIST OF CALVERT COUNTY, MARYLAND
Second District

Name	# of whites	Tract Name	# acres
Levin Mackale	1	Copartnership	182
		pt. Hallowing Point	10
		pt. Trouble	27
		pt. Morocco	50
		pt. 2 chances	150
		pt. Reds	17
William Marcus	7		
John Marcus	8	pt. Newington	211
Richard Moreland	6	pt. Islington	100
John Mitchell	6	pt. Hatchcomb	62
James Morsell	7	Rattle Snake Hill	120
		pt. Mary's Green	76 1/2
		pt. Chance	70
James Merrett	5	pt. Littleworth	60
Levin Marshall	1	Copartnership	182
		pt. Hallowing Point	10
		pt. Trouble	27
		pt. Morocco	50
		pt. 2 chances	150
		pt. Reds	17
Benjamin Mackall(at H.Point)	11	pt. Hallowing Point	390
		pt. Seamores Neck	382
		pt. R_____ & Magruder	46 1/2
		pt. Coursey & Re___	92 1/2
		pt. Two Chances	157
		pt. Dividing Branch	179
Benjamin Mackall 4th	0	pt. Gods Graces	525
		Weem's Delight	42
John Norfold	7	pt. Ridge	64
Thomas Norfold Jr.	3	pt. Ridge	64
William Norwell	4		
John Norfolk Jr.	4		
Thomas Norfolk	2		
John Norwell	6	pt Coxes Freehold	100
James Norfolk	4		
		pt. Refuge,pt Kids Swils &	
		pt. Ireland	100
John Norfolk of James	0	pt. Peakens Nest	50
Ogden Moses	5		
Aaron Ogden	6		
John Ogden	4	pt. Wood's Adventure	93 1/2

1783 TAX LIST OF CALVERT COUNTY, MARYLAND
Second District

Name	# of whites	Tract Name	# acres
Alexander Ogg	4	Meadow Land	6
		pt. Tillington	333
James Owens	4		
Edmund Poole	9		
Elizabeth Price	4	Busseys Orchard	50
Brian Price	8		
Mary Parker	1	Clay Hammond	317 1/2
		Wilsons Commons	29
Peter Paster	7		
Tayman Philpott	6		
Allen Roberts	0		
Edward Reynolds	0	pt. Thatchcomb	35
Mary Read	2	pt. Islington	50
Edward Randall	8		
William Reynolds	3	pt. Abbington	769
		Thomas' & William's Chance	101
		Reserve	300
		The Meadows	132
		Cox's Inclosure	70
		Brooke's Discovery	64
Abraham Rhodes	10	pt. Islington	100 1/2
		pt. Blind Tom	40
		pt. Taney's Right	121
James Rigby	6	lott at Courthouse	
Richard Roberts	0	pt. Tillington	73
		pt. Littleton	77
William Ramsey	5	pt. Arnolds Purchase	50
Joshua Robertson	3		
John Robertson	10		
John Standforth	9	pt. Poor Land	104
Patrick Smith Jr.	0		
Thomas Simmons	1		
Ellis Slater	9	pt. Lowrey's Reserve	70
Ann Strickling	5		
Benjamin Stallings	9		
James Scarth	4		
John Spicknall	8	pt. Henry Chew	400
Phinehas Stallings	8	pt. Thatchcomb	124
William Stallings	2		
John Spicknall Jr.	3		
Richard Stallings	0	lott in Lower Marlboro	

1783 TAX LIST OF CALVERT COUNTY, MARYLAND
Second District

Name	# of whites	Tract Name	# acres
Dr. John H. Smith	8	Bradford	208
		pt. Hardesty's Choice	50
		Dodsdale Manor	435
		pt. Henry Chew	53
		Chew's Manor	60
		Bullings Right	610
		Water & Mill	
Basil Spicknall	3		
James Stone	0	2 lotts in Lower Marlboro	
John Shears	8		
Newman Stallings	14		
Isaac Simmons	11	pt. Borders Enlarged &	
		pt. Reserve	146
John Skinner	11	pt, Newington	94
James John Skinner	0	pt Busseys Orchard	50
		pt. Chance	108
		Dotsons Desire	98
Frances Skinner	6		
Rachel Skinner	0		
Martha Skinner	0		
Ann Skinner	0		
Mary Skinner	0		
Frederick Skinner	7		
Elizabeth Skinner	5	pt. Taney's Right	150
		pt. Scrap	62
		pt. Reserve	121
		William's Purchase	26
Samuel Skinner	0		
James Skinner	6	pt. Borders Enlarged & Reserve-200	
John Stone	2		
William Strickling	6	pt. Hardesty	150
John Slye	6		
James Somervill	0	pt. Stoakley	229 1/2
Susanna Somervill	8		
Joseph Strickling	9	pt. Robinsons Rest	50
William Sewell	3	pt. Cup Haw	80
		pt. Maidens Delight	50
James Sewell	10	pt. Maidens Delight	125
		pt. of Deer Quarter	62 1/2
		pt. Chance	72 1/2
		Lott at Hunting Town	

1783 TAX LIST OF CALVERT COUNTY, MARYLAND
Second District

Name	# of whites	Tract Name	# acres
Francis Spencer	12		
Richard Turner	5		
William Turner	7		
Dilah Taylor	6	pt. Ridge	5 1/2
John Taylor	8		
Jacob Tilliskey	1		
Thomas Tucker	7		
John Tucker of Dorrumple	6		
John Tucker of William	9		
Thomas Talbott	5	Exchange	97
Edward Talbott	3		
Michael Taney	8	pt. Berry	540
		Wooden Point	25
		pt. Angle	3
		Long Point	100
		pt. Berry	60
Thomas Taney	0	pt. Littleworth	25
Joseph Taney	0	pt. Littleworth	25
Col. Joseph Wilkinson	6	pt. Brumale	350
		Piney Point	44
		Water Mill	
Benjamin Wood	7	pt. Wood's Adventure	97
Jonathan Wood	4	pt. Wood's Adventure	100
William Wood Jr.	1		
Elizabeth Wood	2		
Joseph Wood	5		
James Whittington	7	pt. Abbington	250
Philip Wilkinson	10		
Richard Wilkinson	8	pt. Henry Chew	75
John Weems Jr.	6	pt. Dodsdale Manor	1000
		pt. Chance	100
		pt. Islington	26
		Tinleys L. & H. (lott & house?)	46
		pt. Purchase	23
		2 L. & H. in Hunting Town	
Elias Woolf	4	pt. Young Coxes Lane	194
Henry Williamson	7	pt. The Den	362 1/2
John Wiley	6	pt. Newington	98 3/4
John Wiley Jr.	0		
William Watson	5	pt. Islington	40 1/2
		pt. Newington	50

1783 TAX LIST OF CALVERT COUNTY, MARYLAND
Second District

Name	# whites	Tract Name	# acres
Francis Williams	8	pt. Island	101
		pt. Borders Enlarged	102 3/4
		Chance	50
		pt. Orchard	40
John Woolfe	7	lott at Court House	
John Wilkinson	9	pt. Young's Attempt	100
Betty Wilkinson	3	pt. Godsgrace	150
		pt. Stoakley	70
Sabrit Wood	6		
James Wood	7		
John Wood	7		
Dunbar Williams	7		
Talbott Williams	2	pt. Swinsons Adventure &	
		pt. Friendship Rectified	82 3/4
Francis Williams Jr.	0	pt. Marble Stone	56
Aaron Williams	3	pt. Williams Hardship	175
		pt. Williams Right	50
		pt. Winsons Adventure	50
		pt. Friendship Rectified	25
Aaron Williams Jr.	7	pt. Friendship Rectified	151
		Swinsons Adventure	100
		pt. Youngs Desire	50
		pt. Borders Enlarged	29
		pt. Marble Stone	212 3/4
Francis Wheatley	3		
James Weems	7	pt. Stoakley & Taneys Ease	200
		pt. Cuecolds Miss	60
		Success	50
		Hogg Haunt	50
		pt. Busseys Orchard	400
		Mauldons Luck	25
		Meadows Preserved	46
		Youngs Attempt	62
		Youngs Fortune	60
		Youngs Desire	25
		Hard Venture	17
		Partnership	75
		Water Mill	
		Lott at Court House	
		Lott at Lower Marlboro	

1783 TAX LIST OF CALVERT COUNTY, MARYLAND
Second District

Name	# whites	Tract Name	# acres
William Lock Weems	0	pt. Magruder	410
		Penmans Manure	50
		pt. Reserve	50
		Hard Venture	22
Edward Wood Jr.	8	pt. Magruder	150
William Wood	4		
Edward Wood	2		
Henry Wilson (Baltimore)	0	Lott at Hunting Town	
Nathaniel Wilson	-	Stones Lott	50
		no name	99
		Huckleberry	50
Young Wilkinson	0		
Philemon Young's heirs	0	1 lott Lower Marlboro	
Parker Youngs	0	Punch	150
		Hop Yard	150
		pt. Youngs Desire	25
Benjamin Younger	4		
William Younger	4		
John Younger Jr.	7		
George Younger	7		
John Younger	6		
John Younger 3rd	1		

Third District

Name	# whites	Tract Name	# acres
John Askew	1		
Davis Avis	6	pt. Elton Head Manor	143
Robert Addison	7	pt. Devils Woodyard	78
Jarvis Avis	5		
James Avis	3		
John Avis	3	pt. Elton Head Manor	72
Richard Allen	8	Hogskin Clifts	100
Charles Allen	6	pt. Short Hills	41
		Rich Bottom	25
William Allen	5		
Mary Brooke	4	pt. Brooke Place Manor	246
Jesse Jacob Bourne	7	pt. Elton Head Manor	200
		Surplus Land	364
Jesse Bourne	6	Surplus Land	967
		Surplus Land	733

1783 TAX LIST OF CALVERT COUNTY, MARYLAND
Third District

Name	# Whites	Tract Name	# acres
Margaret Bourne	3	pt. Elton Head Manor	200
Christopher Baker	5		
Nathaniel Baker Jr.	3	pt. Devils Woodyard	60
Isaac Roysten Baker	9	pt. Elton Head Manor	50
Isaac Baker	5	pt. Elton Head Manor	50
Joseph Breeder	5	pt. Elton Head Manor	100
Thomas Binion	5		
James Bouquette	5		
Ann Bond	4	Fuller	200
		Middle Fuller	200
		land unnamed	50
Benjamin Blackburn	11	The Back Pasture	96
David Blackburn	7		
Hooper Brome (St. Mary's)	0	Rich Neck	52
		Mary's Widowhood	30
		Add. to Island Neck	30
Nathaniel Buckmaster	8		
Ann Brome	3	pt. Austins Addition	88
		pt. Bread Point	10
		pt. Letchworth	10
John Buckingham	5		
Thomas Brome	2	pt. Bread Point	10
		pt. Neighborhood	82
		pt. Austins Addition	25
		Brooke Battle	124
Alexander Brome	0	pt. Island Neck	220
Betty Heigh	5	pt. Stonerly	200
		pt. Lower Bennett	250
Leonard Barrs	5		
Basil Brooke	3	pt. Brooks Place Manor	276
John Brooke	1	pt. Brooks Place Manor	430
Elizabeth Brooke	2	pt. Brooks Place Manor	304
Charles Blackburn	5	pt. Donington & Doningtons Enlargement	30
Zachariah Blackburn	1		
Thomas Boney	4		
William Barber	5	pt. Donington	462
Ann Binion	7	pt. Round Pond	50
Benjamin Binion	4		
John Beveridge	0	Dear Bought	21
William D. Brome	1	pt. Howard & Letchworth	200

1783 TAX LIST OF CALVERT COUNTY, MARYLAND
Third District

Name	# whites	Tract Name	# acres
Isaac Baker Jr.	5	pt. The Devils Woodyard	120
John Baker	3	pt. The Devils Woodyard	50
Nathaniel Baker	7	pt. The Devils Woodyard	140
Nathaniel Cullember	2		
John Cullember	5		
Benjamin Cullember	3		
Jeremiah Cullember	5		
Elizabeth Culpepper	7	pt. Woolfes Hole	15
		pt. Woolfes Quarter	40
		Venture	16
Frances Clagett	2		
William Crane	5	pt. Elton Head Manor	30
John Clare Jr.	9	pt. Elton Head Manor	65
Elizabeth Clare	0		
John Clare	9	pt. Hard Travell	191
Isaac Clare	2	Horse Path	200
		Addition to Horse Path	40
		Surplus land	50
		pt. Johnsons Lot	71
		pt. Hap Hazard	76
		pt. Concord	98
Jeremiah Catterton	7	pt. Elton Head Manor	50
John Conwill	5	Goldstones Inheritance	150
John Cotton	6		
Jesse Cullember	6		
Henry Cullember	6		
John Coster	6		
John Chesly	1	Point Patience	360
		Addition	6
Richard Conwill	2	Crumton	75
		Rawlings Purchase	60
		pt. Addition	13
Samuel Coe	4	Golden Folly	75
Daniel Day	6		
Robert Day	4	pt. Elisha Halls Resurvey	150
Jane Day	4	pt. unnamed land	100
Nathaniel Day	1		
Thomas Denton	7		
George Denton	5	Peddington	50
		pt. Island Neck	90

1783 TAX LIST OF CALVERT COUNTY, MARYLAND
Third District

Name	# whites	Tract Name	# acres
Charles Dawkins	6	pt. Josephs Place	179 1/2
		Dick's Cabbin	50
		pt. Hucklebury Quarter	8 1/2
		pt. Taylors Joy	114
		pt. Allen's Neck	36
		pt. Friendship	25
James Dawkins	1	pt. Bachelors Hall	280
Jesse Dawkins	4	pt. Gumby Quarter Enlarged	43
Alexander Dawkins	2		
Charles Dawkins Jr.	1		
William Dawkins Jr.	1	pt. Blinkhorne	300
		Surplus land	58
		pt. Foxes Road	42
		Joseph's Reserve	196
Joseph Dawkins	1		
John Denton	2		
Mary Duke	4	pt. Brooke Place Manor	192
		pt. Bachelors Hall	20
Andrew Duke	9	pt. Elton Head Manor	20
		pt. Middlesex	86
		pt. Gideon & Cleverly's Right	19
Moses Parran Duke	6	pt. Brooke Place Manor	300
		pt. Howard & Letchworth	203
		Mill land & Water mill	20
Ann Duke	1		
Rachel Day	0		
Henry Dixon	0	pt. Huckelberry Neck	13 1/2
		Add. to Middlesex	95
		Foxes Walk	5
Benjamin Dixon	7	Allens Neck	26
Thomas Dixon	0		
Joseph Davis	5	pt. Elton Head Manor	50
Peter Dever	5		
Nathaniel Dare	9	pt. Gideon & Cleverly's Rights	472
John Dare	2	pt. Gideon & Cleverly's Rights	170
Gideon Dare	1		
Samuel Dare	3	pt. Smith's Purchase	119 1/3
		pt. Gideon & Cleverly's Right	502
		pt. The Angle	140
Philip Dossey	1		
Jesse Dorrumple	1		
James Dotson	5		

1783 TAX LIST OF CALVERT COUNTY, MARYLAND
Third District

Name	# whites	Tract Name	# acres
Robert Day	1		
William Dorrumple	2	pt. Hap at a Venture	50
		pt. Foxes Road	50
		Water Mill	
John Dotson Jr.	4		
Benjamin Ellt	3	pt. Elton Head Manor	036
		Leaches & Smiths Hill	100
Richard Everest	1		
Esom Edmonds	7	pt. Neighborhood	74
Thomas Everest	2	pt. Island Neck	30
Richard Everest Jr.	4		
Henereitta Egan	5	pt. Brooke Place Manor	575
Dr. John R. Egan	1	pt. Brooke Place Manor	575
Littleton Fleet	5		
Col. William Fitzhugh	0	pt. Elton Head Manor	2200
		pt. Round Pond	100
		Grist & Fulling Mill	
		Mill & Distillery	
Thomas Freeman	6	pt. Rock Hole	135
Pattison Freeman	4		
John Freeman	5	pt. Nortens Chance	105
		Labour In Vain	123
Thomas Freeman Jr.	6		
Catharine Frazier	4	Hills Hall	100
		White Marsh	68
		Lott at Leonard Creek	
William Fryar	0	pt. Round Pond	50
Robert Greeves	7	pt. Elton Head Manor	100
Ann Greeves	2	pt. Stephens Plains	25
Driver Greeves	4	pt. Greeves Rehoboth	36
		Surplus land	9
Absalom Greeves	3		
Ann Gardner	5	pt. Johnsons Lott	65 1/2
		pt. Woolf's Hole	12 1/2
Isaac Gardner Jr.	3	pt. Johnsons Lott	38
Kinny Gardner	7	pt. Johnsons Lott	57
John Gardner of John	8		
John Gardner	5	pt. Johnsons Lott	179
		pt. Short Neck	234
William Gardner Jr.	5		
Robert Gardner	0		

1783 TAX LIST OF CALVERT COUNTY, MARYLAND
Third District

Name	# whites	Tract Name	# acres
Isaac Gardner	5	pt. Round Pond	100
		pt. The Desert	52
Edward Griffin	9		
Dorcas Gray	3	pt. Austins Chance & Add.	91
		Norwood	200
		2 lotts Leonard Creek	2
Dr. James Gray	1		
John Gray	1	pt. Hebbush Manning	40
Thomas Gray, sheriff	1		
Thomas Gray	5	pt. Wootton	101
		pt. Holch	50
		The Scraps	12 1/4
		pt. Trowbridge & Brooks Choice-180	
Thomas Gray of William	5	Gray's Addition	109
		Creeds Chance	64
Richard Gray	1		
Elizabeth Goodwin	11		
James Henley	5	Smuggs Folly	80
William Hunt	4	Brandom	50
		Framton	57
Richard Hellen 3rd	2	pt. Chilton	7
James Hellen	2	pt. Trueswell	150
Searth Hellen	1	pt. Trueswell, pt. Milton Lott,	
		pt Harrow the Hill, pt. Persia,	
		pt. Rich Levele	272 1/4
Rebecca Hellen	1		
Daniel Hellen	1	pt. Persia & Melton Lott	50
		The Gully	63 1/2
David Hellen	7	pt. Persia, pt. Trueswell &	
		pt. Rich Levele	94 3/4
Edmund Hellen	5	Warren	121
		pt. Bowdles Chance	75
		Busseys Lott	75
		Hellens Lott	12
		Veaches Rest	50
Richard Hellen	1		
Peter Hellen	4	pt. Huckleberry Quarter Enlarged-118 3/4	
		pt. Josephs Place	5 1/2
Jacob Hellen	3	pt. Donington & Donington	
		Enlarged	48 3/4
James Hellen Jr.	5		

1783 TAX LIST OF CALVERT COUNTY, MARYLAND
Third District

Name	# whites	Tract Name	# acres
Mary Hellen	5	pt. Hoopers Neck	275
David Hunter Jr.	6	pt. Elton Head Manor	200
David Hunter	5		
William Hillhouse	1		
William Hall	9	pt. Grimby	158 1/2
Isaac Hooper	11	pt. Toby's Quarter	79 1/2
		pt. The Swamp	6 1/2
		pt. Narrow Neck & Gore	7
Abram Hooper	5	pt. Taylors Joy	356
Joseph Harris	3	pt. Fishers Orchard	126
William Hornby	9		
Jonas Hinter	3		
John Hungerford	4	pt. Gumby Quarter Enlarged	100
		pt. Elton Head Manor	100
James Hungerford	1	Hogskins Neck	100
		Shepherd Land	100
		pt. The Desert	100
		Doe Hill	25
		Purchase	24
William Hellen	4	pt. Brewhouse	117 1/3
Ann Hellen	2		
Edward Hall (Frederick Co.)	0	1 lott Leonard Creek	1
Samuel Hance	0	pt. Theobush Manning	189
John Ivey	4	pt. Greve's Rehoboth	42
		pt. Stephens Plains	25
James Heighe	0	Cole Kirby	200
		pt. Coles Clifts	150
		pt. Gumby	30
		pt. Theobush Manning	100
		pt. Prestons Clifts	63
William Johnson	1		
Thomas Johnson	5	The Gift	314
		pt. Prestons Clifts	100
		pt. Gideon & Cleverlys Right	888 1/2
Joseph Johnson Jr.	1		
Joseph Johnson (carpt.)	6	Brians Tree	117
Samuel Johnson	1	Elizabeth	200
		The Gift	70
		Lott Leonard Creek	1
Sarah Johnson	1		
Benjamin Johnson	0		
James Ivey	1		

1783 TAX LIST OF CALVERT COUNTY, MARYLAND
Third District

Name	# whites	Tract Name	# acres
Mary Ireland	3	pt. Elton Head Manor	200
		land not named	100
Richard Ireland	5	pt. The Desart	230
		pt. Prestons Clifts	75
		pt. The Angle	54
		pt. The Mill Marsh	63
		Irelands Hope	50
Gideon Ireland	1		
John Kent	8	pt. Rock Hole	160
Sarah Kirshaw	3	pt. Prevent Danger	50
James Kirshaw	4	pt. Prevent Danger	75
Francis Kirshaw	5	pt. Sharps Outlet	100
		pt. Concord	63
Francis Kirshaw Jr.	1		
Isaac Kent	1		
William Francis Lewis	2		
Thomas Lynes	5	pt. Elton Head Manor	50
Daniel Laville	8		
James Melley	1		
John Melley	8	Hattons Cove	70
		Staffords Freehold	70
		The Gore	70
Isaac Monnett	7	Gerar	12 1/2
Thomas Mackall	3	pt. Evans land	200
		pt. Stonesby	225
		Cold Harbour	100
		pt. Brooke Place Manor	432
John Mackall (A.A.Co.)	0		
Benjamin Mackall of John	0	Brigandines Adventure	24
		School House	100
		Shelton Resurveyed	183
John Mackall of James	1	pt. The Cage	166 2/3
		pt. Perry Neck	66 2/3
		pt. Mackall's Desire	6 2/3
Hannah Mackall	1	pt. The Cage	83 1/2
		pt. Perry Neck	33 1/3
		pt. Mackalls Desire	3 1/3
John Mackall (St. Mary's)	0	pt. Clagett's Desire	276 1/4
		pt. The Desart	332 3/4
Levin Mills	5	pt. Huckleberry Neck	205
Alexander McAlester	4		

1783 TAX LIST OF CALVERT COUNTY, MARYLAND
Third District

Name	# whites	Tract Name	# acres
Leonard Mills	4	pt. Rich Levell	130
		pt. Wooten	101
		pt. Ketch	50
James Mills	5	pt. Fishers Orchard	126
John McDowell	7	pt. Coles Clifts	50
John Manning	5	pt. Theobush Manning	74 1/4
Elizabeth Morgan	2	pt. Garey	160
John McKenney	8		
David Millar	8		
Brian Mayhew	3		
John McKenney Jr.	4		
William Millar	1		
John Mills	4	pt. Towbridge	125
		pt. Brooke Choice	41
Mary Mackall	3	pt. Lower Bennett	500
		pt. Foxes Walk	40
Benjamin Mackall Esq.	0	pt. Horse Range	165
		Sharp Outlet	133 1/2
		Addition to Sharp Outlett	112
Samuel Norfolk	4		
Ward Newton	10		
James Poole	5	pt. Elton Head Manor	200
James Poole Jr.	2		
John Pantry	8	pt. Hap Hazard	84
		Johnsons Lott	13
Francis Paster	4		
Niley Pattison	2	pt. Stonesby	75
		pt. Evans Land	65
Jeremy Pattison	1		
William Pattison	3		
John Parran	4	pt. Fishing Creek	82 1/2
		pt. Chaplain	50
		pt. East Chaplain	50
		pt. Necks Clifts	75
		pt. East Fishing Creek	25
Charles Somerset Parran Jr.	2	The Discovery	99
Alexander Parran	5	pt. Birmingham	50
		Parrans Park	300
		pt. Brooke Plains	100
Thomas Parran Jr.	1		
Charles Somerset Parran	3		
Dr. Thomas Parran	0		

1783 TAX LIST OF CALVERT COUNTY, MARYLAND
Third District

Name	# whites	Tract Name	# acres
Samuel Parran	—	pt. Parrans Park	150
		pt. Winfields Resurvey	207
		pt. Birmingham	25
		pt. Morgan	45
		pt. land without name	100
		pt. Halls Resurvey	4
George Plater, Esq.	0	Miles Run	150
		Miles End	391 1/4
William Powell	5	pt. Gideon & Cleverlys Right-5 1/2	
		Short Hills	23 1/2
John Pardoe	9	pt. Rocky Neck	50
		pt. Foxes Walk	50
		pt. Rich Levell	93
		pt. Brians Tree & Fishers Orchard-33	
Samuel Pitcher	9		
Christian Paster	3		
Sarah Parran	6	pt. The Desart	366 1/4
		pt. Neglect	200
		pt. Clagetts Desire	99 3/4
		Preston	400
John Parran Jr. heirs	0		
John Pattison	4	Timber Neck	50
		Clares Littleworth	43
David Platford	9		
John Rawling	11	pt. Elton Head Manor	300
		Water Mill	
Elizabeth Rawling	3		
Isaac Rawling	1		
Daniel Rawling	10	pt. Elton Head Manor	200
		Bathams Loss	200
		Dear Bought	50
John Rigby	1		
William Rigby	3		
Richard Roberts	0		
Allen Roberts	9	Garey	158
		pt. Lower Bennett	200
Mary Rriley	1	pt. Smith's Joy	33 1/3
Jeremiah Randall	3		
William Stallings	7	pt. Elton Head Manor	100
Henry Stallings	3		
William Smith	5		

1783 TAX LIST OF CALVERT COUNTY, MARYLAND
Third District

Name	# whites	Tract Name	# acres
Thomas Stallings	7	pt. Elton Head Manor	50
William Walter Smith	0	pt. Elton Head Manor	33
Daniel Smith	5		
Benjamin Shield	0		
Henry Sax?	2		
Rebecca Somervell	5	pt. The Gore	100
		Surplus Lane	300
		pt. Smiths Purchase	119 1/3
		Bartholemew's Neck	50
		pt. Woolfes Hole	21 1/3
		Lott Leonard Creek	1
Thomas Somervell	1		
Susanna Somervell	0	The Gore	100
		Surplus Land	200
		pt. Rocky Neck	50
		pt. Toby's Quarter	21
		pt. Allens Neck	12
		pt. The Swamp	60
John Sedwick	7	pt. Neighborhood	176
		Adjander	50
		pt. Hard Travell	191
		pt. Horse Range	16 3/4
		Water Mill	
Joshua Sedwick	6	pt. Brewhouse	6
Benjamin Stinnett	5		
Samuel Slye	9		
Patience Slye	7		
James M. Sollers	6	Prospect	189 1/4
		Smiths Island	60
		Mill, land, & Water mill	20
James Stewart	1		
Walter Smith	7	Taylors Disposal	270
		Leonards	300
		Stones Hills	51
		Purchase	20
		Bullmores Branch	50
		Smiths Hog pen	309
		pt. Woolfes Quarter	300
		pt. Parkers Gift	100
		pt. Rock Hole	100
Henry Tanner	5		
Benjamin Tucker	5		

1783 TAX LIST OF CALVERT COUNTY, MARYLAND
Third District

Name	# whites	Tract Name	# acres
John Tucker (B.C.)	3	pt. Neighborhood	82 1/2
Thomas Tucker	1		
Elizabeth Tucker	2		
Elizabeth Turner	1		
Brian Taylor	6	pt. Foxes Road	255
		Reedby	100
		pt. Smiths Purchase	119 2/3
		1 lott on Leonards Creek	
Mary Wilson	1		
Andrew Wilson	4	pt. Gideon & Cleaverlys Right-214	
Benjamin Wilson	1	pt. Horse Range	100
Ann Wilson	7	pt. Lower Bennett	100
		Mackall's Devise	76
Nathaniel Wilson	4	pt. Island Neck	40
Col. Joseph Wilkinson	0	pt. Garey's Chance	200
William White	10	pt. Smiths Joy	66 2/3
Jesse Wood	5	pt. Friendship	75
		pt. Allens Neck	
Lydia Winnull	7	pt. Norton's Chance	161
John Williams	6	pt. Prevent Danger	97
		pt. Foxes Walk	6
David Wilkinson	9	pt. Donington & Bowdles Chance-53 3/4	
		pt. Donington & Donington's Enlargement	40
George Wheelers heirs	0	pt. Fishing Creek	82 1/2
		pt. Chaplain	50
		pt. East Fishing Creek	25
		pt. Necks Clifts	75
		pt. East Chaplain	50
Edward Willen	4	Jerusalem	108
		pt. Rich Bottom	25
		Willens Swamp	11
		The Content	6 1/2
Thomas Willen	3		
Francis Woolfe	8	pt. Theobush Manning	40
		pt. Gareys Change	75
Susanna Young	8	pt. Harrow The Hill & Truesville	30
George Young	5		
Benjamin H. Young	9		
Parker Young	6		

1783 TAX LIST OF CALVERT COUNTY, MARYLAND
Third District

Name	# whites	Tract Name	# acres
John Yoe	2	Rattle Snake Hill	100
David Younger	3		
William Dawkins	1	Mary's Dukedom	100
		Hughes Fancy	79 1/2
Francis King	6	pt. Mears,	
		pt. Selbys Clifts,	
		pt. Blind Tom,	460
John Somervill	1	pt. Stoakley	189 1/2
		pt. Gunterton	40
John Turner	6	pt. Bowdles Chance	91
		pt. Hap at a Venture	12
		The Fig Tree	50
		Surplus Land	147

Signed by: Thomas Blake
          Joseph Wilkinson
          Thomas Mackall

Lyons Creek Hundred

Name	Tract Name & Acres	# white males	# white Females	# white males 10-50yrs.
Aldridge Allien	Alliens Purchase-290 1/2	2	4	1
Rachel Anderson	pt. Grammers Chance-100	-	1	-
____ Armager	pt. Birkheads Chance-101	6	1	2
(Willi)am Allein	Lott Pig Point	1	3	1
Robert Atwell		2	1	1
John Arnold		4	2	1
Devoll? Brashears	pt. Lott & Manor-100	8	3	2
Benjamin Brashears	Brashears Purchase-124 1/4	1	-	1
Jonathan Brashears	Brashears Purchase-124 1/4	2	2	1
Wilkinson? Brashears	Wilkinsons Folly-84	3	2	1
Mary? Mack Brashears	Grammars Parrett-152 1/2	5	3	1
Richard Brown	Wrighton?-150	5	4	1
____ Burgess	pt. Burkheads Lott-120	3	5	1
Saml. Burgess (Estate)	pt. Burkheads Lott-115	-	-	-
Martha Ball		1	3	-
Abraham Birkhead		6	7	1
Sarah Carr		-	2	-
John Carr Sr.		1	5	-
John Carr Jr.	pt. Burkheads Addition-35	2	1	1
John Chew of John	pt. Harrisons Security-101	2	4	1

1783 TAX LIST OF CALVERT COUNTY, MARYLAND
Lyons Creek Hundred

Name	Tract Name & # acres	# white males	# white females	# white males 10-50yrs.
___ Childs	Childs Addition-100	1	1	-
Joseph Childs		1	1	-
___ima Childs	pt. Polland Manor-162 1/2	-	3	-
Sarah Cowley	Sarah's Purchase-97 1/2	2	1	1
Charles Cowley	pt. Barrett's Purchase-70 1/2	1	1	
_____Cowley	pt. Barrett's Purchase-35	3	1	1
___Crandell	Pleasant Prospect-158	2	2	1
___Chesney		4	4	2
Joseph Cowman		5	3	1
___Henry Darnall		-	-	-
Bennett? Darnall	Darnall's Puncture-2674	1	-	1
Philip Darnall Sr.	pt. Portland Manor-516	1	-	-
	pt. Portland Manor-516			
	pt. Landing-200			
Philip Darnall	Add. to St. James-349	1	-	-
Richard Darnall	Portland Manor-724	2	-	-
	pt. Birkhead-743			
	2 lotts Pig Point-2			
Saml.? Drury	Birkheads Chance-147	1	3	1
Charles? Drury	pt. Portland Manor-96	4	3	1
_____Drury	Gullacks Folly-147	5	1	1
Mary Drury	Birkheads Chance-147	1	2	1
Joseph Deaks	pt. Birkheads Parcel-219 1/2	4	4	-
John Davis	Toogoods Lott-58	1	-	1
___Davis		1	-	1
Wm.? Fitzhugh, Esq.-Billingham-400		-	-	-
Lewis Fisher	Birkhead's Chance-150	2	2	2
Richard Green	Green's Purchase-831	1	-	-
	2 lotts Pig Point			
John Griffin	Ann Wells Purchase-170	2	3	1
John Gardner	Ann Wells Purchase-66	4	4	1
John Gardner Sr.	Gardners Purchase-100 1/2	-	-	-
John Gardner Jr.		3	2	1
John Galwood		5	3	2
Edward Griffith		1	1	1
___ry Griffith		2	4	1
David Griffith		4	3	1
Mary Gover?	Batchelors Choice-412	-	-	-
Elizabeth Hopkins	Hopkins Fancy-204	-	2	-
William Hopkins		1	-	1
Charles Henwood		3	4	2
Joseph Hutton	Beattys Purchase-120	3	7	-

1783 TAX LIST OF CALVERT COUNTY, MARYLAND
Lyons Creek Hundred

Name	Tract Name & # acres	# white males	# white females	# white males 10-50yrs.
Sam. Harrison	Harrison's Security-494	3	3	1
Capt. John Harrison		2	1	1
William Hutton		2	2	1
Abell Hill	pt. Birkheads Chance-274	2	2	1
John G. Hamilton		1	-	1
Sarah Hill	pt. Birkheads Parcel-150	-	-	-
John Harper		2	2	1
James Hutton		2	2	-
Henry D. Hill		1	-	1
Philip Harrison		1	-	1
Sarah Jones	pt. Quicksale-70		6	
Jonathan? Jones		1	-	1
Joseph Jee?		1	1	1
Capt. John Kelly	Strawberry-307	1	1	-
Capt. John Lambeth		4	5	1
John Lambeth of Wm.		5	2	1
Richard Lane	Grammers Chance-261	2	1	1
Stephen Lambeth		3	4	1
John Lane Sr.	pt. Grammers Chance-200	1	1	1
John Lane Jr.	pt. Grammers Chance-133 1/2	4	2	2
Saml. Lane, Esq.	Purnals? Angle-1901 lott at Pig Point	-	-	-
Henry Lambeth		1	-	1
Capt. Saml. Maynard-Delight-156		5	4	1
Sarah Macceney	____Bottom-25 1/2	1	1	1
Zachariah Macceney		1	-	1
Jacob Macceney		1	-	1
Mary Miles	Miles Claim?-222	2	5	2
Thomas Miles	pt. Grammers Parrott-100	1	-	1
William Miles		3	2	1
Samuel Mead	Birkheads ____-135	7	4	-
Rev. Walter Morgavan?		-	-	-
Gilbert Norvell		3	7	1
James Owens Sr.	Owens Fancy-339 1/4	4	5	-
James Owens Jr.		4	3	1
Isaac Owens	Isaac's Purchase-197 1/2			
Benjamin Owens		1	-	1
Jane Owens		1	4	1
John Ogle		1	-	-
Leonard Piles		3	6	1
Thomas Powell	Birkheads Meadows-109 1/2	4	4	1
Henry Powell	pt. Birkheads Meadows-35	3	2	1
Josiah Parker		1	1	1

1783 TAX LIST OF CALVERT COUNTY, MARYLAND
Lyons Creek Hundred

Name	Tract Name & # acres	# white males	# white females	# white males 10-50yrs.
Martha Parker		1	2	-
John Parslow		1	--	1
William Powell		1	2	1
George Ross		2	3	1
Benjamin Russell		3	5	1
Rachel Rattliff		2	4	1
Capt. Wm. Simmons	Greenoch Park-404	6	3	1
Samuel Shekolts	Shekolts Chance-105 1/4	3	2	1
Prissy Simmons	pt. Birkheads Chance-150	2	1	-
William Simmons Jr.		-	3	1
John Scrivenor	pt. Birkheads Woods-125	3	6	1
Charles & Wm. Steuart	Greenoch Park-373 3/4	-	--	-
Thomas Shields	House at Pig Point	2	-	--
Stephen Steward	pt. Lord's Manor-95	-	-	-
John Shekolts of Thos.		4	3	1
Abraham Sollars		4	4	1
Samuel Shekolts		1	-	1
William Simmons		3	4	-
William Tillard	Gravelly Hill-309 1/4	2	3	1
Thomas Tillard	Barshaby-156	3	2	1
Edward Tillard	pt. Fox ___-50	1	2	1
Zachariah Turner		3	2	1
John Welch	Welches Folly-242 1/4	3	4	1
James Walker		1	1	1
John Williams		2	5	1
Abraham White		3	3	1
Duke Wyvill	Quick Sale-200	4	8	1
Josiah Wingfield		1	2	1
Samuel Verhon		1	3	1
John Wood		1	2	-
Samuel Wood		1	-	1
Zebedie Wood		2	1	1
Capt. Aaron Welch		2	2	1
David Williams		--	-	-
Joseph Williams		1	-	1
Stephen Wood	Lot at Pig Point-100	-	-	-
Henry Walker	2 lotts at Pig Point	-	-	-
Ezekiel Gott	Brothers Purchase-197 3/4	3	3	2

THE END

INDEX

Abbott 1,5,65,68
Abram 26
Adair 14
Adams 20,68,102,130,148
Adare 10
Addington 167
Addinton 167
Addison 187
Adkerson 129
Adley 66
Adnerson 20
Ady 95,102,114
Agnew 20
Ailen 1
Aion 20
Airs 79
Akens 29
Akeright 101
Akers 66,68
Akins 31
Albert 161
Alcock 34
Aldredge 44
Aldridge 20,24
Aldron 34
Alexander 10,14,16,26,28, 29,31,65,69,161
Allein 176,199
Allen 1,11,27,34,50,64, 102,120,137,154,160, 187
Allender 125,161
Allford 20
Allien 199
Allin 27
Allinder 102
Allman 5
Allnutt 167,176
Allsop 167
Allton 176
Allum 120
Almony 79
Ammons 120,147
Amoss 79,92,102,103, 114,125,153
Amshir 64

Anderson 5,10,16,24,27,34, 62,66,79,92,137,147,161, 166,199
Andrews 103,117,125,137
Annen 129
Antill 121
Antriam 27
Apleton 116
Applegarth 44,47
Arbuckle 29,31
Archer 10,154
Ardery 66
Arglergee 10
Arlett 117
Armager 199
Armitage 80
Armstrong 10,14,16,19,20, 24,44,66,103,114,121, 126,136,137
Arnet 20
Arnold 116,137,176,199
Arrants 10,20
Arrendal 66
Arrington 66,69
Ash 16
Ashbaugh 20,24
Ashcroft 34
Ashmead 80
Ashmore 161,165,166
Ashy 136
Askew 167,187
Askin 16
Aston 95,101,103,116
Atkin 14
Atkinson 44,47,69
Atwell 199
Auld 34,44,47,48
Aulderson 44
Austen 62
Austin 34,44,49,167
Avis 187
Ayres 94
Badders 19,20
Baden 167
Badthers 120
Bahman 5

Bailes 137,138
Bailey 16,135,137,145
Bailis 137
Bairfoot 20
Baker 10,14,20,26,27, 28,50,64,65,66,80, 92,95,103,137,154, 188,189
Bakman 5
Balderson 161
Baldwin 80,103,115
Baleson 66
Ball 34,44,47,48,199
Ballard 176
Ballarman 5
Banister 62
Bankhead 29,31,80,93, 117
Banning 34,48,50,69
Banns 27,28
Barber 188
Barclay 27,69,147,149, 150,161,166
Barker 167
Barley 28
Barnaby 10,14,69
Barnes 34,47,48,103, 130,137,146,150, 153,154
Barnett 65,66,69,161
Barney 44
Barnhill 10
Barnhouse 154
Barniby 1
Barnsby 5
Barnwell 50,62
Barr 16,20,24
Barrett 29,31,80,138
Barrington 10
Barrock 20
Barrow 34,44,47,49,62
Barrs 188
Barthlay 103
Bartlett 34,65,69
Barton 167
Bateman 14

-203-

Barton 80,92
Barwick 44
Bass 66
Bassett 10
Bateman 29,31
Bathorn 20
Batsey 44
Battensly 101
Baty 80
Baxtor 95,101
Bay 20,95,101
Bay 20,95,102,103
Bayard 10,14
Bayles 10,20,24
Baylis 5
Beal 10
Beale 64
Bean 117   Beam 16
Beard 1,5,20,24,26,27
Bearsley 28
Beaston 10
Beastton 10
Beaty 126,146
Beaver 66,125,161
Beck 5, 20,24,136
Beckett 177
Beden 176
Beedle 1,5,10,20
Belcher 137,146
Bell 31,50,62,80
Ben 125
Benington 147,150
Benjamin 33, 138
Bennet 28
Bennett 29,121,129
Bennitt 33
Benny 35,44,45,50,62,64
Benshaft 161
Benson 4,5,35,47,49,50
Bent 62
Bentley 50
Bently 80
Be.rridge 66
Berry 50,53,64,69,80,104
Bertwhistle 92
Berwick 50
Beswick 50
Beswicke 62

Bevaid 138
Bevard 138,150,153
Beveridge 188
Bevin 80
Bi__e 61
Biddle 10,11,14
Bigam 94
Biggs 10
Bignell 136
Billingsley 80,95,121,125,
   155,161,166
Bind 65,66
Bing 125
Binion 188
Birckhead 69
Bird 10,21
Birk 16
Birkhead 65,104,199
Biscot 45
Black 10,14,17,80
Blackburn 27,121,125,188
Blackstone 104
Blades 35,45,47
Blagdon 104
Blake 1,9,33,51,62,64,66,
   137,146,167,199
Blakoney 47
Blanch 66
Blanchfeld 10
Blanchford 10
Blany 80,92,94,121
Blev 101
Blew 5
Boardman 137
Bodkin 147,150
Bodle 5
Body 136
Boggs 16,28
Bohaimen 10
Bohannon 20
Boils 62
Boler 146
Bolfield 35
Bolster 129
Bonar 138,145
Bond 16,64,80,81,92,95,96,
   104,121,135,161,176,188
Boney 188

Bonion 5
Bonsal 16
Bonsly 64
Bontis 146
Booker 61,62,69
Boon 5,29,31
Booth 16,51
Bordley 8,45,51,104
Borland 27
Borly 137
Boshong 161
Bosly 81,117
Boswick 61,64
Both 104
Botts 137,138
Bouchell 10,14
Boulden 10,11
Bouldin 14,21,22
Boulding 14
Bouquette 188
Bourne 176,187,188
Bowdle 65,66,69
Bowen 11,21,176,177
Bowie 69
Bowings 5
Bowley 62
Bowlis 137
Bowman 51,64,137,146
Bowyer 130
Boyd 16,21,29,31,147
Boyer 5,21,24
Bozman 69,70
Bracco 5,62
Brackley 27
Brackly 28
Bradey 176
Bradford 95,102,121,154
Bradley 16,21
Bradly 125
Bradshaw 66
Brady 5,6,8,136
Brannan 5
Brannon 137
Brashears 199
Brasher 150
Brassaw 167
Brassays 45
Brassey 48

-204-

Bravard 11,14
Brazer 5
Brazier 1,104
Breeder 188
Brerely 47
Brewer 45
Briarly 81,92,93,155
Brice 1,5,161,165
Bridges 35,45,62
Bridget 49
Brimfield 66
Bristow 21,24
Briun 11
Broadway 51
Brome 188
Bromwell 45, 70
Bronn 125   Brook 125
Brooke 177,187,188
Brookins 26
Brooks 104,121
Broom 16,19
Brown 1,5,11,16,20,21,
   24,27,28,49,66,70,
   81,92,95,96,101,104,
   116,121,126,129,130,
   135,136,137,138,150,
   155,199
Brownen 95
Browning 70
Brownly 104,155,160
Broxon 5
Bruaid 6
Bruce 150
Brucebanks 130
Bruff 35,62,64,70
Brumfield 26,28
Bryan 11,33
Buchanan 14
Buck 21
Buckingham 188
Buckleight 138
Bucklor 47
Buckly 66,129
Buckmaster 188
Buckworth 11
Budd 130
Budgis 154

Budkley 65
Bull 96,104,114,121,125,
   155
Bullen 62,70
Bullock 117
Bullon 64
Buntel 21
Bunting 70,96
Burgess 45,51,64,66,199
Burk 35,49,51,117
Burkett 176
Burkham 61,62,65
Burkin 161
Burnham 11
Burns 21,27
Burton 81,137
Busey 167
Bush 64,81
Busney 62
Bussey 81,93
Butell 24
Butler 62
Butterfield 27,28
Byards 137
Byford 95,101
Byfott 124
Byrne 176
Cade 45,48
Cahall 114
Cahey 31
Cain 155
Calahan 29,31
Calder 114
Caldwell 26,27
Calender 101
Callaghan 120
Callahan 62,64
Callahans 55
Callender 66
Calley 161
Calwell 104,121
Cambden 168
Cambel 19
Cambell 29,45
Cambill 16
Camble 161
Camblett 177

Cameron 26
Camlin 11,14
Cammell 116
Campbell 6,11,16,21,
   28,81,121,124
Camper 45,48
Canby 9
Cane 66
Canker 145
Cann 6
Canner 70
Cannon 31,117
Carbire 135
Carcand 168   Card 168
Cardiff 35,45
Carey 6,62,65,66
Carionear 16
Carlile 104
Carlon 93,155
Carlong 81
Carmichael 138
Carnan 6
Carney 81
Carperla 11   Carrold 20
Carr 29,31,65,70,81
   138,167,199
Carslakes 54
Carson 114,138
Carswill 26
Carter 48,81,94,117,150
Cartlon 161
Cartlow 6
Cartwright 6
Carty 11,115,135
Caruthers 16
Cary 81
Cashman 104
Cashore 11
Casky 147
Casly 138
Casseldine 130
Cataneck 6
Cates 17
Cather 27,29
Cathor 24,28
Catrel 124
Catrop 51
* Carroll 35,45,81,96,104,
   114,138,146

Catrup 33,48,51,64,65
Catterton 168,189
Catty 136
Caulk 1,6,35,47
Cazeir 20
Cazier 21,24
Chain 6
Chalk 81
Chamberlain 75
Chamberlaine 35,36,51,65, 66,70
Chambers 11,13,14,16,45, 48,61,62,104,167
Chance 62
Chancy 126,130
Chandlee 16
Chandler 31
Chandly 145
Chaney 130,168
Chaniel 21
Channel 19
Channels 27
Chaplain 70,71
Chaplin 65
Chapman 62,64,66
Charlton 168
Check 11,14
Chelson 104
Cherry 82,92,93
Chesney 200 Chesley 168
Chesny 105
Chevers 62
Chew 1,6,21,24,28,29,31, 150,154,167,168,177, 199
Childes 168
Childs 6,200
Chiles 1
China 177
Chinworth 101
Choosly 48
Christian 51
Christie 130,135
Chuck 11
Churchman 16,19,27
Churn 11
Clagett 177,189

Clare 189
Claremont 66
Clark 26,36,51,52,62,64, 65,66,71,82,105,146, 154,155,161,162,166, 167
Clash 65,66
Clayland 52
Clear 135
Clement 155
Clemons 92
Clenaougham 20
Clendenen 11
Clendening 155,160
Cline 6
Clogg 62
Close 21,138
Closly 45
Cloud 105
Cloward 20
Coale 138,150,153,154
Coalman 82,96,101
Coats 62
Coburn 45,66,71
Cockran 11,16,21,52
Cochron 105
Cockayne 45
Cockey 66
Cockroll 62
Coe 189
Cohorn 31
Colb 136
Colbert 62
Colburn 49
Cole 16,27,29,31,49,62
Coleston 45
Colhoun 138
Colling 115
Collingham 129
Collins 28,66,96,102,124 130,135,136
Collinson 36,45
Colner 62
Colosdy 27
Colston 36,48
Combest 130
Comegys 1,6

Commens 66
Condon 49
Condron 82,92,145
Conely 6,161
Conn 105,115
Connant 167
Connard 105
Connell 117
Connelly 162
Connolly 49,71
Connoly 82,121
Connor 93
Conoly 11
Conrod 31
Conwill 177,189
Cook 21,62,65,66,82, 96,115,120,150,177
Cooley 20,62,93
Cooly 82,93,138
Coonrod 29
Coop 82,93,160
Cooper 6,36,45,52, 62,96,105,147,155
Cooty 160
Copeland 121,126
Coppen 1
Coppin 6
Corbaley 11
Corbett 28,29,31,82,93
Corbin 105
Corbott 26
Cord 26,27,28,130, 135,136,145
Corman 1
Corner 66,71
Corry 138
Cosden 1,6,24
Cosly 146
Cothan 27
Cothon 31
Cotner 62
Cotty 136
Couden 21
Coudon 45
Coulson 27
Coultor 28
Courtney 138

Coventon 64
Covey 45
Cowan 82,105,107,124,
    138,177
Coward 66,71
Cowarding 2,6
Cowley 136,200
Cowman 200
Cox 2,5,6,66,71,82,105,
    138,139,146,147,167,
    168,177
Craddick 66
Craddock 6
Craig 2,6,11,12,29,31
Crail 62
Cralstone 26
Cramphin 177
Crandell 200
Crane 168,189
Cranford 167
Cratts 115
Craven 92
Crawford 27,82,150,154
Cray 45,48
Creadock 6
Creal 120
Creamer 21
Creaton 155
Credock 6
Creighton 96
Creswell 138,146,156
Cresswell 29,31
Cretin 138
Crier 45
Crighton 117
Crinstone 115
Crisp 49
Criswell 96
Crockett 29,31,166
Crompton 177
Cromwell 29,31,105,120,
    150
Crookshanks 26,45,52,71
Crosby 101,124,168
Cross 16,64
Crosson 27
Crouch 6,21,24,48

Crow 11
Crowder 62
Crozier 11
Cruse 138
Cruson 146
Crutchley 168
Cuddy 96,154
Culearth 77
Cullember 177,189
Cully 16
Culpepper 189
Cultraugh 146
Culver 138
Cumerford 52
Cummins 16,27,36,45,48,
    49,138,156,160,166
Cuncoa 16
Cuningham 105
Cunningham 2,6,16,26,28,
    96,101,115
Curlet 21
Currer 21,26
Currey 19
Currier 24,29,31
Curry 82,93,121,125,147
Dabson 21
Daffin 36,37
Dags 147
Dailey 121
Daily 105
Dales 105
Dallam 130,135,136,139,
    150,151,153
Dallas 130
Dandy 66
Danny 117
Darden 66,71
Dardens 52
Dare 168,169,190
Darnall 105,139,200
Darumple 21
Daugherty 96,130,136,139,
    156
David 169,177
Davidson 27
Davis 2,6,11,19,37,45,
    49,62,82,94,121,125,
    151,162,190,200

Davison 16
Dawkins 190,199
Daws 105,115
Dawson 11,21,37,45,
    48,49,52,64,71,92
    117,121,177
Day 16,101,105,115,
    116,189,190,191
Deaks 200
Deale 169,177 Deamon 101
Dearmott 93
Death 29,31
Deaver 96,117,126,
    130,131,136,151
Deavos 129
Debruler 105,124
DeCoursey 2,6
Delahay 65,66,71
DeMoss 82
Denbow 83,94
Denney 168
Denning 105
Dennis 6
Denny 66,71,156,160
Denton 178,189,190
Dever 190
Devins 105
Dewberry 117
Deyoung 83
Disk 83,136
Dickenson 52,71,72
Dickison 31
Dickson 27,120,124
Dier 96
Diggins 162
Dillion 116,139
Dimmett 102
Dines 83
Ditto 83,93
Divan 154
Divas 121
Divine 116
Dixon 11,21,29,31,37,
    45,64,121,126,136,
    178,190
Dobbins 96
Dobson 24,52,62,64,65
* Dickinson 65,66,72,96

Dockett 177
Dodson 45
Domahoy 72
Domey 105
Domigan 26
Donahoo 83
Donavin 131,139,145,146,147
Donning 150
Donoho 24
Donohs 21
Donoly 11
Dooly 135
Doran 117
Doren 177
Dorgin 37
Dorrit 49
Dorrumple 190,191
Dorsey 83,106,130,131,135
Dorvele 169
Dossey 168,169,177,178,190
Doterage 106
Dotson 169,178,190,191
Dougharty 27,48
Dougherty 28,31,37
Douglas 161
Douglass 16,19
Dowland 83
Downey 16,37,45
Downing 11,147,151
Downs 105,156
Downy 37
Draper 92
Drew 126,136
Drimer 121
Drummond 66
Drury 200
Duberry 120
Dudley 52,58,61,62,65
Duff 16
Dugan 21
Duke 190
Duling 45,67
Dulre 106
Dunbarr 29,31
Duncan 72,101,124,147
*Durham 83,96,102,106,116,117

Dungan 106 Dunn 131
Dunning 55
Dunsmore 162
Duran 136
Durant 130
Durbin 29,31,106,139
Dutton 106 Durgan 45
Dwiggins 62
Dwire 126
Dyer 106
Eads 169
Eagin 27
Eakin 16,19,147,150
Eakins 27
Earle 2,6
Easkins 117
Eason 67
Eaton 45,106
Eavens 17
Edgar 48,49
Edmiston 27
Edmonds 191
Edmondson 62,66,72,178
Edmunds 169
Edmunson 26
Edwards 67
Elbert 52,62
Elburn 11
Egan 191
Elisha 169
Ellgis 17
Elliott 21,37,48,83,106,120,162
Ellis 11,14,121,124,125,136,145
Ellt 191
Ellwood 11
Elsbury 11
Ely 151,153
Emmitt 17
Empsom 6
England 17,26,27,83,93
Ensor 11,15,121,125
Ephraim 9
Erven 67,106
Ervin 92
Erwin 156

Erzbey 19
Esgate 37
Essex 178
Etherington 2,6
Eubanks 49,52
Evans 17,21,24,27,28,29,31,83,124,136,178
Everest 178,191
Everet 20
Everett 94,97,106,131,136,139
Everie 129
Everitt 115,135
Evertson 2,6
Evitt 139,145,146
Ewing 17,29,31,62,139,147,166
Ewley 67
Fackney 6
Faddin 143
Fagan 6
Fairbanks 37,38,45,49,62
Fairhurst 67
Fallen 62
Farbad 6
Farmer 139
Farroll 83
Fashney 2
Faulkner 38,45,48,52,62
Fauntleroy 52,53
Fedis 6
Fee 17
Fendall 62
Ferguson 28,32,62,67,139
Ferns 53
Ferus 62
Fideman 38
Fie 131
Field 131
Fields 14
Fife 17
Finley 17,29,32,83
Finnagan 106,115
Finney 28

Fip 106
Fisher 2,6,151,153,162, 200
Fitzgerald 6,83
Fitzgerrald 136
Fitzhugh 178,191,200
Fitzpatrick 53,62,136
Flanagan 32,106,156
Flatt 117
Flearty 83
Fleet 191
Fleetwood 139
Flemming 48,67
Fletcher 19
Flintham 11
Flowers 147
Floyd 62
Fontain 136
Ford 6,11,13,14,15,106, 115,131,139,146,153
Foreson 38,62
Forguson 27
Forman 2,6
Forsythe 120
Forter 166
Forwood 131,156,160
Fory 116
Foster 11,15,20,21,22,24, 29,32,53,62,72,83,117, 120,139,162
Fountleroy 53
Fourt 147
Fowler 11,131,136,139, 178
Fraily 156
Frampton 53,62,65,67
France 106,115
Frasher 120
Frazier 150,169,191
Frazor 32
Freazer 29
Freel 32
Freeland 169,178
Freeman 45,67,116,169 178,191
French 11,169
Frew 21,24
Frisby 2,6,64

Frull 145
Fryar 191
Fryer 121
Fullard 117
Fulton 11,21,24,29,32, 97,102
Gafton 6
Gaines 124
Galaspy 83
Gallahan 64
Gallion 97,121,125,126, 131,140,166
Galloway 178
Galwood 200
Games 178
Gannon 62
Gantt 169
Garden 15
Gardiner 62
Gardner 27,62,151,176, 178,179,191,192,200
Gardnor 27
Garey 52,53,62,64,65
Garland 45,53
Garretson 83,106,115,126, 131,132,134
Garrett 17,132
Garrettson 131
Garritson 106
Garritt 115
Gartrill 19
Gash 120,157
Gatchel 17
Gatchell 17
Gates 156
Gawly 129,147
Gay 29,32
Geer 10
Geers 6,7
Gehogan 140
George 7,11,15,21,24, 53,62
Gerish 21
Gest 120
Gibb 156
Gibson 17,28,53,64,83, 93,106,117,156,160, 162,178

Giffen 124
Gilbert 125,136,139,140, 156,162
Gill 83 - Gild 62
Gillespie 21,29,32
Gillespy 93,115
Gillis 21
Gilmore 11,28,126,129
Gilpin 17,20,21,24,65
Gilse 153
Ginn 17
Ginthor 28
Gisom 140
Gittear 17
Giving 83
Gladdin 93
Glascow 26,27,29
Glass 17,21,32
Glassco 29
Glassford 7
Glenn 11,15,29,32,83, 93,121
Godwin 97
Goggins 93
Gold 7,20
Goldsborough 38,45,53, 54,61,67,72,78
Golloughor 26
Goodin 145
Gooding 2,7
Goodwin 140,192
Gooland 45
Gordan 2,7
Gordon 11,54,72,117 132,139,162
Gore 54,62,65
Gorrell 140,145,151,153
Gorrish 28
Gorsage 45,48
Gorthorp 106
Gossage 45
Gott 202
Gough 106,107
Gouldsmith 107
Goutz 139
Gover 140,146,151, 153,169,200
Grace 21,45,48,62,131
*Giles 17,65,126,132,140 151

Grafton 156,157,160
Graham 169,178
Granger 21
Grant 33,136
Graves 107
Gray 17,62,84,121,169,179,192
Grayham 62
Grayson 62
Green 26,84,97,102,157,200
Greenaugh 49
Greenfield 92,179
Greenhawk 45,54,64
Greenland 140
Greer 32
Greeves 191
Gregory 54,64,107
Griben 7
Gribon 6
Grier 29
Griffen 30,32
Griffin 64,169,192,200
Griffith 120,131,132,135,145,169,179,200
Grimes 30
Groceman 97
Groves 38,107
Grubb 28
Guffoy 26 -Guileland 17
Guinea 33
Guiton 84
Gulbraugh 140
Gulley 67
Gullifer 84
Gurn 107
Haddaway 38,45,48,49,140
Haddoway 45,48
Hadgion 7
Hagan 157
Hagany 26
Hague 7
Halbert 162
Haley 120,162
Hall 2,7,11,15,17,21,24,26,27,30,32,48,54,62,97,120,121,125,126,127,132,133,136,140,141,147,153,170,179,193

Haltham 11
Hambleton 17,38,39,45,67
Hamby 32,84,136
Hamelton 28
Hamilton 28,97,148,201
Hamlin 102
Hamnor 97
Hampton 136
Hance 170,179,180,193
Hancock 72
Handy 153
Haney 97
Hankey 7 Hanlin 97,102
Hanna 20,125
Hannah 84,121,140,146,157
Hanover 84,107
Hanson 122,126,127,129,132,141
Harbert 122,141,146
Hardacre 179
Hardcastle 62,65
Harden 17
Hardesty 170,171,179
Hardikin 67
Harding 67
Hare 7
Hargrove 141
Harkly 120
Harley 12
Harmon 179
Harper 84,92,93,102,148
Harrey 33
Harrington 39,45,48,61,62,65
Harriott 122
Harris 45,48,151,153,157,170,179,180,193
Harrison 39,45,48,49,67,71,72,73,142,170,171,179,201
Harriss 17,39
Harrowood 2
Harry 107
Hart 6,21,24,29,39,62,65,122,157
Hartley 54
Hartshorn 32

Hartshorne 26
Harvey 21,27,84,170
Harvy 101
Harwood 39,45,46,179
Hasking 84
Hassen 28
Hassett 107
Hatfield 170
Hathorn 97
Hattham 15
Hatton 12
Hawbanks 46
Hawkins 30,32,84,117,140,141,151
Hayes 2,7
Hayhurst 107
Haynes 27
Hays 97,120,157
Hayward 54,65,67,73
Haywood 12,19
Hazeldine 62,65
He____ 48
Headney 7
Heaps 84,94
Hearsey 15
Heath 2,6,7 Hedges 7
Hedrick 26
Heigh 188,193
Heighe 170,171
Hellen 180,192,193
Helm 30,32
Helsby 73
Hemmingway 170
Hemmingsworth 179
Hempfield 21
Hemsley 54
Henderion 7
Henderson 12,15,30,32,33,84,94,127
Hendrickson 2,5,6,7
Henly 192
Henny 21
Henry 12,148
Henwood 200
Heron 73
Hersch 28
Hershey 12
Hervey 17,24

-210-

Hewey 48
Hibbett 17
Hicks 54,107
Hickson 73
Higgins 32,62,67,73
Higgons 30
Higgs 54
Hill 17,20,21,26,33,65,67, 84,107,115,136,157,201
Hillhouse 193
Hillis 30,32
Hindman 27,39,45,55,73
Hines 32
Hinesley 62
Hinks 125
Hinter 193
Hinton 170
Hitchcock 21,24,84,93
Hobbs 45,84,145
Hodgson 12
Hokes 20
Holbert 166
Holland 15,107,115,170
Hollandshead 170
Hollinger 157
Hollings 7,12
Hollingsworth 12,15,17,132
Hollins 12
Hollis 127,129
Holloday 48
Holloway 115,160
Hollowood 7
Hollyday 39,46,48,73,170, 180
Holmes 65,67,73,122
Holmon 150
Holonels 78
Holsby 65,67
Holt 21,179
Homer 116
Honey 46
Hook 46
Hooper 12,39,40,46,170,193
Hoopman 132,135
Hoops 2,142
Hope 84,94
Hopewell 67

Hopkins 20,21,40,46,47, 48,49,55,65,67,73,151, 153,154,157,200
Hopper 46
Hornby 193
Horner 17,33,107,116,141, 146
Horney 49,67
Horton 132
Hott 7,24
Houching 107
How 65
Howard 85,94,97,101,116, 140,170
Howe 148
Howell 29,140
Howerton 179
Howey 65
Howlett 148,162
Howse 179
Huches 2
Huddabuck 28
Hudson 12,26,127,157, 179,180
Huet 17
Huff 17,140,146
Hufman 147
Hugg 12
Huggans 107
Huggins 17
Hughes 2,7,11,12,17,40, 46,63,85,107,141,157, 160
Hughston 107,115
Hukill 7,11,12,21
Hull 17,49
Humble 161
Humphrey 7
Hungerford 193
Hunnell 85
Hunt 12,40,46,48,97,170, 171,192
Hunter 12,20,30,32,65, 108,170,193
Husband 141,151,154
Husbands 141,154
Huskins 85

Husler 7
Huss 15
Huston 21,85,94,116, 122
Hutchason 162
Hutchens 170,179,180
Hutchings 60,170
Hutchingson 26
Hutchins 85,108,115
Hutchinson 2
Hutchison 7,15
Hutchman 30,32
Hutson 93,117
Hutton 200,201
Hyland 21,24
Hynott 20
Hynson 2,7,132,136
Iller 27
Ingram 85,108,142,146
Ireland 21,171,180, 181,194
Irons 108
Irwin 27
Isaac 171
Isacke 171
Ivey 193
Jack 26,27
Jackson 2,7,12,21,22, 24,28,30,32,46,49, 55,67,161,162
Jacobs 15,17,73
Jadwin 55
James 65,73,85,108, 126,151,162
Jameson 19
Jamison 146
Jaquith 28
Jarrett 85,86,92
Jarritt 94
Jarvis 97
Jay 148
Jeans 17
Jee 201
Jefferson 46,181
Jeffery 122,125,136
Jefferys 115
Jehu 143

Jenkens 108
Jenkins 67,73,86,108,153,
    162,164,181
Jennings 7
Jervis 157
Jewell 17,86
Jewells 162
Jewitt 124
Jiner 108
Job 17,27,49
Jobion 12
Jobson 15 Johnny 26
Johns 55,142,147,151,181
Johnson 17,19,22,23,24,27,
    30,32,55,67,73,86,94,
    120,127,129,136,147,
    148,150,157,158,160,
    162,171,180,193
Jolly 101,151,153
Jones 2,7,12,22,24,46,48,
    63,67,73,86,93,97,98,
    108,115,118,129,133,
    136,148,151,162,171,
    180,201
Jonnsey 171
Jordan 17,73,74,92,120
Joshua 143
Judd 136,142
Justice 26
Kadel 94
Kane 65
Kanky 22,24
Karnay 108
Karr 148
Kean 86,93,141,146,147
Kee 7
Keets 55
Keithly 46
Keitley 22
Kell 108
Kelly 22,27,30,32,65,115,
    127,142,145,166,201
Kemp 40,46,48,49,55,61,
    63,67,74
Kendale 171
Kendrick 63
Kenedy 118,120,122,125

Kenly 152
Kennady 40,63,67
Kennard 46,93,133
Kent 63,98,118,181,194
Kerby 40,46,55,61,63,65,
    67
Kerk 7
Kerney 19
Kerns 86
Kerr 74,108
Kersey 40,67
Kevin 32
Keys 46
Kidd 30,32,86
Kilgore 17
Kilmore 49
Kilpatrick 28
Kimble 133,136
Kimly 135
King 46,65,171,181,199
Kinly 162
Kinnamont 63
Kinnard 54,63,65
Kinnemont 63
Kinnman 32
Kirby 46,55,63,65
Kirk 7,12,27
Kirkpatrick 122,125
Kirkwood 86,94
Kirsh 17
Kirshaw 194
Kitely 98,108
Kitpatrick 27
Kleinhoff 12
Knight 12,15,22,27,98,
    127,133,142,145,146
Knott 154
Knowlman 115
Knox 32
Krosby 65
Lacky 122
LaCompt 40
Lacy 86,108
Lafferty 32
Lambard 28
Lambden 46
Lambdin 46,48

Lambdon 63
Lambeth 201
Lamdin 40
Lancashire 49
Lancaster 12,108,115,
    132
Lane 171,201
Landrum 142
Landsdale 171
Lane 55
Lang 7
Lansly 120
Lapel 7
Larkin 120
Larramore 46
Larremore 48,49,63
Larrimore 30,32
Lashley 32
Latham 12,15
Lattimore 86,93
Laughlin 142
Laurence 142
Laurenee 181
Laveille 171
Laville 194
Lawrence 124
Lawrenson 12
Lawson 12,15,17
Leach 17,92,171,181
Leason 20
Leddenham 46
Lee 7,27,63,67,108,
    115,152,158,163,181
Leeds 41
Leet 145
Legoe 108
Leins 20
Lemmon 12,154
Leonard 41,46,48,118
Leonare 48
Leslie 7,26
Lesloy 26
Lester 7,129,132
Lewin 108
Lewis 7,12,17,22,25,86,
    98,108,162,166,171,
    194

Liddle 49
Linch 25
Lincicome 48
Linsay 163
Linsmore 49
Linton 32
Little 22,32,127
Littleton 74
Litton 142,146,148
Lloyd 41,55,56,57,74
Lobe 115
Lockard 163
Lockwood 32
Log 63
Logan 7,17,26,32
Logue 12,161
London 158
Londrum 146
Loney 133,135
Long 2,32,86,93,94,146
Longwill 17
Lonnberth 171
Lore 171
Lort 22
Lotherman 63
Louraign 17
Loutit 19
Louttit 2,7
Love 27,30,32,67,158
Loveday 57,61,63
Loverton 63
Lovit 136
Low 22,32
Lowe 41,48
Lowrey 41,46
Lowry 20,22,46,48,161
Lowther 57
Lucas 63,67
Lucky 142
Lukins 118
Lum 22,25
Lundergin 63
Lundrogon 129
Lurty 41,74
Lusby 2,7,41,108,122
Lutton 22,25
Lyles 67,171,172

Lynch 12,15,22,32,108,163
Lynes 194
Lyon 30,32,87,181
Lytle 87,108,122
McAdon 122
McAldon 125
McAlester 194
McAnnick 149
McAtee 163
McBride 12,22
McCall 30,32
McCallam 7
McCallum 57,74
McCan 32
McCandlass 87
McCandless 122,148
McCandley 32
McCann 32,102
McCart 120
McCarting 20
McCarty 67,133,136,145
McCasland 158
McClain 27,28,30
McClane 32
McClary 12,26,
McClasky 87,94
McClave 118
McClay 7,160
McClayland 65,67
McCleary 146
McClehany 93
McCleland 7
McClintock 122,158
McClintough 17
McClorg 15
McCloud 7
McClung 92
McClure 22,33,87,92,125
McColister 2
McColley 22
McCollough 27,28
McComas 87,93,94,98,101,
 108,127,129,152
McCombs 12
McCord 87
McCorg 12
McCormack 26

McCormick 63
McCota 145
McCowen 17,22
McCoy 12,17,30,32,33,
 158,160
McCracken 153
McCraken 22,25
McCray 22
McCreary 118
McCreery 22,23,25
McCue 116
McCullough 26,27,32,
 87,163
McCuncoa 17
McCurdy 143
McCutchen 18
McDaniel 41,160,161
McDonald 87,93
McDowell 22,30,32,145,
 195
McElroy 19
McFaddin 146,163,166
McGaugh 118
McGaw 93,120
McGay 122,125,133,136
McGill 87
McGilton 87
McGinney 74
McGloughlin 122
McGlocklin 12,22
McGoven 87
McGowan 2,7,12
McGown 25
McGregory 7
McGriffin 22
McGuire 63,87,93
McHarrey 30
McHarry 32
McHealey 32
McHenry 12
McIlhaney 158
McIntire 124
McKeever 32
McKenney 195
McKenny 152
McKenzie 172
McKeown 26

McKesson 150
McKew 18
McKibbin 18
McKim 63,109
McKimmey 7
McKimms 12
McKinney 22
McKinnis 57,63
McKinsey 67,161
McKisson 149,150
McKitridge 12
McKneel 20
McKnight 18
McKay 172
McLary 32
McLaughlin 163
McLean 136
McMahan 74
McMahon 67
McManuss 72
McMaster 30,32
McMilligan 7
McMullen 32
McMullin 28,30,32
McNabb 134,148,150
McNair 28,166
McNamarra 163
McNeal 46
McNealey 30
McNinch 22,25
McNulty 48,49
McPhail 98
McQual 63
McQuay 41,48,63,65
McVay 146
McVey 26,27,146
McWorton 22
Mabbitt 129
Macceney 201
Mackale 181,182
Mackall 172,182,194,195,199
Mackey 12,15,18
Mackie 67,74
Maddin 87,93
Maddox 98
Maddree 63,65

Maffitt 22,25
Magill 142
Magnus 108
Mahan 32,33
Mahon 142,143,146
Mahony 49
Major 136
Majors 163
Mallack 92
Malone 101
Malsby 98,109
Manadier 65
Manhorn 125
Manley 22,25
Manning 195
Mansfield 12,46,48,63,67
Manuel 18
Marchant 65
Marcus 30,32,33,172,182
Mardon 145
Marens 33
Marford 109,166
Markland 74
Marr 2,9,172
Marrett 116
Marsh 87,128
Marshall 46,48,67,87,128, 172,182
Martin 7,27,57,63,67,69, 73,74,75,77,109,124, 136,142,146,160
Mason 20,49,67,109
Massey 46,151
Mather 98
Mathews 2,3
Mathis 22
Matthews 7,8,46,49,61,63, 98,122,133,136
Maul 109
Maulden 22,25
Maxwell 27,57,111
May 18
Maybon 18
Mayhew 195
Maynadier 75
Maynard 41,48,201

Mead 201
Meads 65,87,109,116
Means 20,22
Mears 75
Meek 30,32
Mehaffy 18
Meiny 67
Mekins 12
Melley 194
Meluy 65
Melward 46
Mercer 3,8
Merchant 27,63
Merrett 182
Merrick 65,67
Middle 15
Mifflin 27
Milburn 136
Miles 22,88,118,201
Millar 195
Miller 3,8,12,15,22,27, 30,32,33,49,53,54, 57,134,148,181
Millers 25
Milligan 3,8,26
Millington 63,64,65
Millor 15
Mills 19,20,109,194, 195
Milltonton 57
Milton 63
Mitchel 18,28
Mitchell 12,15,30,33, 65,67,101,109,122, 142,143,145,146,182
Moffett 28
Molton 146
Monaghon 161
Money 5,8,22
Monk 109,134,136
Monnett 194
Monohon 101,142,146
Montgomery 12,15,17, 29,88,118,148
Monwow 28
Mooberry 134

-214-

Moody 22,25
Moor 22
Moore 12,33,88,98,102,134
Moorgniss 28
Moratto 160
More 18,28,67
Moreland 182
Morgan 3,8,33,57,63,65,
    118,136,153,163,164,
    195
Morgavan 201
Morling 41,57
Morris 88,99,122,125,133,
    136
Morrison 12,99,122,148,166
Morrow 22,25,33,116
Morsall 109
Morsell 182
Morsoll 41
Mortan 3
Morton 29
Moses 182
Mossly 65
Motton 146
Muckclose 22
Mules 172
Mulherren 109
Mullan 13,18
Mullen 18
Muller 13
Mullican 75
Mullikin 65,67
Munn 164
Murnahon 122
Murnohon 125
Murphew 65
Murphey 13
Murphy 8,22,25,26,30,33,
    63,109,134,135,136
Murray 67,92,152,164
Murry 18
Nabb 63,64
Nail 164
Nash 13,15,22,46,65,67
Navill 164
Neal 65,66,75
Neale 88

Neavil 8,22
Needle 57,58
Neel 19
Neighbours 46
Neill 118
Nelson 3,8,9,88,109
Nesbitt 28,30,33
Nesmith 41,48
Newcomb 41
Newell 26,27
Newill 8,33 Newman 65
Newnam 63
Newton 88,195
Nicholas 8
Nichols 36,41,58,61,
    63,67,71,75,109
Nisbitt 33
Noble 58,146
Noconam 67
Noels 67
Norfold 182
Norfolk 182,195
Norrington 88,109,115
Norris 58,67,88,93,94,99,
    101,102,109,118,172
North 63
Northerman 28
Northwood 66,67
Norton 8,28,63,152
Norvell 172,201
Norwell 182
Norwland 13
Norwood 46,48
Nower 122
Nowland 3,8,18
Nubraugh 109
Nuburk 125
Nudee 15
Nudie 13
Nugeant 99
Nusence 172
Nutt 20
Nutterwell 122
Nutwell 63,65
Oaks 116
O'Flinn 30
Ogan 116

Ogden 46,182
Ogg 183
Ogle 15,201
Oglesby 136
Oglevee 18
Oldham 18,19,27,75,
    109
Oliver 129,136
Onion 109,110
Oram 58
Orem 41,42,46
Orr 26,143
Orrick 26
Osborn 129
Osborne 99,110,128,
    129,134,136,143
Otherson 8
Owens 8,26,29,172,
    183,201
Owings 18,22
Oxenham 58
Ozment 58
Ozmont 65
Paca 99,110,134
Paddison 67
Palmer 28,58,88,164
Pamphilion 75
Panan 172
Pantry 195
Pardoe 156
Parisett 13
Parker 18,20,28,88,110,
    115,122,172,183,
    201,202
Parkinson 63
Parks 149
Parr 88
Parran 195,196
Parriott 58
Parrish 46
Parrott 19,58,63,65,
    66,75,76
Parsley 8
Parslow 202
Parsons 67,88,110,115
Parvin 76
Passmore 18,20,22,25

Paster 183,195,196
Patrick 28,30,33,110,152
Patten 30,33
Patterson 3,8,13,20,23,30,
  33,88,128,143
Pattison 172,195,196
Patton 28,88
Peacock 152,164,166
Peak 18
Pearce 3,8,9,13,15
Pearch 13
Pearsay 46
Pearson 46,48
Pemberton 76
Pennington 3,8
Penny 124
Perkins 46,143,164
Perry 18,66,67,76,145,164
Perryman 122,125
Peter 28,136
Peters 172
Pew 27
Phelps 129
Philips 23,25,122,128,149
Phillips 20
Philpott 183
Phipps 110
Phips 116
Pickering 49,58,65,66,76
Pierce 110
Pike 122
Piles 160,201
Pinkind 63
Pinock 154
Pitcher 196
Pitt 129
Plater 196
Platford 196
Plaxico 30,33,143
Plummer 46,48,58,63
Pocock 88,94
Pointworth 8
Pike 30,33
Pompy 149
Ponock 143
Pook 28
Poole 172,183,195

Poor 143
Porter 3,8,30,33,42,48,49,
  58,63,65,67,146,149
Post 18,63
Poteet 88,89,93,110,115
Potts 28,42,122,123
Pouge 110
Poulson 89,93
Pourson 63
Powell 8,58,76,196,201,202
Pratt 63
Pregory 9
Presbury 110,111,158
Preston 99,111,158
Price 3,7,8,13,23,25,30
  61,63,65,66,67,68,89,
  111,118,123,146,183
Priestly 68
Prigg 164,166
Princil 19
Prindowell 172
Prine 89,93
Pringle 134
Pritchard 28,66,68,76,
  143,160
Proctor 23,66,166
Prout 172
Pruitt 115
Pugh 12
Purvail 152
Pybus 172
Pyles 158,159
Quigley 13,15
Quinlin 159,160,161
Rachel 159
Rakes 66,68,76
Ralition 18
Ralston 164
Ramply 118
Ramsey 18,25,28,111,
  143,183
Randall 173,183,196
Randolph 15
Ratcliff 37,42
Rathel 58
Rathol 68
Ratholl 61

Ratliff 13,202
Rattican 102
Rawling 196
Rawlings 13
Ray 59,65,143
Reace 111
Read 18,20,23,25,183
Reader 66,68
Reagh 28
Reardon 93,134,136
Reash 28
Reason 136
Reat 28
Reaves 93
Reddish 48
Redgrave 23,25
Redman 23,128
Reed 128,149
Reese 115,136,143,145,
  149,161
Register 59,65
Reid 45,59,63,68
Reise 101
Renshaw 89,99,115,
  146,159,164
Reso 161
Reyley 33
Reynolds 8,13,18,28,30,
  33,173,183
Rhey 30
Rhoads 99
Rhodes 183
Rich 8,28,145
Richards 164
Richardson 13,15,23,25,
  42,46,47,48,68,76
  111,116,118,123,
  145,160
Richmond 111
Ricketts 18,19,20,111,
  115
Riddish 49
Riddle 134
Rider 13
Ridgeway 63
Ridgway 42,63
Riestly 68

Rigar 28
Rigbie 147,152,153,154
Rigby 42,46,48,183,196
Rigdon 118,119,120,143,
    146,159,160,164
Rightston 107
Rigs 8
Riley 99,123
Rummer 49
Ringgold 59
Ringrose 46,63
Ritchard 68
Roach 23,25,68
Road 8
Roaugh 42
Robb 13
Robert 8,76
Roberts 8,13,59,63,64,89,
    111,115,173,183,196
Robertson 123,173,183
Robinett 8
Robins 56,61
Robinson 18,20,46,47,64,
    68,76,89,93,99,102,111,
    115,123,129,134,149,159
Robison 13
Robson 42,47,48,68
Roby 124
Rock 89,93
Rockhold 89,94
Roe 59,89
Rogers 18,19,28,68,99,
    123,128,152,159,164,
    166
Roles 101,143
Rolle 42
Rollins 160
Rolston 13
Roney 99,102
Rose 102,111
Ross 13,23,42,59,94,
    173,202
Roste 94
Roughton 173
Rowland 30,33
Rowls 9,18

Royals 64,65
Rriley 196
Rudolph 13,18,23,25
Rue 9
Ruff 111,123,125,128,159,
    160,173
Ruley 3,9
Rumsay 23
Rumsey 3,13,15,18,23,25,
    111,112,143
Ruscorn 89
Rush 112
Russell 23,26,89,202
Ruth 119,149
Rutledge 89,94
Rutman 164
Rutter 23,25,134
Ryan 33
Ryland 3,9.30
Sage 143
St.Clair 136
Salelay 152
Sampson 116
Sands 42,47
Saugston 64,76
Sansbury 174
Sappington 3,9,13,15
Saunders 100,112
Saverson 9
Savin 3,4,9,13,15,23,25
Sax 197
Scarborough 164
Scarf 173
Scarff 89,112
Sciffington 89
Scofield 164
Scott 9,13,15,18,23,28,33,48
    89,94,100,112
Scrivenor 202
Seagers 23,25
Seale 143
Sealy 94
Sears 4,9,47,48
Sedwell 28
Sedwick 173,197
See 9,23

Seivele 173
Seth 46,76
Severe 64,68
Severson 27
Sewell 42,47,48,64,65,
    68,112,115,184
Seymore 47,48,49
Sham 161
Shanahan 42,48,64
Shane 89
Shannahane 59
Shannon 144
Sharp 13,18,76,77,89,
    94
Shaw 9,48
Shawhann 61
Shea 124
Shears 173,174,184
Shekolts 202
Shepherd 18,129,161
Shepperd 9,65
Sheran 13
Sheredine 123,147,153,
    154
Sherewood 123
Sheron 64
Sherwood 42,43,47,59,
    65,66,77
Shield 197
Shields 13,49,64,101,
    120,202
Shinton 123,125
Shipley 30,33
Shiply 89
Shoemaker 174
Shores 94
Short 23
Sidwell 33
Silivain 9
Silva 116
Silvers 143
Simcoe 26
Simmonds 13
Simmons 174,183,184,
    202
Simms 89,149

Simpers 13,18,23,25
Simpson 89,174
Sinclair 89,90,94
Sinclear 47,48
Singleton 18,68
Sivars 153
Skinner 43,59,68,112,173,
    174,184
Slack 66,77,152,161
Slade 90,94
Slater 183
Slone 164
Slow 68
Sly 125
Slye 184,197
Slygar 93
Sluyter 13,15
Slycer 26
Small 48,64,68
Smith 4,9,13,19,23,25,29,
    30,33,43,47,49,59,64,
    65,68,77,90,100,102,
    112,115,116,119,120,
    123,125,128,134,143,
    144,146,147,149,152,
    153,164,165,173,174,
    183,184,196,197
Smithers 174
Smithson 90,100,112
Snelling 48,49
Snody 146
Sollars 202
Sollers 197
Somervell 197
Somervill 184,199
South 18
Sparowgrove 23
Sparrow 159
Spear 30,33
Specknall 174
Spedding 66,68
Spence 147,152,154
Spencer 43,47,48,65,100,
    112,115,119,125,143,
    144,185
Spicknall 183,184
Springer 19

Sprosol 13
Spry 43,47,48
Soaper 9
Soper 9
Spencer 9
Springer 19
Sporat 9
Sprole 75
Stainer 51
Stains 49
Stalcup 23
Stall 18
Stallings 174,183,184,196,
    197
Stallion 123
Stamp 173,174
Standforth 183
Standiford 90,100,112
Standly 123
Stanley 68
Stanfield 47
Stansbury 112
Stapleford 68
Stapleton 144
Starkey 9
Start 64,65,68
Stedman 23,25
Steel 13,18,30,33,134,136,
    149
Stephens 4,9
Stephenson 123,125,134,144,
    154
Sterling 13
Stern 13
Sterrett 30,33
Steuart 202
Stevens 65,68,77
Steward 94,202
Stewart 43,47,64,90,94,113,
    115,129,134,144,149,197
Stiles 123
Stinnett 197
Stinson 26
Stockdail 100,102
Stocker 47
Stockton 4,9
Stoke 136

Stoker 47
Stokes 49,130,134,165
Stokesbury 100,101
Stone 174,184
Stones 149
Stoops 4,9,10,13,15
Strawhan 64
Street 90,94
Strepeck 143
Strickland 116
Strickling 183,184
Strode 154
Strong 113
Stroud 159
Stuart 9,13
Stub 66
Stump 30,33,144,147
    152,153
Stunstill 13
Sturgis 9
Suitor 49
Sullivan 136
Sullivant 174
Sunderland 173,174
Sutter 9
Suttin 30
Sutton 9
Swan 47,49,90
Swany 116
Sweat 64
Sweatman 47
Sweeny 149,150
Sylvester 59,64,68
Taggard 9
Talbott 90,113,175,185
Taney 185
Taneyhill 175
Tanner 197
Tannor 18
Tanquary 174
Tar 47,49
Tardy 120
Tarney 90
Tasker 154
Tate 90,93,113
Taylor 9,10,13,15,18,19,
    23,25,30,33,64,102,
    cont.

-218-

Taylor (cont.)
    113,115,119,129,134,
    135,144,145,152,165,
    166,185,198
Tease 123
Tebbs 28
Temple 9
Tennant 43
Terry 4,9,19
Testor 23
Thacknay 23
Thackray 25
Thomas 12,13,15,18,23,
    25,26,31,33,43,47,
    48,59,60,68,77,78,
    112,129,136,144,149,
    159,160
Thompson 4,5,7,9,11,12,
    13,14,15,26,33,43,48,
    90,91,92,100,101,102,
    113,123,125,144,146,
    159
Thomson 15,19,20,64
Thorn 101
Thornton 60,65,125
Thrap 115
Thrift 113
Tibbles 43,47,68
Tibbs 33
Tier 64
Tigart 30,33
Tilbrook 94
Tilgham 43,44,60,64
Tillard 202
Tilliskey 185
Tilton 60
Timmons 113
Tipton 144
Tobin 68
Todd 9
Tolley 134
Tollinger 123
Tolson 136
Tomlinson 65
Toney 125
Toogood 116
Tool 19
Torman 4

Tormoint 65
Tornsly 123
Touchstone 33,161
Toutchstone 19
Tower 33,136
Townsend 44,48,49,113
Toy 113, 160
Trago 144
Trap 115
Trapnall 113,115
Travis 113
Tredway 91,100
Trimble 19
Trippe 44,47,68,78
Trope 48
Troth 60,64,65,68,78
Trott 174
Troupe 64
Troy 31,33,65,68
Truelock 91
Truelove 136
Trulock 129
Truman 9
Trus 115
Tucker 68,78,185,197,198
Tull 9 -   Tue 116
Tullam 33
Tully 4,9
Turbutt 60,64,65
Turk 102
Turner 47,60,64,65,68,91,
    113,159,160,174,185,
    198,199,202
Tyson 113
Umbey 49
Underhill 19,26,116
Valle 9
Valliant 44,49
Vallow 4
Vance 91,100
Vancleaf 160
Vandergreif 144
Vandergrift 12
VanDike 78
Vandleaf 159
Vanhorn 113,116,123,125,
    129
Vansant 9,13,14

Vansickle 135
Varley 152
Varnay 91,94
Veazey 4,9,10,11,12,14,
    20,23,25
Venimon 14
Venkworth 144
Verhon 202
Vickers 4,9,47,50,58,
    60,64
Vinton 47,49
Visage 149
Vogan 91
Waggoner 19
Wainwright 68
Waldrum 100,123
Wales 65
Walker 31,33,66,68,78,
    144,202
Wallace 14,15,19,23,25,
    61
Wallis 31,145,152,147
Walmsley 4,9,14
Waltham 113,115
Waping 125
Ward 4,5,9,14,15,20,
    91,119,152,175
Ware 31,33
Warfield 135
Wark 28
Warner 44,68,152,153,165
Warnock 153
Warram 23,25
Warren 61,64
Warrisin 20
Waruthers 26
Wash 175
Waters 33
Watkins 119,135,136
Watson 14,16,23,31,33,
    64,123,159,175,185
Watt 91,94,119
Watters 100,113,116,123,
    124,159,160
Watts 19,44,49,68
Waver 94
Wayman 44
Weaklin 102

-219-

Weaks 100,115,116
Wear 19
Weaver 5,10,47,49,68
Webb 10,61,66,68,78,119,
    160,165
Webster 113,124,129,135
Weems 175,185,187
Weir 91
Welch 47,68,78,91,136
    145,202
Welcheouk 26
Wellaks 27
Wellingford 136
Wellington 61
Wellocks 26
Wells 28,49,91,145,152
Welsh 10,26,28,31,33
Wert 14,16
West 14,47,49,65,68,91,
    100,120,144,145,146,
    153,159,165
Weston 23,25,47,114
Wetherall 113
Whan 19
Wheatley 186
Wheeler 91,93,103,159,
    160,165,198
Whirington 5
Whitaker 92,100,101,136
    160,161
Whitby 61,64
White 19,26,68,101,135,
    136,144,145,198,202
Whitecar 19
Whiteford 92,113,116,119
    149,165
Whitelock 31,33
Whitley 10
Whittam 14,16
Whittington 175,185
Wickersham 68
Wigfield 116
Wiggins 26,154
Wild 124
Wiley 92,114,115,149,
    150,185

Wilkinson 44,185,186,187,
    198,199
Willard 92
Willen 198
William 10
Williams 10,19,20,26,28,
    33,49,61,64,65,66,92,
    101,114,135,145,146,
    149,150,186,198,202
Williamson 5,10,129,175,
    185
Willowby 47
Willson 19,20,23,59,
    61,64,65,78
Wilmer 114,135
Wilmore 165
Wilmoth 159
Wilmott 124
Wilson 19,26,68,92,101,
    114,115,120,124,125,
    144,145,147,149,150,
    153,154,166,175,187,
    198
Wimble 14
Wimley 136
Winchester 28
Windman 149
Winfield 175
Wingate 5,10,14,23,25
Wingfield 202
Winhut 19
Winnull 198
Winstanley 64
Winterbottom 47,49
Winters 47
Wirt 16
Wise 114
Witherall 116
Witlock 66
Wood 14,33,116,135,144,
    145,153,185,186,187,
    198,202
Woodland 114,128
Woodrow 20
Woods 19,68
Woolen 114

Woolf 185
Woolfe 186,198
Woolon 116
Woolsy 124
Wooley 145
Wooten 124
Wootors 64
Work 19,28
Worlds 47
Worley 26,27
Worrick 94
Worthington 145,146,152
    153,154
Wright 14,16,19,92,
    136,160,165
Wrightson 44
Wroth 5,10
Wyley 10,28
Wyvill 202
Yardly 10
Yates 23,25,114
Yeates 19
Yeldon 120
Yell 61
Yeoman 28
Yoe 199
York 101,114
Young 10,19,23,51,
    114,124,125,
    187,198
Younger 187,199

1783 TAX LIST OF MARYLAND

Addenda

Vachel Terry had tract called Wormost in Cecil Co. 1st District.

Peregine Ward had tracts called Middle Neck & Money Worth in Cecil Co. 1st Dist.

Alexander Williamson had tracts called Civility and James' Addition in Cecil Co. 1st District.

William Buck of Cecil Co. had 5 white inhabitants in his household.

Errata

Isaac Caulk page 6 should read 1 white inhabitant instead of three

Samuel Chew page 6 should read no white inhabitants instead of one.

Miltonton heirs page 57 should read Millington.

Cnnom page 117 should read Cannon.

www.ingramcontent.com/pod-product-compliance
Lightning Source LLC
Chambersburg PA
CBHW051048160426
43193CB00010B/1109